# PUBLISHER'S PREFACE

*The Confessions of a Rum-Runner* was first published in England in the spring of 1928 by the respected publishing house of William Blackwood & Sons, Ltd. While the author wrote it under the assumed name James Barbican, the publisher vouched for the authenticity of the narrative.

When released in the United States later in 1928, the book was championed by those opposed to Prohibition. They claimed that it offered firsthand evidence of the failings of the 18th Amendment, and of the insurmountable odds facing those charged with the enforcement of the Volstead Act.

In the nearly eighty years since it was published, history has given up some of the information buried in *The Confessions of a Rum-Runner*. In a Publisher's Afterword, the editors of this volume attempt to shed light on what "James Barbican" hid so well.

One of the first things to hit a reader of *The Confessions of a Rum-Runner* is the politically incorrect language. Although the author craftily covered up many aspects of his smuggling operations, he retained the racist language that was endemic to the period.

# AUTHOR'S NOTE

During the last few years I have been both on the east and west coasts of North America and in the West Indies.

The names and descriptions of people, places, and myself, mentioned in this book, have been changed sufficiently to hide their identity from those who might wish to find out more than they are meant to know, as although I myself have retired from business for the time being, I do not wish to embarrass those of my friends who are still in it.

I am not a writer, nor is this a novel, so the pages that follow are not a carefully thought out romance, but just a plain record of the ups and downs of a man who found himself at a loose end after leaving the army a few years ago.

# THE CONFESSIONS OF
# A RUM-RUNNER

Flat Hammock Press
5 Church Street
Mystic, CT 06355
(860) 572-2722
www.flathammockpress.com

10 9 8 7 6 5 4 3 2 1

ISBN-10: 0-9773725-5-3
ISBN-13: 978-0-9773725-5-3

# THE CONFESSIONS OF
# A RUM-RUNNER

FLAT HAMMOCK PRESS
MYSTIC, CONNECTICUT

# CONTENTS

# CHAPTER I

## HOW I TURNED SMUGGLER

My career as a smuggler began in Fenchurch Street some three or four years ago. William Tilney had asked me to lunch with him, and I followed him round the corner into a narrow side street and up some cranky old wooden stairs into a large room full of men who were eating fried soles and steak-and-kidney pudding. When we had finished, my host remarked, "I always get my dessert below; come along down."

We descended to the street, and walking up to a costermonger's barrow, he bought four large rosy apples. Handing two of them to me, he began munching the others, spitting out the pips into the gutter.

His lineage is so ancient and his possessions so vast that he can afford to do things which would have blasted forever the reputation of most of the silk-hatted city gentlemen who went hurrying past us.

"What is your job nowadays?" inquired Tilney between bites at his apple.

"Nothing particular," I answered.

"If you are at a loose end, why don't you go whiskey running?" he inquired.

"I wouldn't mind trying," I replied. "What is the best way to start?"

"Are you serious?" he asked, throwing the core of his first apple under the wheels of a passing motor-bus. "There's plenty of money to be picked up, but you've got to go about it the right way and be ready for rough work."

"I'll start tomorrow if you will tell me how," I said.

"See Captain Cook at 1000 Marchurch Street; tell him you are a friend of mine, and he will show you the ropes. But keep all you hear under your hat."

During the afternoon I found my way to 1000 Marchurch Street, and toiled up interminable flights of steep steps until I came to the very top, where there was a solitary door with "Captain Cook" painted on a board.

I entered a room in which more than a score of young men were bending over desks and working as if for their lives.

They were not the pale clerks one would expect to find in such an office, for their bronzed faces and large horny hands showed that they did not earn their living by slinging ink, and I wondered whether Tilney, who was a man of many strange enterprises, had started a school for smugglers.

It transpired, however, that they were nothing so romantic, but respectable merchant marine officers working between voyages for their mates' and captains' certificates, while Captain Cook was the principal of the school.

At one of the desks sat Tilney, labouring at a problem in spherical trigonometry, for being a keen yachtsman, he was rubbing up his navigation before going on a long voyage in his yacht.

In his sumptuous city offices he looked the typical successful city financier, and here his burly form and tanned face was equally in place among the sailors with whom he sat. I always think of him as having been born a few hundred years too late, for he is the type of man who in the days of good Queen Bess used to climb up the sides of Spanish galleons with a cutlass in his teeth and a pistol in his belt, reminding the twenty men behind him that there was no hurry, as the odds were only twenty to one against them.

He introduced me to Captain Cook, and we retired to a dark little cubby hole of an office in a corner of the room, where the stout sea captain told me that he had been offered command of a ship by a city syndicate which was sending out a load of Scotch whiskey to sell to the smugglers on the eastern coast of the United States.

He produced another captain who had been rum running for the last year, and from whom he was gleaning information about the tricks of the trade. This other fellow was a pale-faced, shifty-eyed individual, whose face bore the stamp of drink and loose living, and he looked as villainous a rascal as one could wish to find in a day's march.

Cook and I had several meetings with this man, and a little judicious flattery, combined with the right number of drinks, made him talk freely about the business, which at first sight seemed simple enough.

According to him a ship had to be purchased or chartered, filled with whiskey at fifty-five shillings a case, and anchored off the American coast just outside the three-mile limit. The thirsty Yankees then came flocking out in their little boats with their pockets bulging with green-backs to buy the whiskey at sixty dollars (£12) a case.

In a month the ship would be empty, and sail home with 300 hundred percent profit on the original investment.

All very simple.

He admitted that there were a few flies in the ointment, but they were such little ones that they did not matter much. For example, there was the possibility of the confiscation of the ship and cargo by the United States authorities if she went inside the three-mile limit or was blown inshore by the wind. Then there were pirates who would attack the vessel, and after murdering the crew, make away with the ship, cargo, and cash; dishonest captains and supercargoes who would run off with the money; and wily bootleggers who came out and bought large quantities for cash, paying in counterfeit notes which would not be detected until they were presented at the bank.

But all these little difficulties, he pointed out, merely showed the importance of having a captain of undoubted ability, bravery, and integrity (such as himself, for instance).

As we sat in the Bodega bar and listened to the yarns he told us, they sounded like the boastings of a drink-crazy lunatic, and that is what Cook and I thought they were. Little did I imagine at the time that in a few months I would find out by experience that all these things were true enough.

We agreed, however, that there might after all be something in what he told us, though we both considered the man himself a useless sort of fellow. We therefore got into touch with the city men whom he said were going to back him, and found, somewhat to our surprise, that they actually did exist, and, moreover, really were planning to send out a ship full of whiskey in the hope of making big profits.

For some weeks I discussed schemes with them, and also with other city financiers, reputable and otherwise, who were dallying with the idea of smuggling.

Most of them were so busy arguing about the division of the future profits that they had little time to spare for buying ships or whiskey.

There were directors' fees, managers' salaries, founders' shares, "A" preference shares, "B" preference shares, participating preference shares, ordinary shares, preferred ordinary shares, and all the tricks and wiles of the city shark for ensuring that the promoters should get the lion's share of the profits, while risking nothing save their reputation.

These people never got very far beyond talk and the printing of prospectuses, although one syndicate asked me to run across the Atlantic to look over the ground and report. I did this, and had a nice little scheme worked out for them on the Pacific seaboard; but when it came to the point they had not enough money to see it through. However, they had paid the expenses, and it had been a most interesting trip, so there was nothing to grumble about as far as I was concerned.

Eventually I ran across a group of men of a rather better type than the others; they had imported a tame American, who had a wonderful scheme of money for nothing. His name was Holder, and he was short and fat, with plaintive brown eyes, and a confidentially appealing manner.

He talked them all into a state of enthusiasm, and although my experience of get-rich-quick schemes made me regard him with a certain amount of suspicion, after hearing his tale I joined them in thinking it was worth looking into.

According to his story, there were in bond in a certain American distillery a quarter of a million gallons of rye whiskey which the Government would not release, and he, Roy Holder, alone of America's hundred million citizens, could persuade the powers that were to release it for sale to a certain Central European country for "medicinal purposes."

After it had been exported to the country in question, it was to be re-exported, sent back on a whiskey ship, and sold at sea to the rum-runners at a profit of about 500 percent.

What made the scheme look good was the fact that very little capital was required, as the sellers would ship it on credit, and take payment after it had been sold. In addition to this, Holder was full of hints about relations in Government offices and "protection" from high quarters, while a mass of official documents he produced seemed to bear out what he said.

The ins and outs of the scheme are too tedious and too involved to tell at length; at any rate, it looked sufficiently feasible for a group of businessmen to put up some money and ask me to go out with Holder to investigate the thing.

To cut a long story short, we went to the United States together, and after a land journey, there, sure enough, was a huge storehouse with thousands of barrels of rye whiskey, guarded by armed Government men.

I had secured the services of an English expert, and together we sampled the whiskey and found it good, although the average age, according to the figures stamped on the barrels, was not what Holder had told us.

Whiskey in its original state is white and clear like pure water; in England it is supposed to be matured in sherry barrels, which after some years give it a yellowish colour. The Americans, who do not drink sherry, put it into barrels which have been burned inside, and after three or four years the action of the charred wood on the whiskey turns it a rich amber colour.

I sent a long cable home saying that the whiskey was not so matured as we had been led to believe, but that otherwise the scheme seemed sound enough, and I recommended them to carry on with it. They wired back that as Holder had misrepresented one thing, he might have misrepresented others, and they would not go any further into the scheme.

From what I know now, I think it probable that if they had carried on they might have cleaned up between half a million and a million dollars with a capital expenditure of about seventy-five thousand dollars, and this with very small risk to themselves. But it is easy to be wise after the event!

I returned to New York and took a room in the Palace Hotel. Sitting on my bed and listening to the roar of the traffic far below, I felt rather disgusted with life, for here, nipped in the bud, was a scheme that should have brought both adventure and profit.

"If that fat addle-headed optimist Holder had told the truth to begin with," I thought to myself, "instead of trying to colour his story as he did, we would have the thing well under way by now, and be making a nice little pile."

I cursed him heartily at the time, but now that I know the Americans better, I realise that it was we who were to blame for not understanding him better.

Between the English and the American mentality there is a gulf as wide as the ocean that separates us. The American is first and last an enthusiast; he has some scheme or theory which he follows up with such speed and zest that he over-runs himself and treads on his own tail. The "pros" fill his whole horizon to the exclusion of the "cons." His eagerness to impress his point of view on somebody is so great that he hypnotises himself into believing his own arguments, even though he knows they are unsound. His ducks are geese, his geese are swans, his milk is cream and his cream "double cream."

The Americans generally are the world's greatest adepts at the art of kidding themselves into believing what they want to believe, and due allowance has to be made for this when dealing with them.

But perhaps it is this very enthusiasm and refusal to see difficulties ahead which enables them to tackle things which more prudent people would leave alone, and thus they make their huge successes and their equally huge failures. If they come a cropper once, they are all the more ready to take a flier next time in the hopes of recouping their losses.

My meditations were disturbed by the ringing of the telephone bell, and the cheery voice of an Englishman I knew called out, "Is that you, Barbican? Come and gnaw a bone with me at the Lunch Club at one o'clock." It was Frank Elderson, a prosperous London broker who was on a business trip to the United States, and as he would take no denial, I went downtown and inquired the way to the club.

The Lunch Club, as everyone knows, is the midday rendezvous of many of the big financiers and businessmen of the city. The fine old engravings, the excellent cooking, and the solid comfort of the place remind one of a London club, although there is a genial camaraderie among the members which is certainly not typical of English club life.

My friend Elderson was waiting in the entrance hall, and introduced me to our host, Peter Clave. He was a black-haired man of about forty-eight, with a dead white face and a gentle, almost suave manner.

We sat at a long table with a dozen other men, who seemed on terms of closest intimacy; their conversation ranged from European politics to Montana copper, from aeronautics to gardening, and there is probably no luncheon table in the world where more solid wisdom and sound finance is talked.

My right-hand neighbour remarked, "You don't know Peter well, do you? He is one of the characters of the city. Every afternoon he comes here at three o'clock, sits in the same chair in the smoking-room down below, and there dispenses wisdom and whiskey to all comers. People come to consult him about the markets, racing, politics, or anything else about which they want advice, and they always go away the better for having seen him, as his advice is usually good, and his Scotch always."

An enthusiastic conversation was going on farther up the table between Elderson and some of the members sitting near him. He was a judge of dogs and whiskey, and it appeared that several of those present, when in London, had admired his kennels, and still more his whiskey.

"Elderson, old friend," remarked the man on my right, an enormously fat cheery fellow named Rallice, "send us over a few thousand cases of that famous 'Cheviot' of yours, and the riches of the Shah of Persia will be naught compared to yours." "On behalf of the Lunch Club," he added, "I would promise you our heartfelt gratitude, and when our admiring nation puts up a statue of Mr. Volstead alongside the graven image of Liberty, we will erect one to you alongside, higher and wider."

The rest of lunch was spent in discussing the merits of various brands of whiskey and, more important still, how to obtain them. I knew nothing about the workings of prohibition, so asked Rallice to tell me something about it.

"Well, it's like this," he said; "while most of us were away soldiering, the women and the men who stopped at home put one over us, and we came home and found it done.

"The temperance people were worked up to a frenzy by an astute political gang, who used them as a stalking-horse. It's all so complicated that it would take a week to explain it properly. The long and short of it is that a man named Volstead was put up to promote a Federal Prohibition law, which was passed, and it is now illegal to import, make, sell, or transport alcoholic drinks.

"If you want to hiccough, you've got to get a Government permit.

"An exception is made in the case of wines and spirits for sacramental and medicinal purposes, so now if you want to get a drink you've got to pay a rabbi, a doctor, or a bootlegger."

"I've heard a lot about bootleggers. What exactly are the animals?" I inquired.

"The word was first used in this country for the Kentucky men who made moonshine whiskey in hidden stills in the mountains, like your Irish do in the bogs and bills. They wore big thigh-boots and slipped a couple of bottles down each boot when they went to call on their customers. Now the word is used of any of the million and one men in this country who make their living by selling liquor illegally.

"Many of these fellows are immensely wealthy and as far as turnover goes, the bootlegging is said to be the third largest industry in the country.

"We have to pay sixty or seventy dollars a case for whiskey which costs a sixth of that in Scotland, so between Glasgow and our houses there is a nice little profit of 400 or 500 percent for somebody. Even then we are not sure what we are getting, for after it gets here it is faked and adulterated, so that now the number of deaths from alcoholic poisoning is greater than before prohibition. It is a rotten law, and the sooner it is repealed the better for everybody."

"I'm not so sure about that," remarked an Englishman on the other side of the table. "I have been out west looking at some big engineering works, and I was told that since prohibition there has been a drop in the number of working hours lost per week, especially on Monday mornings, and a general upward trend in the efficiency of the men and the well-being of their families."

"Sometime when I have a few weeks to spare I will have an argument with you about it," answered Rallice good-humouredly, rising from the table.

As Elderson and I left the club together, I remarked to him, "The sun begins to shine through the clouds. You and I will bring out a shipload of that Cheviot and make our fortunes. You shall have the privilege of finding the money while I do the work over here. Your sole duty will be to sit at home in an easy-chair adding up the credit side of our pass-book, while I run in five hundred cases every dark night for these poor thirsty souls."

"You can count me out of your nefarious schemes," he replied ungraciously. "I have quite enough honest business of my own without resorting to crime."

I dined with him that night, and succeeded in making him promise a certain amount of help, although he stubbornly refused to put up any money or to have to do with breaking the law.

"You are a wild buccaneering sort of fellow, without wives, children, or responsibilities," he remarked "so if you are really bent on seeing the inside of a Yankee jail, I might help you to get there out of consideration for your family. It will be comforting for them to know that you are housed, clothed, fed, and out of mischief for a period exceeding ten, but not exceeding twenty, years."

"You really are too kind," I murmured.

"I will go so far," he continued, "as to give you introductions to some of the men with whom I do business. I would tell them that, as far as I know and up to a point, I believe you to be honest. Even if you were not, I doubt if you would have sufficient brains to swindle an American, so they will be moderately safe in dealing with you in any case. Also I will tell you the name of the people who make Cheviot. But don't blame me when you get into trouble."

"All right, you old Pharisee!" I answered. "Go ahead and give me the letters and names."

Next morning, armed with Elderson's introductions, I sallied forth from the hotel to beard certain big businessmen of the city, to sell them whiskey I had not got, and did not know how to get to them (even if I had it).

On the whole they were very civil, although some of them showed by their behaviour that they considered every one in the "liquor business" quite outside the pale; but as I was not particularly interested in the Yankee pale, I did not lose any sleep over this.

At the end of a few days there were provisional orders for about five hundred cases, although most people expressed their doubts as to the possibility of getting it to them. After some palaver I usually ended up by saying, "Well, if the whiskey does get here in six or eight weeks, you will be good for fifty cases?"

They usually agreed, and some ordered ten, and others twenty-five or fifty cases. The figure I quoted was rather above the current price; but Elderson's introduction, the reputation of the whiskey, and the fact that they knew it really was coming from Scotland, made them willing to pay the extra amount.

It seemed that there would be no difficulty in disposing of a thousand or more cases once they arrived.

But it is one thing to promise a man fifty cases of whiskey in America, and another to get them there from Scotland. Having got so far, the next step was to find out how to spirit them from Glasgow into the houses of the different people who wanted them. As Rallice, the man by whom I had sat at the Lunch Club, struck me as being a knowledgeable sort of fellow, I sought him out to ask for his advice.

"Do you remember saying to Elderson at lunch the other day that you would like some of that Cheviot you used to drink at his house? If you will tell me how to get it here, I will send you some along."

"That's easier said than done," he answered, "for if it were easy, every flat-footed boob in the country would be doing it, and there would be no profit. Take my advice and leave the whole darned business alone. You would be up against the law, and would likely end in jail. Being a foreigner, they would hand it you good and plenty.

"Your whiskey would probably be caught by the coastguard. If it escaped them, the prohibition agents would get it on shore. Besides this there are pirates, or hijackers as they are called, who would rob you, and there is no redress against them, for it is a case of 'dog eat dog.' If they are outside the law, so are you."

"You would be an outsider butting into a semi-criminal business, in which all the rough-necks of America are engaged. I don't know much about you, but if you will pardon me saying so, you look the sort of Englishman whose ancestors for several hundred years have shot partridges and ruled niggers, but never done any work or earned any money. How can you hope to compete with the cleverest brains in the American underworld?

"Do you think they are going to stand by and watch you take away their business? No, siree, not by a jugful! If you are not found drowned or lying on the beach with a bullet in your back, they will frame you up and send you across the road for the longest holiday you ever had in your life. Besides all this, we have an ancient American saying, 'He that lyeth down with dogs shall rise with fleas.' You take my advice, young fellow, and leave it alone."

All this was rather depressing, for Rallice seemed to be a level-headed sort of man who would not give warning lightly.

"Well," I replied, "I am going to have a dip at it, and if you can give me some sort of a starting point, it would be a great help."

"I don't know any more about the inside working of things than you do, but if you are really bent on going ahead, I can give you the address of bootleggers. They might be able to put you in touch with the right people. They are two brothers who are a bit above the ordinary run of men in the business. They live in East Sixty-first Street, and their name is Currant."

After thanking Rallice for his help, I went back to my hotel and telephoned to the Currants, who said they would come round to see me at once.

While waiting for their arrival, I wondered what a live bootlegger would look like. I was prepared to see anything blow in, from a furtive-looking individual with blue spectacles and a large Gladstone bag, to an unshaven desperado with high boots and a gun on each hip.

But when they did arrive, instead of the heavy stage villains I had pictured, there entered two immaculately dressed young men, with the very latest things in the way of cashmere half-hose and gents' silk shirtings. At first they were rather reticent about business affairs; but when they understood that it was Rallice who had recommended them to me, they became quite chatty and opened out their hearts.

"Yes, sir, we supply liquor to all the most exclusive clubs in the city. You see, we have exceptional qualifications such as no one else in the liquor business possesses. We happen by an accident of birth to be on a different social plane to the others, so we can meet the Astorbilts and the Vanderheims and the aristocracy of the country in their clubs on terms of perfect equality. We do our business as gentlemen among gentlemen. We never sell anything but the very best; we could not afford to do it, as our trade is built up on the reputation we have gained for giving a fair and square deal to everyone.

"But what can we supply you with?

"We have a little pre-war Johnnie Walker Black Label in stock, though it is going fast."

As soon as I could get a word in edgeways, I said, "As a matter of fact I don't want to buy anything, but to sell. I have orders for a very special whiskey from certain people who want it delivered to their houses, and I need someone who will buy it off the ship and deliver it to them. Can you arrange that?"

"Sure we can," answered the little Currant, who did most of the talking; "we have a complete organisation of boats and trucks and men and warehouses. How much a case would it cost off the ship?"

As I knew absolutely nothing about prices, my chief idea was to extract information from them before getting down to business.

It is an excellent maxim in life to let the other fellow do the talking, and, as a general rule, there is little difficulty in doing this, since the average man is far more pleased to find a sympathetic listener than he is to meet a fluent talker.

In this case the Currants chatted freely, and unconsciously gave away a lot of information that I needed before we got down to discussing prices.

The scheme that they drew up finally was that they would buy for cash from the ship outside the three-mile limit, and pay thirty dollars a case if they could sell it to the consumer for seventy-five dollars.

"We figure it out like this," the younger one remarked, jotting down the following figures on the back of an envelope:—

> "$30 to be paid to you on the ship,
>   5 for the boatman who runs it ashore,
>   3 for the truckman who brings it up to the city,
>   2 for storage when it gets here,
>   3 for 'protection,'
>   2 for the man who delivers it to the customer's house,
>  30 for ourselves for handling the job and
>       the risk to our capital,
>  ___
> $75 to the consumer."

Passing lightly over the question of figures, I said, "Before buying the whiskey and shipping it out from England, I should require a guarantee that you would take delivery of it when it arrived—a deposit of, say, five dollars a case, to be sent to a bank in London when the goods were ready to ship."

"Certainly that could be arranged," replied the accommodating little Currant. "Of course, we can't put anything in writing, as the transaction would not be legally enforceable. But you yourself are a gentleman, and you are dealing with gentlemen, so we will make a gentleman's agreement to send you a deposit of five dollars a case when the goods are ready to start. Positively you may rely on us to handle the whole thing to your entire satisfaction, and we will make a pile of money working together."

We then went into detailed arrangements about sending the money to a certain London bank, whence it was not to be released until various conditions had been complied with by both parties.

As they were leaving, one of them suddenly asked the name of the ship on which the whiskey was coming out. Not having the remotest idea myself, I side-tracked the question, and hoped that they were not bluffing me to the same extent that I was bluffing them.

After much hand-shaking and many expressions of goodwill, the two young exquisites took their departure, leaving behind them an atmosphere of integrity, gentlemanliness, and efficiency, tinged with a slight aroma of lily-of-the-valley scent.

# CHAPTER II

## A VISIT TO A RUM-SHIP

BEFORE leaving London I had received an introduction to the owner of a rum running ship called the *Mermaid*, which was then lying off the coast not very far from the city. Roy Holder knew the man, whose name was Swivel, and offered to take me out to him.

He was very despondent about the failure of his rye whiskey scheme, although, as I had pointed out to him, if he had stuck to the truth all would have been well. It appeared that he wanted to get some whiskey from the *Mermaid* on credit, to help him to build up his crumbling fortunes.

Nobody seems to know why the vessels in the whiskey business are called "rum-runners," for they seldom have rum on board, and when they do, it is in very small quantities; probably it is one of the many words used by the American journalist in his love of alliteration.

There are several other words used in the trade which need explanation.

The "rum-runner" is the aristocrat of the profession. He is the man on the ship which lies anchored on the ocean, and he has to contend with storms, pirates, mutiny, and the other perils of the sea. He is the owner of the small boat which goes out in all weathers to run in a load of contraband, he and his mate playing a lone hand against storms, fogs, revenue cutters, prohibition agents, police, and hijackers. By day and night he drives cars and great motor-trucks at breakneck speed for hundreds of miles at a stretch, and stays for no man. He runs big risks, and often dies in his boots under the sky; but he is a real man, for no weakling can survive.

"Bootleggers" are the retail merchants who sell by the case, or even by the bottle, and for some reason the word is a term of reproach even in the trade itself, and small wonder, for among them there are some pretty slippery gentlemen.

The big wholesalers, who organise and finance the business, are known as "operators"; they often put through deals involving hundreds of thousands of dollars, and always by word of mouth, as it is not safe to put anything in writing.

"Hijackers" are the desperadoes who prey on the rum-runners, robbing them at the point of the revolver; they are often closely connected with the legitimate operators, and usually sell to them the booty they have wrested from others. They themselves are usually unsuccessful rum-runners whom misfortune has rendered desperate.

Early one morning I met Holder at the railway station, and we took train to a little sea-side town, where we hailed a taxi and went bumping and lurching through the ill-kept streets, and then across some desolate marsh-lands.

The driver pulled up beside a collection of tumble-down wooden houses which stood on the muddy brink of a tidal estuary, and we entered a rickety building, which announced itself as "Claridge's Hotel, first-class accommodation for tourists, hunters, fishermen, and sportsmen; bait provided."

Mine host was a tough-looking citizen, with fair hair and a battered face, and he answered to the name of Fritz. He received us in a rather surly manner until my presence was explained by Holder, whereupon he became more cordial, and ushered us into a bar, where a dozen gentlemen of the smuggling profession were drinking neat whiskey from little glasses at half a dollar a shot. Only soft drinks were in evidence behind the bar, but there were bottles of "hard stuff" on a shelf underneath the counter, and apparently anyone who walked in could get a drink by asking for it.

The Americans drink spirits very much like the Russians drink vodka; they fill up a small glass, throw back their heads, and toss it down at one gulp, following it by a "chaser" of water from a tumbler. So quickly does drink succeed drink that often they can be heard to splash on the top of the previous one.

The ordinary American has very little appreciation of the flavour of what he is drinking, but judges it by the amount of "kick" there is to it. If it burns the throat on the way down, or has evil after-effects, it is called "raw," and is not liked; if it has neither of these qualities it is called "smooth," and meets with approval; but it must always have plenty of kick to it, whether it be whiskey, port, or beer.

Even a new-comer like myself could sort out the assembly into their various branches of the profession. The bronzed hard-featured men, lolling against the bar, doing more in the way of chewing than drinking, were obviously the rum-runners, and their conversation was of boats, motors, and revenue cutters. Two fat Jews, with rotund bellies and creases of fat hanging over the backs of their collars, were talking boastfully of big deals they were putting through, one of them apparently owning a schooner which was anchored off-shore. I put them down as operators, and the mixed lot of minor fry that hovered round the two Israelites were apparently bootleggers, who had come down from the city to buy their wares.

Holder sidled up to one of the rum-runners, a good-looking young fellow with regular features, and after standing him a drink, began to dicker with him to take us out on his boat to the *Mermaid*. Finally he agreed to do this for the sum of seventy-five dollars, so we trooped out of the bar and embarked in a boat about thirty feet long with a large motor amidships.

Our boatman, whose name was Archie, started up the motor, which roared like an aeroplane engine; the boat shot from the dock, and went scudding along the creek between flat marshy meadows, leaving a trail of foam and bubbles behind. She vibrated from end to end, and the noise of the 100 horsepower engine was so great that conversation was impossible. Besides Holder and Archie, there was the engineer, a thin little rat of a fellow, whose pale blue eyes squinted painfully.

After some miles the ocean came into sight, and a line of white-capped breakers stretched in front of us; Archie slowed down the engine, and made for a gap in the long line of waves. The boat hit the first breaker with a resounding whack, which made her quiver like a nervous horse; she hit each wave with a thud as though it were solid, and sent a cloud of spray into the air. After half a minute of this we were through the breakers and in the smooth open sea.

Archie rammed the throttle open, and we shot forward with such a jerk that I was thrown on my back in the bottom of the boat. The bows lifted themselves in the air as we roared along at thirty knots. The sun was shining, the sky was blue, and the warm wind, laden with salt spray, whipped against our faces; next to flying or skiing down the glistening side of a Swiss mountain, it was the most pleasurable sensation I had ever enjoyed.

Holder pointed to a ship some eight miles away on the horizon, and as we came nearer she proved to be a large three-masted yacht of graceful lines, painted white, with a golden figure-head of a mermaid under the bowsprit.

After a while we drew up alongside and clambered up the rope-ladder that had been let down by the crew.

Instead of the ruffianly crowd of semi-pirate which I had expected to find on a rum ship, we were greeted by several smartly dressed officers in yachting caps, and there was an air of orderliness and discipline everywhere which seemed more in keeping with a man-of-war than with a smuggler.

After many puffings and blowings, Holder hoisted his plump carcass up the side of the ship, and was greeted by a tall stout man in a navy blue suit, whose cap bore the badge of a well-known British yacht club. He had the assured manner of a naval officer, and after giving an order or making a statement, he would snap his jaws together as though he were thinking to himself, "I am a man whose word is like the Rock of Gibraltar."

Brisbane Swivel took us all into a comfortably furnished deck-house, which apparently had been the smoking-room of the ship when she had been a yacht. Shelves of books, an open fireplace, comfortably upholstered seats, and a magnificent electrically-driven gramophone gave the place an air of comfort and even luxury.

We all sat round the table while a little steward in a white coat poured out drinks. After a time I took Swivel aside to give him various messages from our mutual friend in London, and he gave me some telegrams to send off for him when I got back to shore.

He said that he was averaging about thirty dollars a case, and that although sales were rather slower than he had expected, he hoped to be home in a few weeks with his cargo all sold, and to bring out fresh consignment.

"How much would you want to freight out a thousand cases for me?" I asked him.

"Ten dollars a case," he replied instantly, "to be paid as they leave the ship, and, of course, they would come at your risk, and you would have to take out your own insurance."

He definitely promised to do this, and I shelved the question of price, remarking that we would leave that to be discussed when we met at home. He then showed me over his ship. Most of the saloons and cabins below deck had been torn out, and the space was piled with thousands of cases of whiskey of many brands.

After having tea on board, we climbed down into the little boat and sped for the shore, which was plainly visible.

Holder had apparently transacted some satisfactory business with Swivel, and this, together with several drinks before tea, during his tea, in his tea, and after tea, had put him in good fettle; the vibration of the engine made his fat neck and cheeks shake like a jelly on a Great Eastern Railway dining car, but the more he shook, the more he smiled.

"Who is the pale-eyed fellow?" I asked him, nodding towards the engineer, who was oiling the clutch with his back turned towards us.

"He's all right," Holder shouted back, making his voice heard with difficulty above the din of the engine. "He's quite a good scout, though he's in a bit of trouble just now, poor boy."

I wondered whether he had lost his wife, or what the trouble was, and questioned Holder more closely.

"Oh, he's had a bit of hard luck, and they are looking for him. But he will be all right in a few weeks; it will all blow over."

Holder was so reticent about the exact nature of the "trouble" that he aroused my curiosity, and after he had taken a few more drinks from a bottle which Swivel had slipped into his pocket as he was leaving, I questioned him further.

"Well, you know, he had a buddy, and they went into a liquor deal together, and the other fellow double-crossed him; they had some sort of an argument on the beach one night, and the other fellow's widow got rather nasty about it, so Sam has had to cop a sneak and keep out of the way for a bit."

For some reason which they did not explain, the boatmen would not return to "Claridge's" until after dusk, so having reached the desolate marsh-land, they moored the boat to the bank, and we all settled down to snooze. The accommodation in the little cabin was rather restricted, and we had to lie at close quarters. I found my head pillowed on the arm of the gentleman who was said to have slipped a knife into his buddy's gizzard not so long ago, but the keen salt air had made me sleepy, as it would have taken more than this to disturb my slumbers. The journey was resumed at dusk, we arrived chez Fritz an hour later, creeping alongside the wharf with the engine barely ticking over, making no more noise than a water rat.

"Lend me seventy-five bucks to pay the boatman," whispered Holder, as we clambered ashore, thus accounting for his kindness in offering to escort me to the *Mermaid*.

After a good supper of fish and "hen-fruit," as Holder called the eggs, we took a taxi back to the station and trained to the city.

As I lay awake that night thinking of the day's doings, it looked as though things were beginning to shape themselves pretty well, for what a few days ago had been merely a wild-cat scheme in my head was now within the realm of practical polities.

Firstly, there were the buyers waiting in the city.

Secondly, there were the Currants, who would pay for the whiskey on the ship and transport it to the buyers.

Thirdly, Swivel would bring the cases from Scotland to the three-mile limit.

The missing link so far was the cash wherewith to buy the Cheviot from the distillery, but this was a ditch to be crossed when we came to it.

I returned to England a few days later, and with some misgivings went to Charing Cross to see my good friend Cox, who told me that there was not enough cash left to do the thing on the scale I intended, and he appeared to be so busy moving house that I did not care to trouble him about such trivial matter as a loan of a few thousand pounds (without security). So now I had to tackle the question of finance.

The scheme was explained to some sporting friends, who agreed to put up the money, and enough was subscribed to buy a thousand cases.

Swivel had now returned with his ship empty, and when I met him in his club in Pall Mall he was full of success and good spirits.

He eventually agreed to take the Cheviot across for seven dollars a case, which was a very high price; but the other rum-runners with whom I had parleyed, although willing to do it much cheaper, were tough-looking customers, who might have drunk the whiskey and knocked me on the head when I came out to get it. So it seemed best to send it with Swivel and regard the extra money as being spent on insurance against having the whiskey stolen, for he seemed reliable as compared to the others.

We discussed the whole adventure over an excellent lunch at the Ritz, and he ended by asking me to act as his agent ashore in America, for which be offered to pay a handsome commission on the whole cargo, which was to consist of twenty thousand cases. It sounded too much like easy money to be true, but as we sat there drinking the champagne he had ordered to celebrate the occasion, he was so cheerful and full of hope that it really seemed as though we might pull off some big coups between us.

Swivel was an unusual type of man, with many queer contradictions in his character. When he liked he could be an excellent host and an amusing raconteur, whose tales, however, always centred round himself and his own exploits. His opinion on men and matters was instant and definite, and his self-confidence boundless. As a general rule, suspicious of everyone and everything, he would suddenly take it into his head to trust somebody and often unwisely, for, like most egotists, he was neither quick nor accurate at summing up other people. A born gambler and bluffer, he was always ready to take risks, in the city, on the sea, or anywhere else.

It was arranged that he would pick up the Cheviot at the Continental port where he was going to load, and he showed me how to use the cipher which he used for communicating with home, so that we could send cables and letters to one another which would be unintelligible to anyone else.

As I was leaving he pulled a couple of envelopes out of his pocket, remarking, "Here are letters from two fellows who say they want to buy from the *Mermaid*; you might see them when you get over there and send them along to the ship. The devil knows how they got hold of my address. And here is a list of what we are bringing out. Get the best prices that you can. We will be anchored off Cape Ozone six weeks from today, and if I make any changes in my plans, I will send you a wireless message. You will have no difficulty in finding us, as every boatman knows the *Mermaid*."

A fortnight later I was on board an Atlantic liner on my way to the United States, having invested in Cheviot literally everything I had in the world. After paying for my ticket, there was a solitary ten-ner left for hotel bills and other expenses while waiting for the arrival of the ship.

"If the *Mermaid* does not turn up, things will be a bit awkward," I could not help thinking to myself. However, this did not worry me overmuch, as things usually come out all right for those who do their damnedest and leave the rest to luck; while, if the worst came to the worst, it would not have been the first time that I had worked my way across the Atlantic.

The only hitch so far had been the fact that the Currants had not sent the deposit they had promised, despite sundry cables I had sent to them asking for it. But if they failed to live up to their promises, I hoped that it might be possible to get Holder or somebody else to do the job.

# CHAPTER III

## BACK IN AMERICA

THE first thing to do was to see the Currants, and they arrived at my hotel as immaculate and gentlemanly as before.

They started with a long story, plausible enough, as to why it had been impossible to send the money they had promised.

"Well, anyway," I answered, "the ship is now on her way here, and we must get on with the job."

"To be quite candid with you, Mr. Barbican," said the elder brother, "we have been talking it over, and we have come to the conclusion that your proposition is not attractive enough for us. You see, we can get any bootlegger to deliver Scotch to our customers for fifty dollars a case; we pay the bootlegger fifty, charge the customer seventy-five, and clear twenty-five dollars with no risk and without having any capital out. We are first and last salesmen.

"Your proposition is that we should pay before we get the merchandise, take all the risk, do four times more work than we do now, and all for the same money.

"Now, as a businessman, Mr. Barbican, you can see that it is not a sound proposition. Of course we are sorry that you should be disappointed, but frankly, as between gentlemen, you would turn it down if you were in our place, wouldn't you?

"But we may be able to work together yet. If you would give us the whiskey for twenty-five dollars a case on credit, we could split the shore profits three ways after the goods had been paid for by the buyer."

I rather thought that the two gentlemanly brothers, guessing that I had no other strings to my bow, were planning to squeeze better terms out of me, so saying that I would think it over, I bade them adieu.

I did not tell them what I thought of them, for in rum running, more than in any other business, it is well to avoid making enemies.

After they had faded away things seemed rather flat, and there were visions of the thousand cases of Cheviot rocking on the ocean week after week, with nobody to take them off the ship. Smuggling may not be difficult for a man in his native land where he knows the people and their habits, but in a strange country, without introductions or friends, it seemed no easy matter to get those thousand cases through the coastguard, the prohibition forces, and the police, and land them safely in houses scattered all over the city.

Holder I could not find; there were rumours that he was in prison, and except for him and the Currants I could not think of a soul that I knew. I then bethought me of the two letters that Swivel had given me on leaving home. One was addressed to him from a street close by my hotel, and ran as follows:—

"*Telephone:* Uptown 5757.                    1444 West 34th Street,
                                                                June 192x.

"DEAR SIR,—Being interested in the class of goods you brought over in the *Mermaid*, and finding their quality satisfactory, I am inclined to purchase from you again, being a large buyer.

"Will you kindly tell me how to get into touch with your American agent, as I shall shortly be in the market for considerable quantities of goods.—Yours faithfully,

                                                                "H. J. BAYNE."

"I suppose this letter is genuine?" I asked myself somewhat doubtfully. "But 'nothing venture, nothing win,' so here's for taking a chance on it. Perhaps it may lead to some starting-point."

The hotel telephone exchange put me through to the number, and a man answered from the other end.

"I have a letter you wrote to a friend of mine in England asking about some goods he is bringing over on a ship," I said. "I am here in the Copley Hotel in case you want to call and see me."

"Yes, yes, I remember perfectly," was the reply. "I will come round to see you within the next half-hour."

The voice, instead of being in the dialect of the country, was that of an educated Englishman, and might easily have belonged to a rather pompous country squire, so I awaited his arrival with some interest, wondering whom he might be.

Presently there was a knock at the door, and in walked a little, shabby, flabby man, with a pasty fish-like face and turned-up nose. He held out a cold limp hand which felt like a dead man's and made me shudder when it touched mine.

In appearance he was beneath contempt, although proficient

21

enough in the way of talking. He professed to be on intimate terms with various whiskey peers whose names are household words, but whose acquaintance I myself had not the honour of claiming.

We both fenced round the subject of business for a time, and I let him do the talking, as I did not intend to say anything to a stranger that might incriminate me.

Eventually he seemed assured that my intentions were honest, and became quite confidential. He said that he knew all the big bootleggers of the city, could put me in touch with them, and sell the whole shipload quickly—for a small commission, of course.

He asked for a list of the cargo, which he wrote down as I gave it to him, repeating each word after he had written it.

> "2500   cases of Dewar.
> 500   "   Four Crowns.
> 4300   "   Peter Dawson.
> 3000   "   Ambassador.
> 2500   "   Old Smuggler.
> 3000   "   Lawson's Liqueur.
> 2400   "   Holt's Pimple Bottles."

"Dimple Bottles," I corrected him.

"Pimple Bottles," he said once more, repeating his mistake, and I did not take the trouble to correct him a second time, but continued with the list of my wares.

For several days the little fellow was assiduous in his attentions, and used to take me round to the offices of various bootleggers, trying to arrange for the sale of the yacht's cargo.

Nothing was accomplished, because most of the men wanted to buy too cheaply or on credit, or else on closer acquaintance proved to be only intermediaries, who hoped to collect a commission for an introduction to somebody else.

The offices in which these men did business were camouflaged under all sorts of names; the commonest seemed to be "Real Estate" and "Theatrical Agents." Their furniture was of the scantiest description; there was seldom more than a couple of telephones, a desk, a few chairs, half a dozen cuspidors, and sometimes one or two good-looking telephone girls.

If they saw signs of an approaching storm they could "up-anchor" and be slipping down the fire-escape stairs inside of five seconds, with the loss of only a few dollars' worth of property.

Little Bayne used to write me long letters containing various "propositions," but none of them was any good; queer typewritten epistles they were, with the lines all crowded together, and the green ink showing through the back of the thin cheap paper.

It did not take long to find out that this little bird was not worth any powder and shot, and as somehow I did not like the look of the other letter Swivel had given me, I was back again in the same position as when I had landed a week ago.

"Well, I must try something else," I thought to myself. "You've got to turn over a thousand stones before you find one worm."

In a strange place the most casual acquaintance is a God-send, and I suddenly remembered the Lunch Club and the two men whom I had met there. I went down that afternoon, and found Peter Clave sitting in the smoking-room, a circle gathered round listening to his dissertation on the question of German reparations.

I could not get a word alone with him, but the cheery Rallice came in, and ponderously taking a seat by my side, remarked, "So you are not taking my advice to leave the thing alone? Well, I think it very sporting of you to try, and here's wishing you the best of luck," he added, tossing off a three-finger tot of Clave's "White Horse."

I told him how the Currants had failed to come up to scratch, and asked him what he would advise me to do next.

"I know the very man to help you," he answered. "Come and dine with me tonight, and I will see if I can produce him for you."

He motored me out to his home in the suburbs, a delightful place which reminded me of an English manor-house, but it was more comfortable, as there was a bathroom for every bedroom.

I felt a little awkward coming to his home and meeting his wife and family, for I had soon learned that everyone connected with the whiskey industry in the United States is looked upon as being an outlaw; but they treated the whole thing as a joke, which they could afford to do, since they belonged to the class which makes conventions rather than follows them.

There were cocktails before dinner, mixed by my host's own skilful hand; sherry and champagne during dinner; port with the dessert and liqueurs with the coffee—all of the very best.

"You seem to do fairly well considering that you live in a prohibition country," I could not help remarking.

"Yes," he replied, "I had a good pre-prohibition stock, and there has not been overmuch difficulty about filling up the gaps in the cellars since then; it is only a question of price. I will go and telephone to that man for you, and see if he can come round; he is sure to be able to help you in one way or another."

In half an hour the butler announced a visitor, and Rallice and I went into the library to see him. He was a tall clean-shaven man with dark hair and a sallow complexion; his arms and shoulders were magnificently proportioned, but, like many city Americans who have passed the thirty mark, he was already running to fat.

"Mr. Barbican, meet Mr. Tom Hoppit," said Rallice, this being the transatlantic way of introducing two people. "You can speak quite plainly to Mr. Hoppit, as he and I are old friends."

I told the visitor briefly what the situation was—that someone was needed to buy the Scotch on the ship and deliver it to the buyers in the city.

He listened attentively, and when I had finished he nodded moodily, remarking, "Sure thing, I can go to work and fix that for you."

He was a difficult man to sum up, for his face never changed its expression, and he had not the flow of words with which so many of his countrymen are gifted. The astute American is a past master in the art of hiding himself when meeting a stranger. Sometimes he assumes the camouflage of silence, and sometimes throws up a smoke-screen of words, and of the two the camouflage is the less easy to penetrate.

It transpired later that Tom Hoppit was born in America of German parents, and I found it an intensely interesting study to watch the struggle between heredity and environment in this first generation of native-born Americans. In a country like the United States, where the different races of which the nation is composed are not yet welded into a homogeneous whole, it is essential for the businessman to understand the psychology of the various peoples of Europe, and make due allowance for these influences when dealing with his cosmopolitan fellow-countrymen.

Having made an appointment to meet me the next day, Hoppit took his leave.

"There he is," remarked Rallice. "I don't know much about him, except that he has to do with the liquor business, so I don't guarantee his honesty. If I were you I would stick to cash transactions; if he is any use to you, use him; if not, drop him."

It was now late, and as Rallice hospitably pressed me to stay the night, I did so, and went up to the city with him in the morning.

Before leaving England I had asked my family solicitor if he would tell me the name of a good lawyer on the other side, one to whom I could confide my business and rely upon to get me out of any difficulties in which I might become involved.

"Yes," said my man of law, "Laurence Finnigan is the man for you, a shrewd hard fellow, of good standing in his profession, and well in with the politicians. In addition to this, I believe he has already been involved in some way with the liquor business. You could not do better than confide in him."

I therefore went to this man's office, which was in an enormous skyscraper downtown. He was a tall, lean, dark man, with a rat-trap mouth set in a long face. He was obviously an able fellow, but his poker face did not give any information beyond this. However, my lawyer knew America, and, moreover, was a pretty shrewd judge of character, so it seemed safe to go on his recommendation.

I told him quite frankly about my business, and wound up by saying, "It is to be hoped that your services will not be required, Mr. Finnigan, but if they are, may I depend on you to see me through?"

"Certainly," he answered. "If there is any trouble the main thing to do is to keep your mouth tight shut and send for me. Remember that many people convict themselves before their attorney can reach them."

So we parted on the best of terms, after he had waived aside my suggestion of a retaining fee.

I came away recalling the words of Benjamin Franklin

"God works Wonders now and then,
Behold a Lawyer, an Honest Man,"

and wondered whether Finnigan was one of God's wonders or not.

The same day Hoppit came to the hotel saying that everything was arranged with his partner, and that they were ready to begin work as soon as the *Mermaid* showed up. After a good deal of talk, the following terms were agreed upon:—

| | |
|---|---|
| $30 | to be paid to me before the Cheviot left the ship. |
| 10 | to be allowed for expenses of landing and delivery. |
| 10 | profit to Hoppit. |
| 10 | profit to his partner. |
| 10 | profit to me. |
| $70 | to be paid by the buyer. |

It was now time that the *Mermaid* should be here, so one day I took train from the city and once more entered the hostelry which catered for "tourists, hunters, fishermen, and sportsmen."

A score of men of the same type as before were standing along the bar drinking spirits at half a dollar a shot, and they looked askance at me until the surly Fritz gave me a condescending nod.

"Looking for the *Mermaid?*" he asked; "I guess she ain't here."

"No, she ain't here," remarked a tall bronzed man, spitting in the stove. "I was out there all morning looking for Bill's schooner with the rye on her, and there ain't no three-masters out there."

The boatman Archie was there, so I asked him to have a drink, which Fritz poured out of a "Peter Dawson" bottle. It was vile stuff, and Archie pulled a long face as be tossed it down.

"Bum hooch," he remarked, "but it's probably some of the phoney stuff off the *Kyletown*. You watch me, Mr. Barbican, and I will show you how to get a 100 percent drink in this one- horse joint."

"Say, Fritz," he called out "this party here wants you to have a drink on him, so come and poison yourself along with us!"

Fritz ambled to our end of the bar and poured out three little glasses of whiskey, also from a "Peter Dawson" bottle; but it was a genuine one, which he kept hidden under the counter for his own private consumption.

I afterwards found out that the *Kyletown* was a large steamer con- taining over fifty thousand cases. A few thousand of these were gen- uine Scotch whiskey, and the rest a spurious whiskey made in Germany, but with the labels, corks, bottles, and cases a perfect imita- tion of the leading Scotch brands. Each of these cases cost about a sixth of the price of the real thing, so the promoters made a colossal profit.

The swindle was largely engineered by an Englishman who unfor- tunately had held a temporary commission in the Royal Navy, and used his very temporary naval rank to inspire the confidence of the Americans. He brought out several shiploads of this "moonshine," and made a lot of money.

[I met him recently in the Strand, and felt no regret when he told me that his German and American confederates had swindled him out of every dollar he had made.]

Nine more days went by without any news of the yacht, and lit- erally my last dollar had been spent in hiring boats to look for her. My assets, although actually liquid, were not realisable while lost on the ocean, and I had gambled my last shilling on the whiskey.

If Swivel had been delayed or anything had gone wrong, he had wireless and could have communicated with me, so I was entirely at a loss to know what had happened.

On the tenth day, having returned to the city, I was stopped in the street by a Jewish gentleman with a large white face.

"Isn't you the party as is looking for the *Mermaid?*" he asked,

Not knowing who he was, I played the village idiot, and asked him what he was talking about.

"You don't remember me? I was at Fritz's when you came back

after looking for the yacht the other day," he said. "I hear she is off Hawkes Point, and has been there for some days."

"I am much obliged to you," I answered, "and shall be even more so if you can tell me how to get there."

"Surely! You take the train to Hawkes Bay, a little one-horse burg down by the sea; if you ain't acquainted there, ask for Josiah Jones. He is a fisherman there, and would likely take you out to the ship; anyways, he will know if she is there or not."

So with rising hopes I borrowed ten dollars from a friendly Englishman I knew, and took the train, for Hawkes Bay.

It was a wearisome journey in an incredibly slow train that seemed to spend all its energies in stopping at small stations and whistling at level crossings.

But at length we arrived at a straggling collection of wooden huts, which crowded one another down to the water's edge. There was not a blade of grass or a tree or a flower in sight; there were no roads, but just cart tracks among the huts, which were surrounded by garbage, tin cans, and fishing gear.

After inquiring of some of the fishermen who were standing about, I found Josiah's house. The door was opened by a sloe-eyed woman, who said that her husband was away, and that she did not know when he would be back.

It was difficult to know what the next move should be, as there was no means of guessing whether the natives, if they knew my business, would be most likely to hand me over to the police as an alien criminal, or receive me with open arms as a brother smuggler.

I wandered down to the little pier, and watched some men landing fish from a smack and loading it on a motor truck.

Offering the driver a cigar, I began chatting with him, and gradually worked the conversation round to what I wanted.

"Could I get a boat to take me out fishing?" I asked.

"Guess so. How far do you want to go?"

"Ten or twelve miles," I answered.

"Looking for a ship?" the man queried knowingly.

"Maybe," I replied non-committally.

"Try John Blake at the green house over there," he said. "I guess he might take you out as a favour."

Strolling over to the house I found a tall bronzed man of about forty working at a carpenter's bench outside his door; a large pair of round horn spectacles made him look like a wise old owl.

"Sure I could take you out," he answered readily enough; "and if the ship is there we'll find her. I know the ocean round here just like you know the back of your hand."

27

In half an hour we were at sea in a ten-ton fishing smack driven by a heavy-duty gasolene engine. We pounded along the coast until we rounded a headland and met the full force of the ocean, unbroken by land for thousands of miles. The little boat rose and fell between the huge rollers, and wallowed so heavily from side to side that I had to cling to the mast to keep my footing.

The sturdy John, clad in brilliant yellow oilskins, stood firmly implanted at the wheel, staring steadfastly ahead, and in half an hour we were in calmer water.

"Even on the calmest day it's rough here," he remarked; "it's a tide-rip. Someday, when you are coming back in a breeze of wind you'd be glad to give fifty cases of booze to be safe ashore. But it don't mean a thing to me. I come out here when the waves are forty feet high."

In another hour there came into sight several schooners anchored in the ocean under bare poles.

"Them's rum-ships," said John. "See that schooner with no top-masts? Your three-master is just to the east'ard of her. I can see her white hull quite plain. I can see farther through my two window-panes than an ordinary guy can without them."

Three hours after leaving the village the little fishing-boat drew up alongside the *Mermaid*, as she rolled lazily on the ocean swell. A long line of heads looked down on us from the deck, some white-topped caps showing where the officers stood.

I climbed the rope-ladder and was met by Swivel who took me to the saloon, where a tall bald-headed man stood with his back to the fireplace. He was introduced as Mr. Robson. His face was white and pouchy, with lines of dissipation on it; his eye was uncertain, and his manners those of a man who was not sure of himself, but who buoyed himself up with an air of aggressive self-assurance. After taking a long drink from a bottle which stood uncorked on the table, he went out on deck.

"I've been looking for you for ten days in the place where you said you would be," I said to Swivel, "and now find you eighty miles away from the rendezvous. You might at any rate have sent me a wire."

"I know, I know," replied Swivel, half apologetically. "I had to call for coal at a Canadian port, where Robson came up to meet me, and said that the market was much better here than off Ozone, so I came straight here, knowing that you would soon hear of our arrival.

"I've made fine arrangements about selling the cargo," he continued. "Robson and his partner Jalleno will buy practically the whole shooting match. They have a boat that is taking four hundred and fifty at a clip, and next week when their new one is ready, they will be taking a thousand every fourth day. Besides that there will be the casual trade from boats that come out 'shopping' and the people you can whip up, so it will not be long before the whole lot is sold and we are on the way home for another load.

"Oh, by the way, as all this is fixed up with Robson and I am paying him and Jalleno a commission, you will be able to look after your Cheviot, and I will pay you commission on any buyers you send out, but not on the whole cargo. I am sure you understand the position, don't you? Come round and have a look at the ship and see how well we are getting her into shape," he added, tactfully changing the conversation when I began to remind him of the agreement he had made at the Ritz. However, I could not afford to quarrel with him as long as he had my thousand cases aboard.

He pressed me to stay the night, so I paid off John Blake, and gave him a bottle of whiskey for himself and a bottle of gin for his wife.

American women are very fond of gin.

No other boat came near us for the rest of the day, although several went to the schooners that were anchored not far away, apparently taking on a load and leaving for the shore about dusk.

I did not know exactly what the business relations were between Swivel and Robson, but from the first moment I set eyes on the latter I disliked him, and he returned the compliment, although he was too diplomatic to show it.

"Well, Brisbane, old fellow," he remarked heartily to Swivel, pouring himself out another drink, "I guess we are all set now. In six weeks you will be homeward bound with half a million dollars in that safe of yours."

About eleven o'clock Swivel took me down to a large comfortable cabin painted in white enamel, with a bathroom attached. The ship was very low in the water, and every time she rolled the port holes dipped right under the waves with gurgling noise which soon lulled me to sleep.

# CHAPTER IV

## RUNNING IN THE FIRST CARGO

THE next morning the cheerful little steward came in at eight o'clock with a cup of tea, took away my suit and shoes to brush them, and prepared a warm bath for me. These ordinary little attentions passed without much notice at the time, but were often remembered in after days when living aboard schooners where a little fresh water in a tin basin was an unusual luxury.

After breakfast in the sunny saloon, Swivel made an inspection of the ship, where everything was in spick-and-span order. He kept almost man-of-war discipline among the crew, of whom there were some forty-four all told, including the captain, three deck officers, wireless operator, electrician, carpenter, boatswain, two stewards, cook, and a stowaway who had been made baker.

The men were kept at work during their watches in painting, polishing, scraping, varnishing, and bringing the yacht back to her former condition, for she had seen war service and showed it.

It was a gorgeous summer day, the sea and the sky were blue, and the white seagulls flew screeching round the ship searching for tit-bits thrown overboard from the galley.

Two or three schooners were anchored within sight, and on the horizon could be seen the bold outline of Hawkes Point, with the white lighthouse on the end of it catching the rays of the sun.

Soon after lunch the lookout shouted, "Boat coming from the point, sir."

A black speck was visible, appearing and disappearing as it crept nearer over the swell, and after an hour Robson called out, "It's our boat with Jim League on board."

In a short time a low black motorboat, without any masts, came silently nosing alongside the *Mermaid*.

The *Tortoise* was about forty feet long, entirely decked over, and had a small wheelhouse up forward. She was old, floated low in the water, and looked dirty and furtive, as though she was ashamed of her occupation.

There were three tough-looking young hooligans on deck, who proceeded to make the boat fast alongside the yacht.

"Get up on the ship, you lousy swine!" said a harsh grating voice from the wheelhouse. "Leave those goddarned lines to me; you blasted landsmen can't tie a knot any more than you can fly."

The three men scrambled up on the ship, followed by the speaker, who was a dark, powerfully built man of about forty, with a wild eye and a big Colt .455 hanging from the front of his belt.

"Barbican, this is Captain League, the best sailor this side the Atlantic," said Swivel, as we all trooped into the saloon.

Here the newcomer formally introduced his crew to me, as I seemed to be the only person present who did not already know them. There was Sandy, the engineer, a cheerful youth with blue eyes and fair curly hair; Tony, a short swarthy young fellow with black eyes, by nationality an Italian and by profession a gunman; and a husky young man named Buster, who was a bruiser of some renown in the Bronx.

Swivel produced bottles and glasses and began pouring them out a drink apiece, whereupon League glared ferociously at his crew.

"Only one drink each, you scum of the earth!" he rasped out. "If I see one of you good-for-nothing sons of dogs take two, I'll sure give him ten hells."

Having delivered himself of this oration, he tossed off a couple of four-finger tots neat; then sitting down at the table, he pulled a huge wad of bills out of his pocket, and turning to Swivel, said, "I'm out for four hundred and fifty cases this time, Mr. Swivel, and when we have the new boat next week, it will be fifteen hundred at a clip."

He counted out $12,500 in yellow-backs, and pushing the pile of notes across to Swivel, he returned his diminished roll to his pocket.

Swivel sent out the steward with a message, and in a few minutes he returned with the chief officer.

"Mr. Tasker, a hundred 'Peter Dawson,' a hundred 'H. and S.,' a hundred 'Old Smuggler,' and a hundred and fifty 'Black and White' on that boat, please," said Swivel.

"Very good, sir," was the reply, and in a few minutes we could hear the crew tramping about below deck getting the cargo ready.

Meanwhile the four rum-runners sat round the saloon, drinking their drinks and listening to Harry Lauder, Caruso, and Melba singing as clearly as though they were in the room, for the gramophone had a marvellously sweet tone.

Whenever their captain was not looking, the three men filled up

31

their glasses, and by the time the steward came in with the tea, they were all in mellow mood.

The idea of tea-drinking in the afternoon tickled their fancy greatly.

"Gee, ain't we just like some Fifth Avenue dudes," exclaimed Sandy, holding his cup aloft and curling his little finger. After his fourth cup he insisted on dancing an Irish jig to the tune of "O Sole Mio," while Tony and Buster had a fierce argument as to the merits of their respective arts.

"Suffering Mike!" said Buster. "If you are close up to a guy, he ain't got a charnst with his iron. You give him one slick wallop on the dial before he can pull his gat like that!" he added, as with a lightning movement his fist whizzed up to Tony's chin, but hit it so gently that if there had been a fly there the blow would not have bent its knees.

When Buster's arm had begun to move, Tony's left hand had been holding a glass containing a modest four-finger drink, and his right had been resting on the table behind him, but by the time Buster's fist had reached his face, his right hand was pressing a .320 automatic into the boxer's stomach.

"Dead heat!" exclaimed Captain League, who had been watching the argument; "but if you lousy toughs had meant business, Buster would have been a stiff and Tony had a busted jaw." His whole aspect suddenly changed, and he turned fiercely on the two men.

"Lay off that booze, you macaroni-chewing Dago, and you Buster, you dirty tapeworm, if you take another drop I'll wring your blasted neck till it looks like a bleeding corkscrew."

"I never let my boys get drunk when they are on the job," he remarked to me mildly, draining his seventh or eighth glass. "Just a drink, or maybe two, to put a stout heart into them. They are good boys but a bit rough, you know, and need keeping in order. They would go through fire and water for me and I love them like my own sons."

When speaking to Swivel or me, his voice was that of an English gentleman, and very different from the foul and forcible tongue with which he berated his crew.

"Now then, you pie-eyed gob, quit drinking that darned hooch!" he barked at Sandy, who was busy pouring himself out another drink.

"All right, Cap, all right," said Mac soothingly; "this is the last one."

"Yes, Mr. Barbican, they are good boys," continued League, "and I need them. I work hard all the time, and every cursed dollar that I make goes to those lawyer crooks to keep me out of the coop.

"Yes, sir, I have the most wonderful lawyer in the city. No

matter what you've done—smuggling, counterfeiting, coke-peddling, shooting, or, as in my own case, murder—he'll get you out on bail somehow. He's not the sort to allow his clients to rot in prison. Not he! Not while they've any money left, at any rate. He's a marvel. Rosco Blumenheim is his name, and though he's a Jew and a crooked one at that, as is natural being a lawyer, he'll stand by you.

"He's friends with more judges and Senators than any man in the country, and I guess he's saved more men from the chair than anyone living. You take my advice, Mr. Barbican, and when you get into trouble, go straight to him. He'll soak you good and plenty, but it's worth it to remain a free man. I have had one dose of the hoosegow, and I can tell you I don't want any more."

I tried to be sympathetic in a mild way, uncertain whether the good captain was trying to pull my leg, or was suffering from alcoholic delusions. It was not until some days later I found out that, although he had been three sheets in the wind when he was speaking, it was the sober truth.

This was my first insight into the extraordinary working of the American criminal law, which enables a man who is accused of any crime, from petty larceny to murder, to remain more or less a free man while awaiting trial. As long as he has sufficient money or influence to work it, he stays at large for months or even years, while his lawyers quibble over one technicality after another, and carry the case from court to court.

If at the end he is finally convicted, he goes to prison, while his political friends get busy with the "Parole Board," a committee which apparently has the power to let out criminals on ticket-of-leave for any reason which seems good to them.

Generally the unfortunate man has been bled dry of his money by this time, in which case he is out of luck. If, however, he still has money or rich relations, long before his sentence is up he is out on "parole" if the strings have been properly pulled and oiled.

The little steward now came in to lay the table for dinner, and the rum-runners did not need much pressing to stay for another meal. I hid the whiskey bottle under the settee, as I intended to go ashore with them, and wanted them to remain at any rate sober enough to steer the boat.

I went out into the dusk on deck and looked down on the black shape of the *Tortoise*. She rose, and fell alongside in the increasing swell; one of the yacht's crew was aboard with an old oar, keeping her from bumping against the side of the *Mermaid*, and up on the bridge there was an officer on watch for the possible approach of a revenue cutter.

Swivel came out on deck and joined me.

"Well," he said, "I shall remain here, and Jalleno and Robson will unload the ship. You had better busy yourself with getting your Cheviot ashore, as I shall be on my way home in a month."

We went into the saloon and began dinner, but half-way through, the officer on watch sent down word that a steamer was approaching.

Everyone crowded out on the dark deck, and waited while Swivel and League examined the approaching ship through their glasses; a red and green light with the white masthead light directly between them, showed that the stranger was heading directly towards us. She appeared to be only two or three miles away, and was approaching fast.

"I guess it's the cutter all right," remarked League quietly. "There's no time for us to get away, as she would be right on top of us with her searchlight before we had gone half a mile."

The danger turned him from a tipsy swashbuckler into a man of action, and he rapped out his orders without a moment's hesitation.

"Sandy, you mangy cur, get down below and start those god-darned engines of yours; Buster, put these matches in your pocket, sprinkle a can of gas about the decks, and stand by for orders; Tony, you garlic-smelling Wopp get down and give that wheel a turn to port, and lash it there."

The three men climbed down into the boat, and each one did his job of work; the engine began to throb, the gasolene was spilt about the deck, and the wheel was lashed.

"All set, sir!" came up Sandy's voice from the boat.

"Tony come back up here. Sandy, stand by, and when I give the word, throw in the clutch and jump for the ship. Buster, when Sandy is clear chuck a match on that gas and hop up here. Mr. Swivel, will you have men at the bow and stern lines ready to cut them? I may lose the boat and cargo, but I'll see myself in hell before those cursed revenue guys pinch her."

For two or three minutes there was dead silence, broken only by the faint humming of the engine and the lapping of the waves against the sides of the yacht; the old *Tortoise* was heaving up and down below us, two pale patches showing where the men's faces were raised upwards as they awaited their captain's orders. The whole of the *Mermaid's* crew lined the rail, while League and Swivel kept their glasses fixed on the approaching lights.

"If she wasn't the cutter, she would never head straight for us like that," remarked League quietly.

"It's not the cutter; probably only some old tramp coming to have a look at us, hoping to get a whiff of whiskey as she passes," answered Swivel, who was the most inveterate optimist that ever trod the deck of a ship.

The stranger came directly towards us until she was about a hundred yards away, and then put over her helm and drew past us, the long rows of lighted port-holes showing that she was a coastal passenger ship.

"She's miles out of her course," grumbled League. "Back to supper, boys."

Sandy stopped the engine, Buster put the half-empty gasolene can up against the pilothouse without troubling to replace the stopper, and we all trooped back to the saloon.

"I guess we've earned a snort after that," said Sandy brightly, producing a bottle of whiskey from heaven knows where. The bottle was dead by the time it had gone once round, and another was produced.

"Here's to the *Mermaid* and Mr. Swivel!" exclaimed League, raising his glass aloft. They all drank no-heelers, and followed this with various other toasts.

"We must be off!" said League suddenly, looking at his watch.

The meal was finished hastily, and the rum-runners clambered down into their little boat. I followed more carefully, for to lower oneself from a ship into a boat rising and falling alongside is no easy task for a landsman.

Sandy went below and started the motor. League took the wheel; while Buster and Tony stood at the bow and stern lines ready to cast off. All of them were half-seas over, but Swivel, who had taken drink for drink with them, was as sober as a judge, nor did I ever see him otherwise, however much he drank.

We rose and fell alongside the yacht, at one moment being almost level with the deck on the top of a wave, and then going down in the trough of the sea until the side of the ship towered above us like a cliff.

"All set in the engine-room?" League called out.

"All set, sir," was the reply.

"Let her go!" roared League, pushing in the clutch.

Tony and Buster cast off the lines, and the old boat, loaded to the gunwales, began to move forward slowly, as if in protest against her heavy load.

Suddenly there was a pop and a splutter as the engine stopped dead. We continued to rise and fall, scraping against the side of the ship, and drifting slowly towards her stern.

Amid a flood of abuse from the captain, Sandy laboured at

cranking up the engine, while we continued to drift slowly backwards, and saw the yacht's stern get more and more above us. I knew that if we got right under her counter the waves would lift us up against it and smash the crazy old *Tortoise* to matchwood. The crew of the *Mermaid* had seen our plight, and threw down lines for us to haul ourselves ahead out of danger; but it was very dark, and Tony and Buster were very drunk, so the ropes slipped back into the water

Looking upwards I could faintly see the long row of faces looking down on us, and then they were lost to sight as we drifted right under the stern, and were caught like a nut in a pair of open nutcrackers between the sea below and the overhang of the stern above. I slipped off my coat and made ready to dive before the crash came.

League remained immovable at the wheel, and I could not help wondering whether his coolness was heroic calm or merely drunken indifference to his fate. Suddenly the engine gave a kick and started again. The boat crept forward, but at that moment a wave lifted us, and we hit the yacht with a crash.

The pilothouse was bent sideways as though it had been made of cardboard. The door was wrenched off its hinges and hurled into the sea, while the steel railings on the starboard side were buckled flat against the deck as though they were wire.

If the wave had lifted us a moment sooner, we would have hit the counter of the yacht fair and square, but, as it was, we only hit it a glancing blow, the engine starting when it did, just saving us.

League circled round the *Mermaid* twice, and I was expecting him to return along to examine the damage.

"Sandy, you addle-headed booze-hound, are we making any water down below?"

There was a long pause, and a voice answered from the depths of the engine-room, "No, sir, not much more than usual."

"I daresay she will get to shore all right," muttered the captain to himself. "And if she doesn't, what's the odds? Only four more darned rum-runners gone to Davy Jones."

He turned the boat away from the ship and headed for the shore.

The engine was now running steadily, and a dark figure appeared from the engine-room.

"I guess we owe ourselves a snort after that," said a voice.

There was the pop of a cork and a bottle was pushed into my hand; I took a pull and handed it on to the captain. Personally I think whiskey an unpleasant beverage, but there are occasions when it is comforting, and this was one of them.

"The old *Tortoise* isn't much to look at, but she's a hard-working lucky old bitch," remarked League. "She's taken more hard knocks and pulled in more booze than any boat in America. Why, the first load Mr. Swivel ever sold was to her!"

The battered old boat went chugging steadily towards a far-distant light, rolling heavily in the swell as she went. She carried no lamps, and the captain would not allow the crew to smoke lest the glow of a cigarette should give away our presence to some prowling cutter. The engine was completely covered in deep down in the boat, while the exhaust came out below the waterline, so she slid up and down the rollers almost as silently as some great fish swimming sluggishly on the surface of the dark sea.

After an hour the crew were all asleep, and the captain was nodding at the wheel. We came to a white light, which seemed to be moving. I pointed it out, asking if it was another boat.

"It might be the gash-buoy or it might be the lighthoush," answered the captain. "Tell me which it is, Mr. Barb'c'n."

He pulled himself together, and lighting a cigarette, began to look round. His left hand was on the wheel, and his right hand with the cigarette in it was resting on the wooden ledge of the pilothouse window. The ashes fell into the open can of petrol that Buster had left there, so I removed it to a safer spot.

"Is that the gash-buoy or the lighthoush?" repeated he.

Now, to tell the truth, at that time I was so profoundly ignorant of matters nautical that I did not know what a "gash-buoy" was, nor had I the slightest idea of where we were, so I could not help the good captain.

"Guesh we'll wait till morning; then we'll know where we are; and the boys are tired, too. Good boys; mustn't work 'em too hard. Sandy, you drunken swob, stop the engine, and tell that squint-eyed guinea to throw the mud-hook overboard."

The engine stopped, the anchor went over with a splash, and we lay there in the pitch darkness, rolling and pitching in the swell. We crawled below and finding about two feet of space between the tops of the whiskey cases and the deck, stretched ourselves out on them.

Suddenly League's voice came out of the darkness.

"Where's Mr. Barb'c'n?"

"Here I am, captain," I answered.

He struck a match, woke up Tony, and made him move some cases and stretch out some coats to make a more comfortable lair for me; they then crawled back to their resting-places, and were soon snoring lustily.

I could not sleep, for although I was new to the game, it seemed to me that the whole proceeding was somewhat lacking in discretion. The old boat, after the terrible battering she had received alongside the ship, was anchored in the open ocean with all the crew asleep below. She would be absolutely at the mercy of any cutter or gang of hijackers which happened along.

So I crawled out and kept watch myself, not liking the idea of being below if the boat sank or we were boarded. Close by was a flashing light, evidently on a buoy; some miles away was a lighthouse throwing its beam for many leagues round, and occasional moving lights showed where ships or boats were passing lug in the dark.

After some hours I fell asleep where I sat, and woke with a start at the first flush of dawn. We lay four or five miles offshore, in full view of the lighthouse and every passing ship, and it seemed as though we must be very conspicuous.

I routed out the captain and crew, who showed no ill-effects from their potations of the night before, and in a very few minutes the anchor was up, the engine running, and the boat continuing her journey.

"Well, I guess we need a little mouth-wash after sleeping down below there," said Sandy's cheery voice. There was the pop of a cork, and an "H. and S." was passed round.

"I haven't got my Kolynos with me this morning," remarked Sandy, "but I guess that will kill the microbes just as well!"

"It will kill you, too, if you don't go easy on it," I could not help remarking. This makes me think of an American I once saw in a typhoid infested country brushing his teeth in bottled beer because he could not get any boiled water.

After this little aperitif, Sandy lighted a small coal stove down below, and soon the good smell of eggs, bacon and coffee overpowered the aroma which pervades every craft carrying a "wet" cargo. The other two boys handed up the breakfast, and I was as well waited upon as if I had been at the St. Francis Hotel, for their hospitality and politeness could not have been outdone by Arabs in the desert, and as the boat ran along parallel with the shore they pointed out places where they had landed cargoes on previous occasions. The sun was shining, a gentle breeze ruffled the blue sea, and the crew lay about on deck smoking cigarettes, singing snatches of music-hall ditties, and yarning to one another about their escapades.

The captain kept a sharp lookout for any suspicious craft, and several times there were alarms of "cutter" which made the captain change his course to avoid getting near the suspect; but they turned out to be false, and we continued on our way undisturbed.

The crew were a hardy lot of young ruffians, and it was amusing when listening to their conversation to notice the difference between them and their confrères in England.

Two things about them struck me specially. One was their supreme contempt for the police. The latter were divided into two categories—"good sports" who would wink at a small misdemeanour and accept bribes for overlooking a large one, and the "bad actors," whose big ideas about graft made it unprofitable to deal with them, or who, from cowardice or greed for promotion, would not accept bribes, but "pinch" anyone without giving him a chance to talk business.

The other outstanding trait was their admiration for achievement of any sort. Whether they approved of a deed or not, they praised it if a man "got away with the goods," whether it was an urchin with a tin can who ran the petrol out of parked cars, or a politician who pilfered millions of the nation's money.

About four hours after sunrise we sighted a long low boat apparently at anchor in the sea, and a man stood in the bows waving his arms.

"It must be Pip-squeak," exclaimed one of the crew.

The *Tortoise* was turned towards her, and, as we drew nearer, the other boat showed herself to be a beautifully finished, fragile little craft, with cabins fore and aft, and a huge engine amidships. League said that originally she had belonged to a millionaire with a mania for speed, but having found something a little faster he had sold her. So League had bought her for rum running, and Pip-squeak was taking her from the city to their base at Hawkes Bay, which we had passed some hours ago.

"What are you doing there, you son of a cross-eyed cow?" he yelled at Pip-squeak as we got within hailing distance.

"Dropped anchor last night to have a sleep. Couldn't pull the blamed thing up this morning. Been waiting here for someone to come along to give me a hand. No water on board; no eats; no cigarettes," he said in an injured tone.

As I wanted to go to Hawkes Bay, and was not over-anxious to take the chance of voyaging all the way into the city with my present companions, I changed over to the speedboat, after bidding farewell to my cheery hosts.

"Goodbye, Mr. Barby, hope to see you again soon," they called out, and I hoped so too, as they were jovial young scoundrels, and their hospitality had been of the best.

So the old *Tortoise* went chugging on her way, and I was amazed at League's hardiness in running through frequented waters like these with a load of whiskey aboard.

Pip-squeak opened the throttle, and we were soon tearing along at about twenty-eight knots with such a high wall of spray on each side of us that people on shore would only see a white cloud skimming over the water and nothing of the boat.

We soon reached Hawkes Bay, and I telephoned to Tom Hoppit in the city to tell him to come down, as we could start work right away. There was no hotel or inn at Hawkes Bay, so John Blake and his kindly wife put me up.

# CHAPTER V

## WE MEET THE HIJACKERS

THE next night Hoppit and his partner arrived; the latter was a short stout man of about thirty-five whose name was Ernest Sankey, and I liked the look of him.

They went straight to the house of Josiah Jones and arranged with him that he would go out next day to bring in two hundred cases and store them in a shed alongside his house. For pay he was to receive five dollars a case freight and one dollar for storage—twelve hundred dollars for twelve hours' work—not bad for a fisherman who formerly was lucky to make that amount after a year's toil at sea.

He often made money like this, sometimes six or seven times a month, but he remained living in the same squalid shack without a stick of decent furniture in it. The only evidence of his prosperity was a luxurious Buick limousine, which he kept in the little out-house, and had to leave in the open when he needed the shack for storing whiskey. When smuggling was stopped for a time in Hawkes Bay, few weeks saw him in debt, and the car went up the spout. Heaven knows what he did with all his money.

Hoppit and Sankey took me aside in John's house, telling me that they would buy a hundred cases of Cheviot from me, and a hundred cases of ordinary Scotch from Swivel; they handed me six-thousand three-hundred dollars in cash, and I gave them a note to Swivel to say that I had received the money for the two hundred cases, which were to be given to the bearer, whoever he might be. The actual figures, and any other information intended for Swivel alone, was put in cipher, so that no one would be able to alter the order *en route*, and as a result we never lost anything from forged orders.

I put the bills in my money-belt, and kept a revolver handy in my jacket pocket, for as yet I did not know whether the natives were honest or not. Later, when I got to know them better, I would some-times leave with John or some other fisherman as much as twenty thousand dollars to look after for me, and it was as safe with them as it would have been in the bank. Mrs. Blake would sometimes roll up the money inside a pair of her stockings and throw them into the drawer among the others.

Next morning there was a dense fog, so thick that houses were invisible at seventy yards. Josiah said that it was impossible to go out, and there were no boats moving in the little harbour.

After lunch I stood at the end of the fish pier, cursing the fog and hoping that it would lift in time for us to go out; but the fishermen were idling about smoking their pipes and cigars, and there were no signs of the weather clearing.

After a time there was the faint chug-chug , a motorboat in the distance, soon a dark patch appeared in the mist, and the *Tortoise* came slipping alongside the dock.

League's face was thrust out of the pilothouse window, and the crew were standing about on deck with ropes ready to moor her.

"So you got home all right, captain?" I asked him.

"Sure thing we did," he answered; "and now we are going out for another load. I've got those hungry lawyers to feed, blast their dirty souls."

"Are you going out in this fog?"

"Of course we are! What's to stop us?" he asked defiantly. "I am not one of these coast-crawling fishermen. Do you know how these Hawkes Bay men navigate? They are dog-watch sailors. They hear a sharp bark and say, 'That's Charlie's collie, so we are off Pinuckle Point.' A terrier yapping shows them they are near Smith's farm, and so on. Away from the dogs and lobster-pot buoys they are lost."

"Hey, you mangy old clam-digger," he shouted to the fisherman who tended the petrol pump, "give us some gas, and look slippy about it!"

The man strolled up and handed the hose-pipe to Sandy, who proceeded to fill the tanks of the *Tortoise*.

"If you go out today, you sure are one plumb crazy guy," remarked the fisherman, spitting in the sea.

"Oh, shucks! You go and spit in your hat, you croaking old bull-frog," was Sandy's polite retort.

Since I had seen Swivel, several cables had come for him from London, and there were one or two other things to talk about, so I asked League if he would take me out with him. He agreed, and I hurried off to John's for my oilskins, stopping on the way at the village store to buy some drawing-pins, which are known in America as "thumb tacks."

Letting down the blinds in my little bedroom and locking the door, I pulled out the bottom drawer from the chest of drawers, turned it upside down, stuck the sixty-three hundred dollars on the bottom with the drawing-pins, and slipped it back into its place. Having done this, I returned to the dock and soon found myself aboard the old *Tortoise* once more.

We slid off into the fog, the captain at the wheel, Sandy in the engine-room, and the other two boys lying flat on their stomachs in the bows trying to pierce the gloom for signs of danger.

To a landsman like me it seemed impossible that the little boat could steer twenty miles through the fog and find the ship far out on the ocean. But League seemed to have no doubts about it. Had he lived a few hundreds years earlier he would probably have made a name for himself on the Spanish Main, but in these prosaic and uneventful days he was merely the captain of a rum-runner keeping himself out of jail with the help of smuggling and a Jew lawyer. He had his little weaknesses, it is true, but he was a man and a fine sailor.

After going full speed ahead for twenty minutes, he slowed down, calling to the two men in the bows, "Look out for the breakers, you pop-eyed mutts!"

In a minute or two they shouted out, "Breakers ahead, sir."

A dim white line could be seen a hundred yards ahead. The captain turned the boat out to sea, and in another half-hour he again slowed down. Immediately after we saw the breakers once more.

"How on earth do you know when we are near the shore?" I asked him, for he appeared to know before anything could be seen or heard above the noise of the sea and the engine.

"Well, it's like this, Mr. Barbican, we have to run along the shore for a good many miles before hitting it out to sea, so I am making a series of arcs, each about two miles across the cord, with the ends resting on the beach. When we get near the shore the water gets shallow; I can feel that from the lift of the swell. I slow down, and if those two drunken gangsters in the bows are still awake they see the breakers before we get among them.

"Our next arc will land us near the lighthouse, and we shall hear the foghorn. I shall take my departure from there, steering N.N.W. When we have run for an hour, I shall give her half a point to the westward, to allow for the change of tide. We make about eight knots going light, so one hour and fifty minutes from the lighthouse I shall stop the engine, and listen for the yacht's bell, which she ought to be ringing all the time in a fog. Of course, in a small boat like this it is difficult to steer exactly on a given course, but there is not much sea on today, and we shall not be far out."

Sure enough, at the end of the next arc, we were right underneath the lighthouse, although we could not see it; but the booming of the foghorn ahead, and apparently above us, showed exactly where it was.

The captain now put the boat's head N.N.W., and he took the time by his watch; the crew went below for a snooze, and I remained on deck to talk with him, for he was a travelled and interesting man, who had seen much of the world.

It appeared that he was not working for himself, but for the Italian, Jalleno, who provided the boat, paid its running expenses, and gave the captain and crew so much a case on each cargo they brought in.

In the midst of our conversation he suddenly glanced over his right shoulder, and called down the hatch in a hoarse whisper, "On deck, boys; quick, with your guns!"

In moment the three men had scrambled out on deck, each with an automatic in his hand.

"Hide your guns and keep still, you lousy toughs," be ordered.

He was steering with his left hand; in his right was a huge .455 Colt, and another lay on a little ledge in front of him.

His eyes were fixed over his right shoulder, where the dim form of a boat could be seen; she was larger and faster than we were, and was rapidly overhauling us.

Without turning his head, League said as quietly as if he were asking me to give him a match, "Mr. Barbican, would you mind putting your hand in my left jacket pocket and getting out a box of shells that are there? Thanks! Now open the box and spread the shells out on that ledge."

Doing as he asked, I put the twenty-five cartridges on the shelf, and not quite knowing what was afoot, I filled my right jacket pocket with my own cartridges, so that there would be no delay in getting at them in case of need.

"Who are they?" I asked the captain.

"Don't know," was the laconic answer.

It was not a very pleasing situation. To witness a friendly shooting match once in a while helps to relieve the monotony of life, but for all I knew these other fellows were coastguardsmen, who, after all, would only be doing their duty, and I had no desire to get mixed up in an affair with them.

League and his crew were a pretty desperate gang, who would stick at nothing; and if there was a skirmish, I was hand in glove with them, and would have to share whatever was coming to them, good or ill.

44

We had no contraband on board, and I was about to suggest to the captain that he should let them search us if they wanted to, when it occurred to me that, after all, he was an old hand at the game, and I was only a novice, so that it would be best to let him take his own course.

I pulled my cap down over my eyes, kept my gun in my hand, and modestly retiring behind the pilothouse, awaited developments.

The other boat had by now almost caught up the *Tortoise*, and was apparently about to run alongside to board her, when the helmsman seemed to change his mind and passed on the starboard side, leaving about ten yards of water between the boats. She was a low boat, about fifty feet long, and made twice our speed; there were three men on her bare deck, and one in the wheelhouse, so she was obviously no fisherman.

There were none of the cheery greetings or hand-waves with which boats passing on these waters invariably salute one another, whether friends or strangers, they passed in dead silence, staring intently at us as we stared at them. "Don't shoot till I give the word," said League to his men.

The strangers saw League's dark ferocious face peering out of the wheelhouse; they saw Sandy, Tony, and Buster standing on deck, each with his right hand held behind his back, and apparently they did not like the look of things, for they put over their helm and disappeared in the fog.

In a few minutes they again shot up alongside, but as before kept several yards of water between the two boats; slowing down, they took another long look at us, then one of them struck a match in his cupped hands and lighted a cigarette.

"He ain't got no gat in his hand," said Tony, contemptuously spitting into the water as the other craft melted away in the fog for the last time.

"Hijackers!" remarked League, slipping the loose cartridges back in his pocket. "I guess they didn't like the look of us. There were likely half a dozen of them down below deck, ready to jump out when they got the word.

"If they stick up a full boat, they get the booze; if they stick up an empty one, they get the brass," he said, pulling a great wad of hundred dollar bills half out of his pocket. "So they score either way till they bump into a bunch of real tough babies like mine.

"Tony, you yellow-faced Dago, show Mr. Barbican how you can shoot!"

Tony dived below and reappeared with an empty bottle, which he threw into the sea. They all began blazing away at it, and the water round was whipped up by the bullets, but their marksmanship was poor, and the bottle remained intact until it disappeared astern.

In an hour and a half the shadowy form of the *Mermaid* appeared right ahead, and even the taciturn League could not resist a dour smile lighting up his face as the *Tortoise* ran alongside without having to alter her course even half a point after sighting the ship.

He took another four hundred and fifty cases, and departed shorewards with a stone-sober crew, leaving me aboard the *Mermaid*.

The next afternoon John Blake arrived in his fishing-boat saying that Josiah's engine had broken down, and that he had come in his place for the two hundred cases.

The ship's crew loaded his boat for him, a hundred and fifty cases down below and fifty on deck. By the time it was all aboard night had fallen, so we set off and steered for the flash of the lighthouse on the horizon. We travelled at about six knots, and made hardly any noise; it was dark, the ocean was large, and we seemed fairly safe.

In about three and a half hours we came within sight of the lights of the village, so John throttled down the engine to quarter-speed, and we crept like a ghost-boat among the other shadowy craft in the little harbour until we picked up John's mooring. So quietly had we come that the men awaiting our arrival on the beach fifty yards away did not know we had arrived, until John rowed ashore in his dory, leaving me on the boat.

He soon returned with some more men, and I handed the cases down to them one at a time until there were about thirty on the dory. Then it melted away into the darkness, and another one pulled quietly alongside.

This went on for an hour in perfect silence, and when the last case had been piled on the bigger of the dories, I sat myself on the top and went ashore. We were within a few yards of the beach when the man backed on his oars, waited for a wave bigger than the others, and rode in on the top of it; several shadowy forms dashed into the water out of the darkness, seized the little boat, and pulled her nose up on the beach.

The cases were taken off and rapidly loaded on to a motor lorry which had been brought almost to the water's edge.

When they were all on board, we jumped on the back of the lorry, and it went slowly and quietly up the main street of the village. On reaching Josiah's house, it was backed against the little broken-down shack, into which the cases were piled.

After the doors had been shut, I went inside with a flashlight and counted the whole two hundred cases neatly piled tier on tier; the door was then locked, and I went home with John to the good supper which the kindly Mrs. Blake had prepared for us.

Next morning at breakfast one of the neighbours came in to see Mrs. Blake and have a bit of gossip.

"Say, Helen," she said, "did you hear of the battle in the fog between the rum-runners and the hijackers the day before yesterday? They were shooting at one another for nearly an hour, and several men were killed, but no one knows who they are. My husband was down by the point and heard the firing. You shouldn't let your John go out there alone; it really ain't safe for decent folks now, what with these gangsters coming down here from the city and all sorts of strangers about."

"I reckon my John can look after himself all right," answered Mrs. Blake placidly; and I lay low and said nothing, remembering that the casualties of the battle had amounted to less than one broken bottle. On such slender foundations are rumours started and stories built up round them.

# CHAPTER VI

## COCKTAILS, CLUBS, AND CHEMISTS

THAT evening the plump Ernest Sankey produced a couple of light motor-vans, or "speed-waggons"; the two hundred cases were loaded on them, and they disappeared into the darkness for some destination known only to the drivers and their employer.

I took the money out of its hiding-place, tucked it into my money-belt, and went up to town with him. The more I saw of him the more I took to him. Like everybody else in the business, he had in his time played many parts, and, unlike some of them, was an honest man turned bootlegger. He had a very complete organisation with head-quarters downtown, where he carried on his business.

His office opened directly out of the public corridor of a huge office building. There were several desks about, each with a telephone on it, and at one of them a man would be carrying on a conversation such as this:—

"That's all right . . . Yes, sir, we'll send you a case of 'Black and White' straight away. Where do you want it sent? . . . Very good. We'll have it there at 146 West 900th Street by four o'clock sure. Thank you, Mr. Spargoni."

The speaker would call over one of the men lounging on a settee in the corner of the room.

"Say, Harold, take a 'B. and W.' to that Hitalian that keeps the candy store, and don't let him have it until he hands you the dough. He still owes me for that case of gin, and I'm not giving him any more on the cuff until he pays for it."

Harold would amble round to the firm's garage, open a case of "Black and White," put the dozen bottles into a suit-case or a cardboard box, which he would place in the back of a Ford car with a number of similar packages for other people, and then drive round to Mr. Spargoni's emporium.

It really was amazing how openly the thing was done, considering that it was illegal. Some firms were more cautious, and were very shy about doing business on the telephone, except with people they knew well, as sometimes the prohibition men would listen in on the wires to get evidence and information.

Occasionally a policeman in plain clothes or some minor prohibition official would come to get a few bottles for nothing, or to collect tribute from the bootlegger, but usually they were more discreet, and transacted their business in some less public spot.

When reading about the trials of the big operators in the newspapers, I had noticed that sometimes they got into trouble by giving or receiving cheques; and if the authorities could not catch them out over smuggling, they would get them for non-payment of income tax or some other charge, which was often proved by tracing their bank accounts.

As far as possible, therefore, I avoided the banks and dealt in cash, although it meant carrying about large sums in my pockets, sometimes as much as thirty or forty thousand dollars at a time. Like most others in the business, I took safe deposit boxes in various banks under different names and used to stow away the money in them.

The next day Ernest Sankey gave me a list of the people to whom the Cheviot had been delivered, and I sent a trustworthy man for the money. They nearly always carried out the transaction themselves, and paid in cash, so that their underlings should not know anything about it.

Occasionally I went to see some of them myself, and they treated the whole business as a great joke, and were much intrigued as to how the whiskey came from England to their houses, but it did not seem prudent to tell them too much.

The big businessmen of America certainly know how to do themselves well, with their sumptuous offices, Turkey carpets, beauteous secretaries, and always the row of bottles and glasses in the safe in the corner.

Many an excellent lunch have I enjoyed at their clubs, where the good fare and their entertaining company used to help me to forget for an hour all the cares and worries of a smuggler's life.

The thoroughbred American is one of the best men in the world—courteous, well-read, hospitable, and efficient to his finger-tips; it is a calamity for America that he is so rare, and that he keeps himself so completely aloof from public life.

Many American clubs are more like busy commercial hotels than clubs, with tape machines rattling away, raucous voiced "bell-hops" howling out members' names, hard-worked spittoons in every corner, and money-making the sole subject of conversation, but the best are as good as our best, and certainly more luxurious.

My first visit to one of these was when calling to see a personal friend of mine, who, by the way, did not know about my present occupation.

I got there rather early, and was waiting in the hall for him to arrive. A genial elderly gentleman came down the staircase; instead of looking at me in the what-the-devil-are-you-doing-here sort of way with which the average Londoner regards the stranger in his club, he walked up to me.

"Are you expecting someone?" he inquired "Yes? Well, you might as well come and have a look round while you are waiting."

He spent a quarter of an hour showing me over the place and telling me about the historic old furniture and the interesting collection of prints. Finally, he took me into a little room at the back of the club, where each member had a small locker specially made to take half a dozen whiskey bottles. These locker rooms are almost universal in American clubs now that the law has made it necessary to drink in secret. One of the club servants mixed an excellent cocktail from the private store of my kindly host, and as we were drinking it, my friend came in and joined us.

This is, I believe, what the Americans call the most "exclusive" club in the country, and yet its president went out of his way like this to entertain, with the most charming courtesy, a stranger whom he had never seen before and would probably never see again—and not a very respectable one either had he only known it!

Occasionally some of the smaller fry were not so pleasant to do business with; sometimes they would even wait to pay until they had sent a sample of the Cheviot to an analyst and received a favourable report to show that it had not been adulterated.

Almost every respectable citizen, besides having his pet bootlegger, who gets the whiskey "direct from the ship," has also his analytical chemist to whom he submits samples of each fresh consignment of liquor he buys, to make sure that the bootlegger really did get it from the ship, and had not mixed it in the bath from homemade ingredients as so many of them do.

From the results of some of these analyses I imagine that many of the chemists just take a drink, and write out their report next morning according to whether they have a headache or not. They charge anything up to five dollars for this, and afterwards probably fill up the bottle with water and sell it for eight dollars, thus making thirteen dollars (and a drink) out of each customer.

Here is an instance of what happened to me once.

A man bought from me fifty cases of Nicholson's gin, which were lying in the farmhouse where they had been stored after being landed.

Soon afterwards he came back with a long story that he had taken a bottle to the E—— Hospital to have it tested, and that their chemist had reported that it was unfit for human consumption. He was very annoyed about it, and so was I, for it was the first time that I had ever been accused of selling anything that was not good; but to prove his contention, he produced a written document confirming what he said.

So I had three samples taken from one bottle, sent them to three different analytical chemists, and paid them their fees. The following are exact copies of their reports, which I have by me as I write, and I only omit the names of the firms for obvious reasons. My name was given as Higgins:—

### CHEMIST No. I.

Reference 713,45. Sample gin.

| | |
|---|---|
| Alcohol (ethyl) by volume . . . . . . | 43.28 |
| Proof . . . . . . . . . . . . . . . | 86.56 |
| Methyl (wood) alcohol . . . . . . . | Present |
| Formaldehyde . . . . . . . . . . . | Absent |
| Acetone . . . . . . . . . . . . . . | " |

Not fit for beverage purposes

(Signed) F. K. M.—

### CHEMIST No. II.

*Certificate of Analysis. Analysis No. 1815A.*

Mr Higgins.

Dear Sir,—Our analysis of the sample submitted to us shows the presence of 42.90 percent alcohol by volume. We fail to find wood alcohol, formaldehyde, or other denaturants.

Respectfully,

(Signed) J. L. M.—

(Chief Chemist)

CHEMIST No. III.

*Certificate of Analysis.*

To Mr Higgins.
We have examined with the following results:—

| | |
|---|---|
| Alcohol by aichometer . . . . | 45% |
| Proof . . . . . . . . . . . . | 90 |
| Absolute alcohol by volume . . | 44.7% |
| Absolute alcohol by weight . . | 37.7% |
| Wood alcohol . . . . . . . . | None |
| Formaldehyde . . . . . . . . | " |
| Added coloring . . . . . . . | " |
| Added sugar . . . . . . . . . | " |
| Added glycerine . . . . . . . | " |
| Total solids . . . . . . . . . | 0.040 |
| Denaturants . . . . . . . . . | None |

*Remarks.*—Nothing spurious found this sample of gin It is a potable dry gin, alcoholic content pure, and of proper strength for a dry gin.

Respectfully submitted,
(Signed) M. F. S.—

Thus it will be seen that the hospital and Chemist No I. found the gin poisonous, while Chemists Nos. II. and III. found it good. As a matter of fact, it was good.

I felt a trifle offended when they sent the Cheviot to be analysed, but perhaps they were wise, for Benjamin Franklin knew his fellow-countrymen well when he remarked, "There's none deceived but him who trusts."

The money for the hundred cases was turned over to Hoppit, and he bought two hundred more from me, which Sankey delivered as before.

I sold some of Swivel's whiskey, but not very much, as just then Hawkes Bay was not popular with the rum-runners.

Jalleno was only taking small quantities, as his new boat was not ready yet, and he and Robson did not fulfill their contract to bring others to buy from the *Mermaid*, for they were getting good whiskey at a low price, and did not wish their competitors to butt in on what they regarded as their preserve. I kept on pointing this out to Swivel, but he had considerable faith in Robson, and would not consent to move to Cape Ozone, where business was good, and there was little trouble from the revenue men.

At last, after wasting some weeks, he threw over Jalleno and Robson, who were doing nothing to justify their pay, and asked me to sell for him the thirteen or fourteen thousand cases that were still left.

After he had decided to do this, I went down to Hawkes Bay to arrange with him about moving the ship to Cape Ozone, and asked John to take me out in his boat.

He rather hesitated, and taking me aside said in a low voice, "This is quite confidential, Mr. Barby, and you mustn't let on that you know. An hour ago I saw that dark Dago, Jalleno. He was loading his gun, and said that he was going to pump your guts full of lead for interfering in his business. Real angry he was, too, and looked as though he meant it."

This was the first time that I had been told that I was going to be "bumped off," and I took it more seriously than I do now that I understand these sort of people better. If an American meant business every time he said he was going to shoot someone, the Indians would soon be shooting buffalo in Broadway.

So I loaded my revolver in all its chambers, made sure that it was working properly, and went out to the yacht in search of Jalleno, thinking that if there was going to be a shooting match, it would be better to have it on the ship with two-score good British sailors on the scene than in the United States with a hundred million Yankees as a background.

As we drew near the ship Jalleno could be seen walking up and down with a glowering face, and a formidable customer he looked, too; short and immensely powerful, with a body like a gorilla and a face like a large black pansy. His complexion was sallow, his eyes dark and moody, and his southern European parents had endowed him with a violent and uncontrollable temper, the fear of which kept the members of his gang in order.

I climbed up on deck, and Swivel appeared on the scene. Being a past master in the art of blarney, he succeeded in mollifying the angry Dago with glowing promises which he never meant to keep, with the result that Jalleno and I parted good friends for the time being.

I went ashore and then straight down to the new pitch at Ozone with Hoppit, and we arrived there late at night; he was in front of me as we walked into the local hotel and wrote our names in the book. Looking over his shoulder, I saw that he had put himself down as "George Knox" and me as "Eldred Wuggins."

"No harm in being careful," he remarked as we walked upstairs to our rooms.

The next morning I stepped out of the hotel with the slightly guilty conscience that a respectable man should have when living under an assumed name. I stood for a few moments on the sidewalk making my plans for the day, when I heard a piping little voice alongside me asking, "Please, are you Mr. Barbican?"

There standing beside me was a pretty little girl of about twelve, who repeated her question.

I did not know a soul in the place, and was rather taken aback.

"What do you want?" I asked her.

"There's someone in that motor-car who wants to speak to you," she answered. I approached rather suspiciously, but there, laughing at me over the steering wheel, were the blue eyes of my friend Margaret, whom I had not seen since we danced together at Lady D.'s in Pont Street a year ago.

"I saw you standing in the door of the hotel and sent the child to ask for you," she said, and then, looking at my dirty old flannel shirt and sheepskin coat, asked inquiringly, "And what are you doing here?"

As she is one of the three discreet women in the world, I told her, and having arranged to meet later, we each went our way.

The next time I went to that hotel the desk clerk evidently remembered me, although some time had elapsed since my last visit. When I came in for dinner, he said, "We have given you the same room as last time and sent your grip upstairs. Will you please register?" he added, dipping a pen in the ink and thrusting it into my hand.

I was about to sign my name, when it flashed across my mind that Hoppit had registered for me the last time, and had put down the first name that had come into his head. For the life of me I could not remember what it was!

"I wonder what Conan Doyle would do in a position like this?" I thought to myself. "An author has hours to think it out, while I have that damned darkie watching me and waiting for me to write."

He stood expectantly, holding the room key in his hand.

To gain time I began to pluck an imaginary hair out of the pen nib, and inquired, "How are the duck this season?"

"Pretty fair, sir, pretty fair; we have had quite a few hunters down here already, and they have had some good sport."

"I wonder if any of my friends have been down?" I asked, turning back the leaves of the book and scanning the names in haste. Keeping up some back-chat about the shooting, I turned back until I came across Hoppit's round bold handwriting, and there was my name as large as life, "Eldred Wuggins."

With a sigh of relief I signed the book and went upstairs to bed.

In this place I was introduced to a nest of local smugglers, and very decent fellows they proved to be. Their headquarters were in a garage, where they used to meet regularly and had their own private telephone. There was a sort of head man whose authority was more or less recognised, one Danny Roper, in whom I had considerable confidence as he seldom let me down in my dealings with him.

These men had a small fleet of Seabright dories with powerful engines, and bootleggers used to come down from the city with a roll of bills, and giving one of the boatmen five or six thousand dollars, send him off to buy a load.

The man would go out to one of the ships lying at anchor outside, buy two or three hundred cases for, perhaps, twenty-five dollars a case, run them ashore in his boat, and store them in a cottage or garage, or perhaps in some lonely shack away in the marshes. He charged five dollars a case for freighting the cases in, and a dollar for storage, so he made six dollars a case for freighting at another man's risk, which was good business for him. Some of them would get the load at twenty-three, and tell the bootlegger that they had paid the full twenty-five, considering the two dollars change their perquisite. But, on the whole, this little gang were fairly honest, and some of them as straightforward and honourable men as could be found anywhere.

My idea was to make friends with them and get them to go to the *Mermaid* in preference to the other ships. It was not easy, because Swivel insisted on keeping up his prices above those of the other ships; but, generally speaking, we did very well, and sold quickly and at a good profit.

I remember going down to the rum-runners' headquarters one evening when the weather was stormy and it was impossible to work. They were just sitting down to a game of poker.

"Come and join us, Mr. Barby," said a jovial red-faced mariner, who was taking down a small mirror and rehanging it face to the wall. "We play a nice little game here. It's the roof off, and it's seldom there's any cheating. Except that old buzzard Rob in the corner there—you want to watch him."

The remark about the cheating was really superfluous, for we all watched one another so closely that it was impossible.

It was with Danny Roper that I made my first trip on a "booze-waggon," and saw the rum-runners at work on land.

There was a friend of Elderson's who wanted seventy-five cases of Cheviot; he told me where to have it sent, but was very worried when he saw me making a pencil note of the address. Finally, he made me promise not to put anything in writing, and to tell nobody of the transaction. It meant a lot of extra trouble, for how could one send a truck of whiskey to a man without telling the driver where to go? It meant going myself, but he was a very pleasant fellow, and a friend of Elderson's, so I gave him the promise.

One dark evening I got Danny to load the seventy-five cases on to a small speed-waggon and we went tearing across country at forty-five miles an hour, through bye-lanes and unfrequented roads.

After about an hour and a half we turned down a lonely avenue of trees, and came to a lighted mansion with many windows.

Switching off the lights, I left the truck standing in the darkness, and, marching boldly up to the front door, rang the bell.

The butler must have been rather surprised to see such a tough-looking customer at the front door at nine in the evening; but if he was, his face showed nothing.

"Some goods for Mr. van Syden," I said.

"Very good, I know about it," he replied. "Will you back your van to the side door?"

I went back to Danny, and he backed the truck silently to a side door which led down to the cellars. Two or three footmen in livery appeared, and with the help of the two men Danny had brought with him, it was not long before the whole lot was unloaded safely into the cellar and the truck back under the trees again.

Mr. van Syden himself appeared to watch the work, while the butler checked the number of cases as they went down. Van Syden thanked my men with great courtesy, as though they had conferred some favour on him by coming.

"Might I give them a drink before we leave?" I asked him, for we had worked hard, and the sweat was running down our faces.

"Certainly, certainly," he answered. "Come along with me."

He led the way up some stairs, and I expected to be led into the butler's pantry, which would have been quite good enough for the likes of us.

Instead of that, he opened a door and ushered us into a huge dining-room, with a large mahogany table, which had evidently just been left by a party of six people. He made us sit down, while footmen flitted round and filled our glasses, handed us nuts and fruit, and lighted our cigars.

Our host, in his faultless evening dress, sat at the head of the table chatting easily and pleasantly to us rum-runners as we sat there with our dirty clothes and grimy faces. The air was filled with the delicious perfume of the hothouse flowers with which the table was decorated, and through the closed doors at the end of the room there came the faint sounds of music and women's voices.

Van Syden himself was a tall fresh-complexioned man of about forty-five, with a clear steady eye—an aristocrat from head to toe, for what product of democracy could have sat in such surroundings and entertained a rough quartette like us with such delightful simplicity, and without the slightest touch of condescension?

Things were going pretty well now, and every evening the little speedboats would come out for their loads of a hundred or two each; some would pay cash on the ship, and others would pay me on shore and get an order. Every time I went out to see Swivel he would give me as much money as I cared to carry, to take to the bank for him.

When the notes were small ones, I could not take more than ten or fifteen thousand dollars without bulging uncomfortably; but when they were mostly for fifty, a hundred, and five hundred dollars, I used to tuck away in my belt and pockets a much as thirty or forty thousand dollars at a time.

It was rather a responsibility to carry so much of another man's money about, for it would have been a sorry business to have to come back one day and say that I had been robbed. This was no unlikely thing in a country where men will risk their lives in holding up a store or a bank on the chance of getting away with a few hundred dollars.

To these gentry, the rum-runners, going to and from their ships, offered a pleasant and lucrative field of endeavour. But I always kept my revolver loaded and well oiled in my jacket pocket, and never told anyone where I was going to land, so I did not get held up on this trip.

The revenue cutters, which were small white steamers, used to come along sometimes and catch the rum-runners, and there were always the prohibition agents working on shore, but at this time the business really went along very happily.

# CHAPTER VII

## WATCHED BY THE POLICE

ABOUT this time I happened to be in the city one evening when Hoppit, who was always a hospitable fellow, asked me to dine with him. We went to a German restaurant, and as we sat down he was hailed by a jovial young man of about thirty-five, who was sitting with half a dozen others at a neighbouring table. After a while Hoppit's friend came over and joined us.

"Jim Barbican, meet Mr. Hank Lean," said Hoppit.

"Pleased to meet you," was the correct reply.

We shook hands, and the cheery Hank sat down and entertained us with his conversation.

He was a big powerful fellow, with dark flashing eyes, a pugnacious face, a huge Roman nose, and an amazing flow of conversation. He was always on the aggressive, and two long, yellow, canine teeth projecting down far over the lower lip gave him the appearance of a big mastiff looking round for someone to attack. Having in his time played many parts, he could talk fluently, and sometimes intelligently, on any subject that was brought up.

"Mr. Barbican and I have gone to work and brought over some wonderful Scotch," marked Hoppit during a pause in the conversation. "I can tell you that it's the real Mackay. It has the Royal Arms of England on every bottle to show that King George and Queen Mary drink nothing else, and they ought to know what's what. I'll send you along a case this week, Hank, and if you don't think it's the best you ever tasted, I'll eat the bottle afterwards."

"Well, Mr. Barbican, and how do you like Hawkes Bay?" asked Hank Lean. "It's a bit out of the way for a Londoner like you, but there's lots of fresh air and sea, if those are any good to you. How is the *Mermaid* getting on? I hear that she is about half unloaded, and will soon be on her way home for another load."

"You seem to know all about me," I remarked with a laugh, as I had not gathered who he was.

"Yes," he replied, with a twinkle in his eye. "I guess I can tell you quite a bit about yourself."

He dived into his breast pocket, and pulling out a mass of papers, started sorting them through. At last he picked out a type-written sheet, and holding it so that I could not overlook it, he began to read,

"You arrived in this country on the 2nd of last month on the Pink Star liner *Piponic*, and went to the Palace Hotel, where you stayed in Room 1142. You are acting on shore as agent for the *Mermaid*, and she hasn't a bad cargo either, though you are standing out for rather high prices.

"There is—    Dewar's.
            Four Crowns.
            Peter Dawson.
            Ambassador.
            Old Smuggler.
            Lawson's Liqueur.
            Black and White.
            Holt's Pimple Bottles, and other brands.

"You saw quite a number of bootleggers before the yacht arrived, but your prices were too high, and you did not do much business.

"There's lots more I could tell you about yourself, but it will have to wait until next time as I must be off," he said, rising and putting on his coat.

"Well, pleased to have met you, Mr. Barbican. Good luck, and be careful," he added meaningly.

I thought I had kept my doings pretty quiet since arriving in the city, and it was disconcerting to find that any one had taken such an interest in them as this man seemed to have done.

"Who's that bird with the big beak?" I asked Hoppit.

"Hank?" he asked. "He's a Department of Justice man. His job is to keep tabs on the rum-runners. He only has to snap his fingers and you would find yourself in the cooler. But he's all right. He and I were at school together, and he won't touch a friend of mine."

That night I had an uneasy sort of feeling as I lay awake thinking that it was not very pleasant to have one's record at police head-quarters like this, and I kept racking my brains to find out how anyone could know so much about me.

I recalled one incident which I had forgotten about.

A few weeks after arriving in the city, one of the girls at the hotel telephone switchboard had begun to make herself very friendly over the wire, and when things were slack with her, she used to ring me up and have a chat, mainly about nothing; she had a pleasant voice, and like most American girls was full of amusing back-chat.

Then one day she called me up about five o'clock.

"Say, Mr. Man, me and Sadie, that's my girlfriend here, is just going off duty, and we are just crazy for a cup of tea like you English have in the afternoons, and we was thinking how nice it would be if we ran into you just outside the restaurant down below. I'm wearing a green hat, and Sadie, she's wearing a yellow one. So long, see you in a minute," and she rang off.

A rum-runner, not many days before, when handing out good advice to me as a beginner, had told me to always make a special point of keeping in with the telephone girls, and said that in his hotel he used to send them a box of candy or a couple of theatre tickets every week. I did not quite see what the girl's game was, but thought there would be no harm in making a reconnaissance, so went down to the restaurant, and was greeted outside the door by two plain but perky damsels.

"Say, Mr. Man, I know that's you all right; you English can't hide yourselves; you've got London writ all over you. Come along and dig us out some eats."

There was no escape now, and I meekly suffered myself to be led into the restaurant, where they ordered their afternoon tea, which began with fried oysters and ended with lemon-pie and dough-nuts.

When they were fully gorged I managed to shake them off, but next morning Cissy rang me up again.

"Well, how's business going? Gee! it's some hot down here. Wish I had a bottle of Scotch. Do you think you could get me one? You must have plenty about. Say, and I've got a hole in my stocking; you'd like to give me a new pair, wouldn't you?"

"I'm too busy now," I answered. "Give me that number I asked for, 'Uptown fife thr-r-r-e-e fife thr-r-r-e-e,' there's a good girl."

In five minutes there was a knock at the door, and a beautiful young woman in a black silk dress presented herself; she had two pairs of silk stockings slung over her arm.

"I'm from the ladies' shop in the hotel; there's a young lady downstairs says you are giving her two pairs of stockings, and she's chosen one pair of black at three dollars and one pair of beige at four dollars; she thought you would like to see what you were giving her. That will be seven dollars, please."

A fast worker was Cissy!

"One pair of black," I said quite firmly, giving her three dollars.

Of course it was obvious that Cissy was listening in to people talking with me, and as some of them spoke with less discretion than I used when speaking to them, she must have had a pretty fair idea of what I was doing.

She might be in the pay of the police, and thought she would make a bit both ends by adding a little blackmail to her pay as spy, or else, with true American enterprise, she was trying a little amateur bluff on her own.

At any rate there was not time to bother about it just then, as I was just off to sea.

A few days later on my return the telephone bell rang.

"Is that you, Mr. Man? I thought you must have gone away. Say, Sadie and me was going to a dance tonight, and being near the end of the week we haven't enough money for the tickets. How's business with you? You would like to come to the dance with us, wouldn't you? We're neither of us too hard to look at, are we? Meet us outside at seven, and say, don't forget that bottle of Scotch. Bring one for Sadie too."

"Delighted," I replied, and since then have often wondered how long they waited, for by seven o'clock I was safely ensconced in another hotel, nor did I leave any forwarding address.

On thinking over the incident, it seemed that, although the big-nosed man might have got some of his information from Cissy, he could not possibly have obtained all that detail. Then like a flash it suddenly dawned on me that he had read out "Holt's Pimple Bottles" instead of "Holt's Dimple Bottles."

Where had I heard that mistake before?

Bayne!

And to add to that, the paper from which Hank Lean had read was very thin, with green type showing through.

Later on I confirmed my suspicions when I found that the little fish-faced man was a "stool-pigeon," as the Americans call an "agent provocateur."

He was in the pay of the authorities, but at the same time, like many others of his kidney, he was a genuine bootlegger, and if he had been able to do business with me which would have brought him in more than giving me away to the police, he would have done so gladly. The little jackal was not an American, nor was he English, Scotch, or Irish.

The first impulse was to go and have it out with him, but there came to mind one of the first principles of contre-espionage, which is that if you find out that the enemy is watching you, do not let him know that you know.

So whenever I ran into little Bayne, which was often, I remained on the most friendly terms, and tried to drag him into some imaginary deal, in which he was going to make thousands of dollars. While talking to him I would casually let slip bits of information, also imaginary, about my doings, and doubtless he would trot off to his typewriter and send off a long report to the good Hank, who would not be very much deceived, as later on I used to confide my real plans to him.

One evening while on board ship, a rum-runner named Johnnie, whom I knew slightly, came alongside in a queer-looking craft; she had once been a sailing yacht, but growing too aged for racing, her masts had been sawed off and an engine fitted into her. She was a clumsy-looking thing, but she was dark-coloured, lay low in the water, and the engine was well muffled, so she was quite suitable for her job.

She took six or seven hundred cases aboard, and as I wanted to go into the city, I asked Johnnie to take me ashore with him, giving him a case of Scotch by way of paying my fare.

As usual, I took my belt of money for the bank, and kept my revolver in a handy pocket, for though I knew Johnnie slightly, I did not know the other men in the boat.

After getting near land we ran beside the shore for many miles; the gentle rolling of the boat and the steady throb of the motor lulled me to sleep.

I was awakened by the slowing down of the engine, and found that we were gliding noiselessly by a wood, with the trees overhanging the water.

The boat was headed for a black mass on shore, which turned out to be a brick boathouse, with several motor launches tied up inside. We went right in; a number of men came forward, and the cases were handed out to them. I stepped ashore among them, and was immediately stopped.

"Say, Johnnie, who's this guy?" someone asked.

"He's all right, he's from off of the *Mermaid*," was the reply, and I was allowed to pass.

Among the trees were hidden a number of motor-trucks on to which the whiskey was loaded, and in a couple of hours the old boat slipped away empty into the darkness, while the motors made ready to start.

The boss of the gang, a young Jew with a careworn face, offered to take me up to the city in his car, and not having the slightest idea of where we were, I accepted gladly.

It was pitch dark in the woods; no lamps were lighted, and the men were not allowed to smoke for fear of attracting attention. Our car took the lead, and went crawling through the trees on the grass track until we came to a carriage drive with imposing iron gates. There was a lodge on each side of them, from one of which there slipped a dark shadow which rolled back the gates.

The little procession passed through without a word being spoken, and once on the high road, the trucks spread out and turned on their head-lights. We stayed behind until the last had gone by, the boss shouting directions to each driver as he passed. Then we shot ahead past them, and travelling at fifty or sixty miles an hour, it was not long before the city was reached.

"That is the X—— estate," remarked the Jew to me, mentioning a name better known than any other on both sides of the Atlantic. "The family are away, and we have fixed the man who looks after the place. A dandy landing it is, too. The cops would no more dare to search that place than they would the gardens of the White House. Don't tell anyone about it. Johnnie didn't ought to have brought anyone in there, but I suppose you are all right," he added thoughtfully, glancing at me in the grey light of the dawn.

He good-naturedly took me right to my apartment, and in a few minutes I was fast asleep in bed, with my money belt still round my waist.

Some months later I came in from sea, and on entering my sitting-room found a note from some friends asking me to dine with them that night. Usually I refused invitations of this sort, for though money will open the doors of society to most people, I had never yet come across the rum-runner rich enough to buy his way in, and I was always afraid of meeting someone who knew what I was doing, and thereby causing embarrassment to my host. But these people, like the Rallices, did not have to worry about what people thought of their guests, so I rang them up and accepted.

When I arrived there, I found that my dinner partner was Miss X., while her mother sat opposite to us. Little had I expected to meet them! Very charming people they were too.

After dinner we went to the opera, which is a wonderful sight in the season; the first tier of boxes is known as the "diamond horseshoe," because the women who sit in them appear to be dripping with diamonds.

The American women certainly do know how to dress, and on such occasions their trappings are the equal of those in any capital in Europe. Perhaps in time to come the men will learn to dress well enough to do justice to their wives.

To enjoy life to the full there must be contrasts, and the greater the contrast the greater the enjoyment. A few hours before I had been unshaven, clad in oily clothes, running in a load of whiskey in broad daylight on a disreputable old boat, a pariah to be haled off to jail by any coastguard or police who could catch me.

I kept well to the rear of the box, for many opera glasses were directed towards it, but apparently my brothers-in-arms did not patronise Wagner for none of them were there that night.

# CHAPTER VIII

## A DEBAUCH

THE *Mermaid* was now nearly empty, and Swivel decided to transfer the remaining few thousand cases to a little steamer which he farmed out to Jalleno and Robson. As I did not wish to have any dealings with these two, there arose the question of what to do with the rest of the Cheviot, as there were still some three hundred cases left on board which Hoppit and Sankey would not buy until they had delivered what was lying on shore.

So I arranged with Danny for him to land the remainder at my risk and store it for me.

Then I went up and down the coast telling the rum-runners that the *Mermaid* was leaving the next day, and was therefore selling cheaply, so that they would get good bargains if they went out at once.

The next morning I went out in a speedboat, and found the crew of the yacht discharging into the little steamer.

Then began a never-to-be-forgotten day in the history of the *Mermaid*.

About lunch-time a boat appeared, heading for us, then another and another, and still more, until the whole sea seemed to be dotted with them. Swivel and I sat in the cabin receiving the money from the boatmen; the crew stopped loading the steamer, and every available man was put to work handing down cases to the small boats. The full ones left, and still more kept coming. About three o'clock I counted fourteen small craft in sight, some coming out empty, some loading, some cruising about awaiting their turn, and the full ones on their way home.

Suddenly the officer on watch called out, "Cutter coming up from the nor'east!"

Swivel went up on the bridge with his glasses, and I followed him. There was a black smudge of smoke on the horizon, and underneath it the white hull of a cutter.

"Beat it, boys!" called out Swivel.

We were about five miles from the beach, and once near the land the small boats were safe, because there was not enough water for the cutter. The slow boats at once made for the shore, while the fast ones awaited developments, for they knew that with a short start they could get away from her.

"To hell with the cutter!" said the burly boatman who had invited me to play poker. "The blasted son-of-a-gun only makes twelve knots, and I make sixteen. What's the scare about?"

So he went on coolly loading his speedboat, leaving his mate on the yacht to watch the movements of the cutter.

She came straight for us, and then, when only about four miles away, turned round and went back the way she had come.

"That fellow's a real gentleman," remarked the boatman.

After the enemy had disappeared over the horizon, the little boats came flocking back again. The two men I had sent out for the Cheviot seemed honest, but as I loaded ten thousand dollars worth of whiskey on to their boats, without a cent of security for it, I had some feeling of misgiving, for this was the first time that I had let anything leave the ship without first receiving the money; but there was nothing else to do unless I sent it back to England on the *Mermaid*, or trusted it to Robson. I had to rely on a guess at the characters of the men, for there was nothing to prevent them from stealing the lot and saying that they had been caught by the revenue men. I knew nothing about them except their nicknames—not even where they lived.

At six o'clock there was again a shout of "cutter"; she was coming up again, and this time the smoke pouring out of her funnel showed that she was going at full speed. She was well inshore of us, evidently with the idea of cutting off the boats from the inlets through which they had to return.

She certainly meant business this time.

Each boat made for the shore as hard as she could go; there were more than a dozen of every shape and sort, from slow old tubs doing their seven knots, to speedboats, specially built for the business, making their twenty-five.

They looked for all the world like a lot of ducks in a pond when a dog dashes in after them.

We stood on deck and watched the race; I was not worried about the Cheviot, for I had chosen the two fastest boats, but it looked as though some of the others were bound to be caught.

The cutter went in as close as she dared, but by the time she reached the buoy which marked the shoals, even the slow boats were in the shallow water, and as far as we could see, they all got away.

The cutter then steamed out to us to make sure that there were no boats tied alongside us. She came within a biscuit throw, and we watched the smartly uniformed officers on deck as they stared at us. There seemed to be a crew of about forty or fifty men, and there were several guns both in the bow and stern, which they did not hesitate to use if a boat would not heave-to when signalled to do so.

I had quite a feeling of respect for these white cutters, for most of them were going honestly about their work, and could not be "got at."

As we were British, and on the high seas, she could not touch us, of course, so after having a good look at us, she went on her way.

When she had gone, several more boats came out, and we found that during the afternoon and evening more than three thousand cases had been sold to these small craft for over sixty thousand dollars.

After dark a tiny motorboat came for a load; there was now nothing left on the yacht, so they took it from the small steamer, and I gave them a case to take me ashore.

They were going to land about twenty or thirty miles along the coast, near "Claridge's" Hotel.

We left at ten o'clock, and skirted the shore about three miles off the beach; it was pitch dark, and the two young fellows on board, who did not seem to know much about a boat, got a little worried, for the wind was rising and the weather began to thicken. Their craft was twenty-five feet long; and was so heavily loaded that there was only about nine inches freeboard.

I gathered from them that they had to find a narrow opening in the surf, and that if they could not find that, there was no shelter within many hours' run.

After a couple of hours they slowed down the motor and began peering about in the darkness for landmarks. For an hour we cruised round, unable to see anything, the roar of the surf on the shore our only guide. At last I spotted some fish-trap stakes in the water, which showed that we were near the inlet, and later on we found a gas-buoy with a revolving light which gave them their position; but they had to admit that the weather was too thick for them to find the way in, so they decided to throw out the anchor and wait for daylight.

When the motor stopped the sound of the unseen surf seemed ten times greater, as it crashed on the beach with the unbroken force of thousands of miles of ocean behind it, and there was nothing but the one little anchor to keep the boat from drifting into it.

A cold and miserable night we spent, broken by spells of pumping, with occasional discussions as to whether some of the cargo should be thrown overboard to lighten the boat, and sometimes we had to start the engine and put out to sea again when the anchor began to drag.

But the worst time must end, and we hung on until the first signs of dawn, when the anchor was pulled up, and we rode in through the inlet on the top of the rollers.

This was one of the many occasions when ignorance is bliss, for knowing what I have since learned about the sea, it is obvious that if the wind had freshened, the boat would never have reached land right side up, for there was no shelter within fifty miles, and the wind was blowing dead on shore.

However, "all's well that ends well," and in a couple of hours we came alongside a muddy bank, where some planks ran down to the water's edge from a little wooden hut.

As far as the eye could reach there were lonely swamplands, with stretches of salt water and mudbanks.

We tied up the boat, throwing a piece of sailcloth over the whiskey cases, and made for the hut. Queer sounds, half-animal and half-human, came through the closed door. We peered in and saw two men and two women lying on the floor sodden drunk; the remains of food lying about and several empty bottles showed that the party had been there since the night before. Occasionally one or other of them would break into song, which usually ended in their taking another drink from a bottle and rolling over to continue their stupefied sleep.

My two boatmen, who were decent young fellows, shrugged their shoulders in disgust at the unpleasant sight, and began to make a rough apology for having brought me there.

"If prohibition can stop this sort of thing, then I'm for prohibition," I could not help remarking.

"That's where you're wrong, brother," answered the elder of the two. "You never saw this sort of thing when people could go and get a drink decent like, without this hole-and-corner business. Disgusting, I call it. This here girl's married, too," he added, stooping down and shaking one of the women. "Hey, Elsie, where's Al? Does he know you're here?"

The woman opened a pair of bleary drink-sodden eyes.

"Dunno; gimme that bottle; it's g— d—— rotten hooch, but better than nothing."

The rum-runner picked up one of the bottles and handed it to me.

"And you can't blame we rum-runners for this, anyways," he added.

It was a claret bottle, with a "Johnnie Walker" label and a "Black and White" cork, and a sniff at the contents brought tears to the eyes.

It was one of those clumsy home-made fakes which the poorer classes drink when the price of genuine smuggled liquor is too high for them.

"Makes you kind of watery in the lamps even to smell it,"remarked one of the men with a grin; "the devil knows what it does to your guts."

"Guess we'll have to stay here till dark," said the other man to me. "We can't run in by daylight, and there is no way for you to get away from here, for we are on an island. We'll see if we can rustle some grub."

Taking no more notice of the four drunks than if they had been dogs, they lighted a stove, routed round the shelves, and before long had a meal of hot coffee, ham and eggs ready, and right welcome it was.

There was nothing to do in this desolate spot but wait for the sun to set, so we ate and slept, and in due course darkness came.

The party in the hut were left to continue their debauch. We slipped away in the dark, and in half an hour came to a sharp bend in the course of the stream. The engine was slowed down until the boat was barely moving through the water; there was no sound to be heard, and no lights were to be seen.

"There's often a prohibition boat up here with that dirty swine Spills on board," whispered one of them to me.

A dark shadow on the water came drifting towards us, and we were all strung up to the highest pitch of listening and looking. There is no thrill in the world to compare with that of man-hunting, whether you are the hunter or the hunted.

At one end of the shadow a match was struck in somebody's cupped hands; then another, and a third.

"That's the O.K. for us," murmured the rum-runner, giving a gentle sigh of relief, and opening up the throttle.

In a few minutes we were slipping silently alongside Fritz's wharf, and in ten minutes the cases were all off the boat, and safely hidden away in a back room.

I took train up to the city, and had a much-needed meal and bath.

Every case given to my two Ozone boatmen had been safely landed and hidden inside a hollow hayrick many miles inland, and were eventually delivered to the buyers.

I now made up the accounts to see how the venture had panned out.

There is always a big leakage when dealing with wet goods, and although theoretically we ought to have made over a 100 percent on the money, in actual fact we cleared 75 percent net on the investment, of which I paid the investors two-thirds as had been agreed, and kept one-third for myself.

They seemed quite satisfied, and I wired to them to send out three times as much next time, which they promised to do.

# CHAPTER IX

## DIFFICULTIES AND FAILURES

Now were this a novel, there would be one success after another, and having surmounted every difficulty, I would finish up a happy millionaire, married to the girl of my dreams.

But it is a plain story of life, and the failures must be recounted as well as the successes. Real life runs in patches, like poker or roulette, although very often a man does not live long enough for the rouge to equalise the noir; that is why some men are unlucky and others lucky, when as far as ability goes they may be equal.

Swivel's partners in London, fired by the success of the *Mermaid*, wired that they had decided to send out another ship, because the yacht could not get back to America in time for the Christmas market. I found a city on the coast where there was a shortage of liquid cheer for the holidays, and arranged with some rum-runners there to take the whole load.

As Christmas came nearer and nearer, there was delay after delay in sending out the ship, and urgent telephone calls and telegrams kept coming in from the dry city asking when the ship was going to arrive. Eventually, ten days before Christmas, they lost patience with us, and sent a man to a place where there were plenty of rum-ships, brought up one of them, and took their stock from her.

On Christmas Eve, after all the holiday supplies had been bought, the *Oldtown Cape* arrived at her anchorage, and I went aboard her with a friend of mine named Binny Dows. We had been friends when undergraduates at Oxford, where he had been one of the first American Rhodes' scholars, and a few months before we had met by accident in Fifth Avenue and recognised one another after many years. He was a perfectly respectable citizen, and had nothing to do with rum running, but being ready for any adventure in sight he said he would like to come out with me to see what a rum-ship was like.

The ship lay about thirty miles away from the nearest port, and we went out in a fishing-boat; it was so rough when we arrived alongside that it was with difficulty we climbed aboard, and as soon as we were there, the fisherman shouted that it was "breezing up," and that he would go home and return for us next day. Without waiting for a reply he headed for the shore, leaving us on the ship.

The supercargo, Sammy Byson, was a man who belonged to a famous British yacht club; the captain was a tough phlegmatic young fellow hailing from Wales, who had already run contraband into other countries. Binny, too, had knocked about the world, so between us we had enough to talk about until next day, when various boats were to come out to take loads, even though the ship had missed the market.

It blew hard all night, and in the morning the decks were several inches deep in frozen spray; the cabin leaked, there were no spare bunks to sleep in, and Binny and I had nothing but the clothes we stood up in, so we woke that Christmas morning not in the best of tempers.

All day it blew and froze, and we wallowed and rolled in the heavy seas, while the ice got thicker and thicker on deck. But the captain had a smile which never came off, Sammy was a good sportsman, and Binny an inveterate optimist, so things were not so bad.

On Boxing Day it still blew, and the next day, and the next, until we imagined ourselves on the *Flying Dutchman*.

One day we dragged anchor and began drifting, so it was necessary to up-anchor and steam out to sea again; but the steam gear was frozen solid, and we had to pull it up by hand. It took several hours for six men to pull up the hundred and ten fathom of chain, and was work as hard as I have ever done. There was not room for more men at the windlass, and as it took their whole efforts to move it one cog at a time, there was not much breathing space.

Day after day the storm continued, and it was not until New Year's Day that the sea went down and a boat arrived with our local bootlegger. He was a Scotch-American, with two wonderful rows of gold teeth, and to avoid rubbing away the gold on the cigar which never left his mouth, he always used a rubber cigar-holder.

He said that he had made two attempts to get out to the ship. On one occasion the boat had been wrecked and the men barely escaped with their lives, and on another the boatman had refused to go on and turned back, still another man who had started by himself had not been so lucky, for his boat had swamped and he had been drowned.

Binny and I went ashore, and there followed weeks of stormy weather when work was impossible; the demand for Scotch was small, the harbours were frozen, and the people with whom we had arranged to work took what goods could be landed from the other schooner, and poor Sammy used to be nearly distraught when he saw the few boats that did come out, loading from this ship.

For six weeks we remained there with the market poor, the weather bad, and the gold-toothed Scotchman failing to live up to his promises. Often at night in our dry warm beds, we used to think of poor Sammy tossing on the icy ocean and looking longingly shorewards for the boats which so seldom came, and probably trying to invent fresh cuss words for us for not sending them out.

Things now looked so hopeless that I went to a place a few hundred miles away to find a fresh market for the cargo in some spot where conditions were better.

I left Binny in charge, and with him my brother, who was spending a few weeks' holiday with me. After a few days I found a man who would take the whole load, and just as I was completing the deal a long-distance telephone call came in from my brother.

"Binny went out to the ship early yesterday morning with some provisions, and nothing has been heard of him since," he said.

I told my brother to send out men to search for him with every boat and tug he could get hold of, and I jumped on the next train to go up myself.

When I arrived there a half day later, he announced that Binny was just back again, which was good news, as he was a game fellow, and I had grown very fond of him.

We found him in our hotel bedroom, haggard and unshaven, seated in his dressing-gown in a chair by the fire, wolfing down eggs, bacon, and coffee, and too much interested in his food to talk.

After he had eaten his fill he leaned back in his chair, lighted his pipe, and told us what had happened. Here is his story.

"It has been almost impossible to get out to the ship because of the ice; the boats are nearly all frozen in, and I could not get one for love or money. But at last that fat Italian Dominik said that he had found one, and would go out to buy a load if I would go with him.

"When I got down to the dock, I did not much like the look of the boat; it was a cranky old tub about thirty-five feet long, with a little cabin three feet high which housed the engine, and had in it a stove the size of a coffee-pot; the motor was kept together with boot-laces, hair-pins, and bits of string. But it was the only boat he could find, and as it was many days since it had been possible to get out to the ship, I was afraid that Sammy might give up hope and sail away, so we had to go ahead.

"The boat was frozen solid in the ice, and the two Italian boat-men, who could barely speak any English, had to break their way out with oars.

"The ship was anchored twenty-seven miles from harbour, and as the boat only made about six knots, it was five hours before we reached the spot where she had been last time.

"It was a rotten trip, for we had to stand on the frozen deck with the wind blowing right through us and freezing the spray on our oil-skins, or else to crawl on hands and knees into the dirty little hutch of a cabin and lie alongside the motor with its horrible smells of exhaust gases, hot oil, bilge water, and unwashed Wopps.

"For two hours we cruised round the place where the ship had been, but never a sign of her could we see; the wind was getting up all the time, and there was quite a sea running by now.

"Dominik, who was as sick as a dog, kept saying we must turn back, and at last it seemed no good staying any longer. We steered for home, but the wind was offshore, and we made scarcely any headway.

"Soon after this, the engine began to splutter, and in spite of the efforts of the two fishermen, it went slower and slower, until it gave a dying kick and stopped dead, leaving us wallowing heavily in the trough of the sea.

"For two hours we sweated away at that miserable heap of scrap-iron, but never a sign of life could we get out of it. At last, after spitting on the cylinders and letting off a string of Dago cusswords, we gave it up in disgust. All this time it was blowing harder and harder, and Dominik was getting more and more sick and excited. We were all huddled together in the little cabin, and he hoisted himself up on his knees, and began praying to all the gods and saints of Italy to come to his aid. Sometimes he prayed in Italian, and sometimes in bad American.

"'Dear God and blessed Virgin, take me back to my poor widow and dear little orphans, and I will give you all I have,' he begged. Then glancing out of the porthole and noticing a momentary lull in the wind, he added hastily under his breath, 'I will give you a hundred dollars.'

"We were being carried out into the Atlantic at about three knots, and as those blighted Wopps did not seem able to do a thing to the engine and there were no masts or sails, things did not look too good.

"One of the men, sweating after still another effort to get the engine going, called out to the other, 'Getta me one drinka water, Tony.'

"'Isn't no goddarned water,' replied Tony; 'dem tapses on dem wharf alla frezza, and me forgetta flila dem demijohns.'

"We searched the boat, but all that we could find was one little stone bottle full of liquid. It was poured out into a cup, and turned out to be ink. Tony shrugged his shoulders.

"'Anyways, we can write to Jesus and tell him we are stuck,' he said.

"It was now getting dark, and we took it in turns to stay on deck to keep watch for some passing ship. After several hours the man on deck gave a shout, and we scrambled out to join him. It was hard to keep our footing on the ice-covered planks, but we clung to the top of the cabin, and as the boat rose on each wave we saw the lights of a ship some miles away. For nearly an hour we waved the lantern and yelled, and I fired my revolver into the air, but she did not see us, and her lights disappeared in the distance; the others went into the cabin, and I remained on deck to keep watch.

"By this time we were getting pretty thirsty, for they had a little fire going in the stove, and the gas fumes and the wood smoke and the stench of the cabin made our mouths as dry as the bottom of a parrot cage, while to stay on deck all the time would have meant freezing to death.

"Later on another ship passed a long way off; we dug out some old lifebelts, soaked them in petrol, tied them to the end of an oar, and threw a match at them. They flared up like a volcano, and it seemed impossible that the other ship would not see us, but they didn't, and they, too, passed out of sight.

"Dominik slept and prayed and cussed all night, and the other two guineas just slept, except when I could get one of them to keep a watch on deck. Tony was a good fellow and kept his heart up, but the other Dago was as yellow as you make 'em, and did nothing but whine.

"At dawn there was nothing to be seen but grey waves and grey sky. At the rate we were drifting we must have been outside the steamer track; we had gone thirty miles under power on the way out, and in fifteen hours' drifting at about three knots must have gone another forty-five miles, so the chances of being picked up were pretty slim. Nobody did much talking now, for our mouths were too dry. The guineas were too fed up to do anything more to the motor, and it looked as though we were for Davy Jones all right.

"I began to think of some of the sea stories I had read where the perishing sailors had drawn lots to see who should be killed for the others to drink his blood. Tony was sitting opposite to me, and I could not help wondering if he was thinking the same thoughts as I was. There was a big knife stuck in the cabin wall just above his head, and a tin cup hanging on a nail; however, I was not very much tempted myself, as the blood of those greasy Italians would probably taste like a mixture of engine-oil, garlic, and tobacco juice.

"At noon we had our hopes raised again when a trawler came in sight, but although they were within a mile or two of us, apparently they did not see our signals, for they kept on their course. One of the men said that he knew the boat and the skipper, and prayed God mercifully to allow him to reach the shore again, so that he might stick a knife in the captain's stomach.

"At last in the afternoon, after two days and a night on the water, we saw a smudge of smoke on the horizon, and an ocean-going tug came into sight. Again we went through all the hopes and fears we had experienced before, but this time we were seen, and the tug came alongside and towed us back to port. The captain was a white man, and treated us well; he said that we might have drifted across to Spain without being seen, for we had crossed the steamer track by many miles, and it was only by chance that he happened to be passing that way.

"That's the last time that I ever go out in a boat without any sails. However, it's all in the day's work!"

With a tired grin he rolled into bed and slept for sixteen hours.

The next morning he was little the worse for his adventure, and said that he was ready to go out again to look for the ship; but a telegram arrived from the owners in England to say that they had received word from the supercargo that the ship had been obliged to leave her anchorage and go to a British port for engine repairs, and that, as business in that part of the world was so slow, they had arranged to sell the cargo elsewhere, and had sent instructions to the captain to that effect. So the three of us trekked back to the city, having put in much hard work, run a good many risks, and spent three thousand dollars without getting one cent in return.

However, it cannot be all beer and skittles in a business like this.

# CHAPTER X

## THE SECRET ROOMS

In the course of our wanderings my brother and I once found ourselves on the ocean in a little twenty-six foot boat off a coast altogether strange to us. Night was coming on, so we made for a landlocked harbour, which we reached about ten o'clock; not a soul was about, and twice in the darkness we ran on the mud, and had a strenuous time in getting off.

Eventually we came alongside a wharf, tied up the boat and went asleep, wondering where we would find ourselves when we woke up in the morning.

The boat was a smart little craft, ship-shape and trim, and next day the natives of the seaside town wandered down to the quay to look her over.

One burly fellow, a hard-looking citizen of about thirty-five, was even more curious than the rest, and at first I was a little suspicious of the interest he took in our doings; but his aggressive devil-may-care swagger seemed to mark him out as one of the tougher type of rum-runner, and after sparring round for a while like two strange dogs, we were each pleased to find that we were brothers-in-arms.

"We thought as you was Federal guys in that slick little dory of yours," he remarked "so I just come down to give you the once over and see what you was doing here. So you are off the *Mermaid*, are you? I took the very first load from off of her the day she arrived here on her first voyage. She surely is one fine ship, and that captain on her is a real gentleman.

"I once tied up alongside her to get a load when it blew up a breeze of wind, my boat sank, the painter broke, and she went to the bottom. Next day when the sea had gone down, the yacht's crew dragged for her and pulled her up. Me and my engineer lived aboard the yacht while they over-hauled the engine and put it in order.

"Treated us like princes they did. A steward in a white coat brought us tea in bed in the morning, there were hot baths, and it was like being on the *Leviathan*.

"Would you like to come to see my boat? Some he-boat she is, too; she has hauled in more booze than any boat on the Atlantic coast."

It was blowing hard out on the ocean, and we could not continue our journey until the sea went down, so we started up our engine and took the boat to a wharf a mile away, where our new-found friend Bud said she would be safe from petty thieves.

After we had tied up, he took us for a run in his thirty-six foot Seabright dory. She had one enormous engine amidships, about two hundred horsepower, I think it was, and we roared over the water at thirty-five knots with our bows right in the air.

Bud was a bold reckless seaman, ready to face any odds of weather, cutters, or hijackers, and, unlike most of his kind, realised that his engine was his life, and treated it accordingly.

His engineer spent his whole time in tending the motor, although it was only used a few times each week; every drop of oil was drained from the engine after each trip; the gasolene was poured into the tank through a chamois leather; the clearances were adjusted to the thousandth of an inch, and there was a complete set of tools neatly stored in the engine-box, with spare plugs, batteries, torches, and other engine parts.

"I guess you'd like to meet Stan Sharp," he said as we landed; "he's the main squeeze round here in the booze business."

Bud guided us up from the sea to a trim little house standing near the road, with garages and outhouses clustered round it. Everything was neat and clean, and lacked the usual garnishings of empty tins and refuse, which so often take the place of gardens on the Western side of the Atlantic.

He entered the house and introduced us to Stan Sharp, a small wiry man with a hard eye, who received us very hospitably, and made us free of his home, which was furnished regardless of expense. He appeared to be one of those exceptional rum-runners who had made a good deal of money, and instead of frittering it away on motor-cars, women, and gambling, had salted it down into something solid.

He had been a rum-runner in the early days, and after making good at the sea end of the business, had settled down as a dealer on shore, where he used to store and sell whiskey for the rum-runners.

At first sight it would seem easy money to store five hundred or a thousand cases, and get a dollar or two a case for doing it, but, like many other things, it is not as simple as it looks.

The storage man has to hire labour and teams and trucks, have them waiting on the beach or wharf ready for the arrival of the boat, and arrange it all without attracting attention. He must know his men personally, for if any of them were to turn nasty and give information to the police or hijackers, the whole concern would be jeopardised.

However well he knows them, he still has to keep a sharp lookout, for men who are honest enough in anything else cease to be so when they have to do with whiskey, whether they be clam diggers or Government officials.

When carrying the cases up from the boat the men are apt to slip one under a bush, or to throw one off a truck into the ditch, and come back for it at daybreak next morning.

I have watched a man who was waiting for one of my boats to come in scratch a hole in the sand about two feet square, leaving what he had scooped out in a little pile beside the hole. His idea was to drop a case in, kick the sand over it, and leave it there until next day, when he would come to collect it.

And suppose he had been caught doing this? A lusty kick behind would be his desserts, but if he got this he would be liable to "tip off" the whole concern.

Truly the successful rum-runner needs one foot like a Tottenham Hotspur forward and the other like King Agag!

If the owner of the liquor finds a shortage in the storehouse, he blames it on the storage man, who in turn blames the truck-driver, who puts it on the men working on the beach, who passes the buck to the boatman, who blames the sailors on the ship, who blame the supercargo, who in turn accuses them of stealing the case to sell to some stray fisherman or to drink themselves.

The landing place and storage place is known as the "drop," whether it is on the beach or in the city, and always has to be guarded, for whiskey left alone invariably disappears in some mysterious way.

The man at the drop must have courage to defend the place against hijackers, and diplomacy to satisfy the demands of the police and prohibition agents as cheaply as possible; also he must be a man of sterling honesty, for many a fisherman and farmer have goods worth fifty-thousand dollars stored in their houses and outbuildings with instructions from the owner to sell at the best prices they can get to any respectable buyer who shows up. There is nothing to prevent them arranging with some friend for a fake "hold-up" and a fifty-fifty split on the booty.

Stan apparently had all these qualities, though possibly his courage outran his discretion, which fact made life a trifle difficult for him at that particular time. There had been a little affair with some hijackers, and although Stan and his gang with a true Christian spirit, had paid for the funeral expenses, and even passed round the hat for the widow, the other people were still rather sore with them. Possibly this accounted for the fact that after dusk every outside door of the house was locked, and every lighted room had the blinds down and the shutters drawn.

"A fellow in the light don't stand much chance against a guy waiting outside to get him," remarked Stan, as he carefully pulled down a blind in the sitting-room before turning up the light.

He himself always had on his hip a bulge which was not the shape of a flask, and in every room of the house there was a shotgun hanging on the wall or a revolver in some handy spot.

It will be a pretty quick man who puts one into Stan before Stan gets one into him.

For a day or two it blew hard, and we remained with him and his wife as their guests—two strangers blown in from the sea, men whom he had never seen before, and would probably never see again. Such hospitality is hospitality indeed.

He put us into a spotlessly clean little bedroom with a bath attached, one of those he kept to house some of the boys who worked for him. On the third day, after we had become very friendly, he made us swear secrecy, and showed us some of the inner workings of the place.

I have been in many Jacobean mansions with secret passages and priest-holes, but Stan, with his sliding panels, concealed vaults, and secret rooms knew more about it than any sixteenth-century architect. Our ancestors made heavy weather about hiding one emaciated priest, whilst he could store two thousand cases and yet have the place searched from cellar to garret without anything being found, as had happened more than once already.

He really was a smart little fellow, and if ever he gets into trouble it will not be from lack of brains or courage, but from the national failing of being unable to resist the temptation of letting the world know it.

# CHAPTER XI

## THE RETURN OF THE *MERMAID*

THE *Mermaid* had left home with the second consignment of Cheviot, and was now due off the American coast.

Swivel had sent a cipher telegram saying when he would arrive and the position where he would anchor, which was to be twenty miles from Cape Ozone, the place where we had done so well at the end of the last trip, and he said he would remain there until I went out to see him.

On the day he was due to arrive, I had arranged for everything to go off like clockwork. I was going out on a fast boat to make sure that he was there, then the boat was to go straight back to take a message to bring out half a dozen other boats for fourteen hundred cases.

But on arriving at Ozone I found there had been a hard frost the last two nights, and the whole place was frozen up, so that none of the speedboats, with their thin planking, would put to sea, and I had to get hold of a man with a heavy old boat to take me out; she had a copper bottom which would not be damaged by the ice.

We smashed our way out for half a mile, breaking the ice ahead with heavy poles, and then charging at the gap so that the bows slid up on the ice and the boat broke through with her own weight.

But after a time we stuck and had to put back again.

On telephoning to a rum-runner at Smithtown, a place on the coast some thirty miles away, I found that conditions there were better, so I went down by the next train. It was evening when I arrived, and as none of the boatmen would cross the bar at night in such weather, I had to wait until next morning. A local bootlegger named Antler offered to put me up for the night and ran me a few miles into the country in his new Buick coupé.

He was a stolid phlegmatic sort of fellow who had once been a contractor, but now found whiskey dealing more lucrative than laying drainpipes. For some time he had been very useful to me in running me about in his car, finding boats, and helping me in other ways.

We drew up in front of a charming little house standing in its own garden, and after parking the motor in a large two-car garage, we entered the house, where Mrs. Antler gave us a good supper, nicely served on a polished mahogany table.

By telephone he arranged with the boatman to make a daylight start next morning, and put me in a large comfortable bedroom, with radiators by the window and a telephone by the bed.

At dawn next morning he motored me down to a boathouse on the estuary, where a small speedboat was waiting ready; it had a tiny cabin over the engine, into which it was possible to crawl on hands and knees

The ice was thin and the powerful engine had little difficulty in pushing its way through, so we were soon scudding over the inland waters on the way to the open sea.

Once over the bar it was pretty choppy, and the spray soon coated us and the boat with ice. Icicles as big as pencils hung all round our sou'westers, so that they looked like black lamp-shades with glass head-fringes.

For two hours we went thumping from wave to wave until we were forty miles from Smithtown, but we could see no sign of the *Mermaid* in the place where she was supposed to be.

After cruising round for an hour we had to give it up and make for land, as the open ocean is no pleasure resort for an open boat in February. If the wind gets fresh, the spray is liable to freeze so thickly over her that she may sink or turn over.

Having frozen in an aeroplane ten thousand feet up, and frozen in an open sleigh on the Russian steppes, and spent a solid hour in a Great Eastern Railway waiting-room, I thought there was nothing that I did not know about the cold, but this was worse than anything I had yet met. However, many years of knocking about the world has shown that heaven has been kind to make a limit beyond which a man cannot suffer either in body or mind, and once this point is reached, it does not matter very much what happens.

After a four hours' journey back, at last we slid into inland waters and approached the boathouse.

The kindly Antler was there waiting for me; and after giving me time to thaw by the stove, he drove me home for another night in his comfortable house.

"Tomorrow you are going to find me something with a stove in the cabin," I said to him after supper, "for it's no picnic in those open boats!"

After telephoning to a number of boatmen he found a boat with a cabin, and arranged with the owner to be ready to start early, the next day.

At dawn the following day he motored me down to what had once been a saloon by the waterside, but was now by way of being a restaurant frequented by fishermen and "bottle-fishermen," as the smugglers are called. A dirty old craft lay alongside the wharf, and after some delay the owners were rounded up and we went chugging towards the sea.

In an hour we reached the ocean, where the great rollers were coming in lazily and breaking with a mighty crash on the bar. It was white water all the way across.

"Maybe it will be better when the tide changes," remarked the boatman, Alf. "Guess we'll wait a while to see. I wouldn't mind hitting the yacht tonight; we would be the first boat out, and the big fellow might give us a case for ourselves. He'll likely remember me, as I was the first guy that ever took a load off of him when he came out the first time."

So the boat was turned round, and we anchored behind a little sandy point in smooth water, and lighting our pipes waited for the change of the tide.

Alf was a pretty rough customer, but he had some very decided views on life; he made his living running whiskey in his boat, and evidently spent the money as fast as he made it. I often wondered what he found to spend it on, for he was dressed in the shabbiest of clothes, lived in the meanest of shacks, and never seemed to have a dime in his pocket, although he would often make a thousand dollars in a night, and could do that several times a month if he wanted to.

He began to meander about his experiences, taking a pull at a bottle every now and then to keep the cold out.

"Yes, sir, this ain't no bad place at all for hauling in the booze. Once you get within a mile of the shore the cutter can't follow you because there ain't enough water for her, and if you load in daylight from a schooner six miles out, you can see the cutter coming in time to get to the bar before she can ketch you.

"Another good thing is that there ain't none of those blasted Wopps down here. Wopps is a darned nuisance; if things don't go just as they want, they get all het up, and out comes guns and knives. Before you know where you are, there's a dead Dago left lying about, down comes the police and troopers, and there's all sorts and kind of trouble.

"We had one knifed down here five months ago, and since then we boatmen have made a sort of gentlemen's agreement not to do no hauling for no Hitalians, and now it is quite peaceful like.

"Our only trouble just now is that long-nosed son-of-a-dog of a prohibition man named Spills who's located down here. He's knocked off two drops and a boat in the last few days, and that sort of thing makes you kind of uncomfortable like. Yes, sir! He's a goddarned rat, and I wouldn't be surprised if he wasn't bumped off one of these days.

"Last week he heard that there was some stuff going to be moved along a lonesome road three miles beyond that point you see over there, so he got some Government guys and waited for it in the dark.

"But one of his men was cousin to the wife of Mike Sullivan, who was going to drive the truck, and he gave Mike the low-down on it, so Mike left the load behind and drove along with an empty truck.

"When he came to the place where Spills and his gang was hiding, they all jumped out on him, and held him up with their guns.

"'Good evening,' said Mike to them, as pleasant as you like.

"'Put 'em up, quick!' says Spills.

"So Mike puts them up and watches them searching the truck with a grin on his face.

"Then they saw as how they had been fooled and got fair mad with him; they pulled him off the truck and beat him up so proper they nearly put his light out."

"Hadn't he got a gun with him?" I asked.

"Sure he had a gun; but what's the good of pulling a gun when there's six fellows with badges up against you? It's just what they want you to do, then they kill you in self-defence and get promotion for it, while if you shoot any of them, like as not you'll find yourself on the way to the chair. Of course, if there's enough of you to clear up the whole blamed bunch and leave no witnesses, that's a different pair of shoes.

"When Mike gets out of hospital he'll go gunning for Spills, and if he gets him, I won't be sending no grapes to the funeral."

"Can't this fellow be fixed?" I inquired.

"Sure he can be fixed, what do you think he is an agent for? To get the few lousy dollars a month that the Government puts in his pay envelope? No, siree, not so as you would notice it! If he was a square-shooter he'd be as lonely as a lawyer in heaven.

"The trouble is that he's new down here, and we don't know how to handle him yet. These new guys always start like that. They come along with the hell of a reputation.

"They wouldn't take a million berries, not if they was dropped into their pockets. So tough, their mother gave 'em a mule's mit for a teething ring, they chew glass and drink iodine.

84

"They makes it that hard the boys can't land nothing. Stuff runs short, prices go up, and it's hard to get at that. Just what they wants.

"Then the next thing you know, one or two of the big guys is working and pulling in a thousand cases several times a week.

"Then the little fellows like me think they will have a try, and they get knocked off every time.

"For why?

"Because the big operators has got close to the prohibition man, and he's getting his dollar or two dollars a case. And he thinks he is entitled to it, having made the price rise because he has acted so tough. And as like as not the big operators is tipping off the little ones so they shan't bring in more goods and drop the price.

"So the agent gets bouquets thrown at him by the Department for catching the small men, and he gets four or five thousand dollars a week from the big ones, though some of this he had to pass on to the guys up above him that gives him the job, and some to the guys below him to keep their traps shut.

"It's a great game being an agent, and the slick ones get away with a wad big enough to choke a cow."

Alf relapsed, into moody silence, and spat in the stove as if to show what he thought about Government officials generally.

The tide changed, and we went down to the bar again, but the waves were breaking as heavily as ever, so we had to return to the ramshackle house by the water.

Having arranged with Alf to try again next day, I persuaded the cook to give me some eggs, and bacon, and after supper I pushed aside the dishes and stretched myself on the table for a night's sleep, there being no other moderately clean spot in the room.

The proprietor of the place was a wheezy old gaffer named Maisoni; he looked in his dotage, but was as sly an old fox as ever sold a case of whiskey. Several times during the night I was awakened by the dogs barking, and the old man came shuffling downstairs to let in mysterious visitors.

There were whispered conversations in the darkness, and one time a strange voice asked, "Who's dat guy dere on de table?"

"It's only de fellow as is looking for de *Mermaid*," Maisoni's voice answered.

They disappeared through a door at the back, and did not return for half an hour. Heaven knows what they were up to, but very likely it was only some affair of buying whiskey, for there was a good deal stored about the premises.

For all its tumble-down appearance the whole place was highly organised for its work; ostensibly it was a rendezvous for fishermen and sportsmen, and was actually used as such. Maisoni used to tell people that he had a lot of valuable fishing tackle and sporting guns about, and was nervous about thieves breaking in.

"So soon as I hears any one foolin' around, I'se goin' to shoot without asking no questions," he used to say. What is more, people knew he meant it; and as he had the reputation of being a dead shot, I have never yet heard of him being troubled by hijackers.

He kept a number of dogs prowling about the place, the approach to which was along a narrow private road; there was a powerful electric searchlight fixed at the top of the house so that if any strangers approached unannounced, he could turn a dazzling beam full in their faces to see who they were.

While the boats were unloading their cargoes at the wharf, their bows would be pointing downstream and the engines left running, so at the first sign of danger they could slip away into the marshes, where nobody could catch them.

He also had confederates scattered about the district, and if there was any special activity on the part of the police or prohibition men, they would telephone a warning to him, with the result that, though the authorities knew pretty well what he was up to, so far he had not been molested.

Talking of old Maisoni reminds me of something that happened in connection with his place some time after this.

I was talking with the prohibition agent, Hank Lean, about a matter in which we were mutually interested, and which involved a visit on his part to a ship lying off the coast.

"Would you like me to take you out?" I asked him.

"Yes, if you can arrange it so that nobody knows about it," he said. "Where is she anchored?"

"South of Smithtown," I answered.

"How about starting from Maisoni's?" he suggested. "It's a nice quiet place, and there is seldom anyone about in the daytime. I suppose the old rascal is storing stuff as usual? It's a pretty good place, too, and hasn't been knocked off yet. I shall have to go down there one of these days and make a pinch, but I think Tom Hoppit has a good bit of stuff there just now, and I'd rather wait until he has sold it, for he's a good scout; his wife is my wife's cousin."

I was a little taken aback at his intimate knowledge of what was going on, but agreed to his suggestion, on condition that he did not "pinch" any one while he was with me.

We had lunch at Smithtown together, and afterwards I walked alone down to Maisoni's and found Alf's sister, who after a long hunt produced Alf, nearly half sober.

"Will you take me out to sea with a friend of mine?" I asked him. "I might," he answered.

After some delay he and his mate brought the boat to the wharf and were ready to start. I telephoned to Hank, and he arrived with his coat collar turned up and his cap pulled well down over his eyes. He slipped into the cabin, and off we went. Poor Alf would have gone stone sober with astonishment if he had known who his passenger was.

It was choppy at sea, and the wind was increasing. Alf's crazy old boat rolled and pitched, but Hank never turned a hair.

"No use to go on, Mr. Barby; we wouldn't be able to get you two aboard even if we did make the ship. We've got to turn back," remarked Alf, poking his head into the cabin.

So back we went, and although he waited for several days, the weather was bad all the time, and eventually he was obliged to leave in order to continue his official duties of exterminating rum-runners.

But I am wandering far from the story.

I then made several attempts to get out to the ship, but they all failed owing to bad weather. At length the wind seemed to be dying down somewhat, and I got hold of a rum-runner who was old in the game, and asked him if there was any harbour from which it was possible to get out without having a bar to cross.

He told me of a place forty miles away, and gave me the name of a boatman named Ericson who had a fast craft.

Rolling up my oilskins and sea-boots in a bundle, I caught the next train, and went to the house at which I was told the Norwegian could be found. People of this sort, and, in fact, nearly everyone connected with bootlegging, seldom give their real addresses, but usually that of some friend or acquaintance, who parleys with anyone inquiring for them until it seems certain that the stranger is bona fide. In this case I found myself at a boat-building yard, and after some palaver and giving the names of various mutual acquaintances in the rum running business, I ran Ericson to earth.

He was a fine-looking fellow, with fair hair, square shoulders, and a fearless blue eye; one could imagine his forefathers crossing the North Sea in a Viking ship and raiding the east coast of Britain.

He agreed to go out at once, as it was a clear night and the lights of a steamer would be visible many miles away. He telephoned to his mate, and the three of us tramped down to the wharf, where a number of boats were tied up.

"That's the *Cigarette*," he said, pointing to a long low shadow in the water below us. "She's the fastest boat in the world and has run more booze ashore than any boat in America; that's our boat tied up alongside her. I know the *Mermaid* well; I ran alongside her before she dropped anchor the first time she was out, and took the first load off her that she ever sold."

We climbed down the steep side of the wharf on to the *Cigarette*, and into a large Seabright dory moored on the other side of her. While the two men began getting the engine ready, I sat down on the edge of the boat, unrolled the bundle of oilskins, and took off my shoes in order to put on my sea-boots. At that moment a bright light suddenly appeared close by, there was noise of water and voices, and a boat shot round the corner of the wharf and came straight for us.

"Beat it!" said Ericson.

We all three jumped across to the *Cigarette*, scrambled up on the wharf and ran down it, as a fast boat full of men, with a searchlight in the bow, came tearing in from the darkness outside and drew up alongside the dory.

"Hide!" whispered Ericson, who apparently was not given to wasting words in an emergency. I had not the foggiest idea what it was all about, but did as he said.

A man without boots is a helpless animal; somehow it seems to destroy his morale altogether, and makes him feel like Samson shorn of his locks.

However, it was too late to go back for them, so, in my socks, I legged it across a piece of remarkably stony wasteland.

A black mass loomed ahead; it appeared to be a sort of wall, and I crawled through a hole in it. When my eyes became more used to the darkness, I found myself in a shed with piles of lumber lying about.

Peering through a crack in the boards, I saw the men who had disturbed us wandering about with flash-lamps and shouting to one another. They came nearer, and I felt my way round the walls until I found another hole through which to bolt if they entered. They came close to my hiding-place, flashing their lights here and there, but walked past, and their footsteps grew fainter and fainter until they disappeared round a corner. Some of them had apparently been left on board their boat, for the engine was started and they went away, throwing their searchlight about as they went.

After they had gone, I crept from my hiding place and climbed cautiously down on to the *Cigarette*, found the two Norwegians back, and my boots still there.

"Who were they?" I asked.

"Harbour police," replied Ericson.

"What were they after?"

"God knows," he muttered, "but once we get agoing the devil himself won't stop us."

The engine started, the mooring ropes were cast off, and running dead slow the boat nosed her way silently out of the dock and into the darkness beyond.

It was pitch dark, except for a mass of confusing lights on the water; some red and some white; some stationary, some moving, and others blinking.

"Let her go, buddy!" said Ericson to his mate.

"To hell with the police and the cutters!" yelled Ericson above the din of the engine, as the boat shot forward. The compass light threw a faint glow over his bronzed face and fair hair, and he looked more than ever like some Norseman of old hurling defiance at his enemies.

The boat was making about thirty knots, and he steered her skillfully between buoys, beacon lights, and anchored craft until we found ourselves in the open sea with a long line of gas-buoys stretching away to the horizon like the lamps of Piccadilly at two o'clock on a wet morning.

He slowed down the engine somewhat and for nearly three hours the boat hummed along until we saw the anchor light of a ship some miles ahead.

As the light got nearer and nearer, I began to think of the *Mermaid* with the open fireplace in the saloon and the little steward handing round the hot coffee which would be so welcome. But when we drew close we could see that it was a schooner, with two speed-boats alongside loading cases of whiskey.

"What's your name?" Ericson shouted.

"The *George M. Cook*," said a big man with a Scotch accent.

"Have you seen the *Mermaid*?"

"No, she ain't anywhere near here."

So we went farther and asked the men on another schooner which was also lying at anchor. They gave us their bearing, so we marked it on the chart and made for the exact position which Swivel had given; on arriving at the spot there was no sign of the ship, though it was possible to see for many miles round.

A thick mist now rolled up over the ocean, and even lights were only visible for a few hundred yards, so for the next two hours we cruised round, and every now and again stopped the engine to listen for the *Mermaid*'s bell, but heard nothing. The ocean is a lonely place in a fog, and in a small boat there is the same sense of being cut off from the world and humanity that there is when flying high above the earth, with nothing visible but cloud and blue sky, or lying cramped up in an eighteen-inch tunnel underground, oppressed by the heavy air and the silence that can almost be touched.

Daylight came, and although we went thirty miles out to sea there was still no sign of the ship, so they turned the boat back, and we arrived in the city about ten next morning, cold, hungry, and disappointed.

# CHAPTER XII

## THE *MERMAID* FOUND

I went back to my little apartment in the city, and after a bath and a meal, got busy on the telephone. I rang up men up and down the coast asking if they knew anything of the yacht; but nobody had heard of her, until Danny Roper answered that he had news.

"Yes, Barby, Lu told me that Ed was out for a load to a schooner off the cape, and saw the *Mermaid* there. She was about ten miles to the east'ard, and he got a load from off of her."

This was some encouragement, although it was only third-hand news. If the ship was where he said, she was some ten miles out of position, which would account for the failure to find her.

Taking the next train down to Smithtown, I hired a man named Lem who had a fast open boat, and we set off on our trip on a Sunday morning, as people were on their way to church. The boat was a Seabright dory, a type of boat much used by the rum-runners, and they are very fine sea-craft indeed. They have square sterns, bluff bows, are wide in the beam for their length, and carry the engine in a box amidships. Their length varies from twenty-five to forty feet, and they are built of very thin wood—about five-eighths of an inch as a rule. This is not much protection between a man and the ocean, especially at night, when a log or piece of wreckage hit end-on will go through the side of one of these boats like a pencil through a piece of paper, and with the immense weight of the engine the boat would sink like a stone. When they gain speed, the bows get up out of the water, until at thirty knots a third or a half of the keel is visible above the sea.

After crossing the bar, Lem suddenly slowed down and pointed to the horizon; there was a smudge of smoke with a speck of white below it, which meant a Revenue cutter, and she was going in the direction in which we wanted to go.

Lem followed her slowly, allowing her to increase her lead until she disappeared on the horizon, when he struck out to sea to look for the yacht.

"What could they do to us if they did catch us?" I asked him, "We have no booze aboard; we're just three honest citizens out for a Sunday morning joy-ride."

"No, they couldn't, but they would. In this business it isn't what the Government guys can do, but what they do do, that counts. If they picked us up now they would hold me if there was the least thing wrong with the boat's papers, and if there wasn't anything wrong they would make them wrong. They would be liable to keep you for examination as to how you came into the country, and would hold on to my dory; by the time I got her back she would be worth about three hundred and fifty dollars, instead of the thirty-five hundred I paid for her, for they would knock her about, run her without oil in the engine, and pinch everything movable. No, sir, it can't help you any to let those white babies get too close to you."

In about an hour I was looking round the horizon, and noticed a trail of smoke inshore of us, where steamers did not usually go, so I asked Lem what it was.

"The crafty son of a gun!" he exclaimed, after examining it with his glasses. "He must have seen us all the while, and now he's got inshore of us to cut us off from the inlets, and chase us out to sea till our gas is all used up. We must beat him to it."

He swung the rudder over, and the boat went round with a rush, and headed back the way she had come. It was twelve miles back to the inlet, and although we were faster than the cutter, she was inside us and nearer to it; she was trying to cut us off, and having a shorter distance to go, she was going to give us a close race.

The smoke began to pour out of her funnel, and the seagulls watched a very pretty race that sunny Sunday morning between the big white cutter with her shining brass and her gold-braided officers, making her fourteen knots, and the little open speedboat skimming along from wave to wave.

The race lasted about half an hour, with the cutter gaining fairly rapidly, for the waves, which were too small to affect her speed, cut down ours considerably. Lem stood quietly at the wheel with a trace of worry on his ruddy good-natured face, glancing over his right shoulder every now and again to see the progress our pursuer was making while the engineer hovered over the throbbing engine with an oil-can.

As we approached our goal the cutter got nearer and nearer to us, until we could see the men moving on deck and a gun pointing aggressively towards us.

"Why doesn't she shoot?" I asked Lem.

"Well, she hasn't anything particular against us, and if she hit us, and we really were some city guys out for a holiday, they might get into trouble."

At last we ran into shallow water where the cutter could not follow, and she came to a standstill a third of a mile behind us.

We anchored behind a spit of land and waited for her to move, but although we were out of her sight, she remained there.

"I guess we had better call it a day, and anyways I doubt if we have enough gas left to make the trip," remarked Lem, so we went back, and by the time we had moored the boat at his wharf the wind had sprung up again.

After several more fruitless trips, which it would be tedious to describe, I sought out Alf again.

"What about it, Alf?" I asked.

"What's it worth?" he asked.

"Eight cases if you put me on board, and nothing if you don't."

"Seen her yet?" he asked.

"Yes, we saw her yesterday, and had to turn back because it breezed up."

"That's Jake for me," he answered.

At six o'clock that evening I started off the seventh time. There was a flat calm, and the waves were not breaking even on the bar.

We ran without lights, of course, but there were several craft in sight, and one in particular which Alf watched very closely; she had a row of lighted portholes, and seemed to be moving about rather aimlessly. Suddenly a white beam shot from her decks and began sweeping the water round her.

"The cutter!" remarked Alf. "Bill MacIntosh's schooner is out there, and the boys were going to pull two-thousand off of her tonight. His crowd have been shouting off their mouths too much and I guess the coastguard heard, and has come down to watch her."

He altered our course and kept nearer the shore. It was another bitterly cold night, and there was ice floating about in the sea. Suddenly, right ahead of us, another searchlight began playing on the water.

"Another of the darned things! They're as thick as fleas in a Chinamen's bed!" remarked Alf, again altering the course. As we watched the first cutter, the searchlight went out, and then every light in the ship was extinguished and there was darkness.

We continued on our way for a quarter of an hour, when without any warning a cutter appeared close by us, with her lights all burning and the searchlight playing on the water. It was evidently the first ship we had seen, and she had put out all her lights and gone cruising round in the hope of catching some boat unawares.

I expected Alf to put about and make for safety, but nothing of the sort; he kept right on and, after playing hide-and-seek with the two cutters for half an hour, finally got clear of them, his hardihood doubtless stimulated by the eight cases he was to get.

At last the lights of the *Mermaid* came into sight, and on this, the seventh attempt, I ran along her and climbed on board. "You've been the hell of a long time coming out," was Swivel's greeting.

Alf and his engineer came on board for food and drinks, and received the eight cases they had been promised for the fare; in addition I gave them ten cases to freight in for me at five dollars a case, so he would clear altogether about five-hundred dollars on the trip. After resting an hour they climbed down into their boat, taking with them a letter to a friend of mine telling him where the ship was, and asking him to send out boats.

Alf's return trip was not without incident, for when they were about half-way back the engineer went into the cabin to do something to the engine, and on coming out found himself alone on the boat with seventeen and eleven-twelfth cases of whiskey. The night was dark, and the ocean large, so the chances of picking up a lost man were about one in a thousand, even if he had not been drowned immediately.

He put the boat about and went back on his tracks, peering intently into the darkness hoping for a sign of his lost skipper. After going some distance he saw a pale blur, and steered towards it. It was Alf, whose new yellow oilskins had held enough air to support him in the water, in spite of his heavy clothing and sea-boots, and their light colour had made him visible when otherwise it would have been impossible to see him.

He was pulled aboard somehow, and their account of the rest of the voyage was somewhat vague; probably in the hopes of averting a chill he had broached cargo more than was wise; they said they were chased by a cutter and had to throw all eighteen cases overboard, and did not get back to Maisoni's until noon next day. One thing at any rate is certain, which is that those ten cases of mine were never seen again, nor did I ever employ the worthy Alf anymore, for however excellent a man is, if he does not know when he has enough liquor aboard, his value, in the smuggling business at any rate, deteriorates about 50 percent.

But to return to the *Mermaid*. It seemed that Swivel, having given his bearing from Ozone, had taken it for granted that I would come out from there, and had steamed in to meet me some ten or twelve miles, hoping thereby to shorten my trip. As it was, I had been obliged owing to the ice to approach from a different point, and arriving at the rendezvous could not find him, as he was many miles inshore of the agreed place.

Swivel casually announced one piece of bad news, which was that owing to faulty arrangements at the port of shipment, two-thirds of the "Cheviot" had been left behind. This was a great blow, as it had all been ordered and the buyers were waiting for it, so it meant a heavy loss to me, to say nothing of the delay.

The next few months were just hard work with many ups and downs; there was the joy of being out in the open and having more work to do than could be done, but otherwise there was little romance or pleasure about it: it was like going up to the trenches—the first few times are an adventure, and give the young soldier quite a thrill, but it soon settles down into the ordinary day's routine. There was the great difficulty of communicating with the ship, and a succession of fruitless trips to sea in small boats; there were days on end, sometimes four or five, without bed or sleep; there was severe competition from other ships and Swivel's refusal to drop his prices sufficiently to meet this competition; worst of all there was the curse of credit, which began to creep into the trade about this time.

From other ships the big dealers were buying hundreds and even thousands of cases on credit, and paid for them after they were sold; buyers naturally went to these ships in preference to the others, so we had reluctantly to follow suit.

Most of the buyers would pay for goods they took on credit provided all went well and they themselves got the money for them; the trouble was that when they took a loss they would claim a rebate, or perhaps be unable to pay, or even disappear altogether from the scene. The whole art of the game now lay in knowing whom to trust and exactly how far to trust them, for most intelligent men will be honest as long as it pays them to be so. When they have built up a reputation for fair dealing, and are able to get large credit, then is the time to watch them, for they are apt to make a big killing and then fade away. I knew Hoppit was this type of man, so fed him continuously on descriptions of the far bigger deals we were going to do in the near future.

"You want to be careful on this credit business, Barby," said a friendly operator to me one day. "It's all very well for us big fellows to give stuff on the cuff, because if a guy don't cough up the dough what he owes, we can make him do it. If he don't pay when we ask him reasonable-like, we just sends along a couple of our tame gorillas, who take him down a cellar and beat the juice out of him with a piece of lead pipe. When he gets out of hospital he's in an almighty hurry to pay up. Supposing he don't and one morning he's found floating in the river, or on a vacant lot with his toes turned up, that's his funeral and he's only got what was coming to him.

"Sometimes if he's a tough guy, he'll keep a few of his own boys tagging along after him all the while to look after him, and then you've got to look out for trouble.

"So if you hasn't got some real tough babies behind you, who are ready for anything from chin music to lead pills, you don't stand much charnst.

"If ever you gets any bad debts, come along and tell me and I'll sure be glad to help you out, if I can, without making nothing on it neither. I've got some real good boys in my outfit, and I'll loan them to you if you'll pay them the same as I do. Ten dollars a day I give them when I want them to trail round after me in case anything turns up, twenty-five dollars extra if they has to hand a fellow a sleep pill with their black-jacks or pull their guns, and fifty bucks if they have to shoot; there's other things they get five centuries for, but that don't come their way every day—not often from me anyways."

Hoppit used to get a good deal of whiskey on credit, and had always paid up. One day, however, the coastguard grabbed a load of about a hundred and fifty cases, for which he owed about three thousand dollars, and for a few days it seemed doubtful whether he would pay or not, for he was terribly close with his money; but when he was asked for it, he produced a great roll of bills and paid every cent, evidently thinking that at the moment his reputation for honesty was worth more to him than three thousand dollars. During this trip and the previous one I sold over a hundred thousand dollars' worth of goods for Swivel on credit and did not make one bad debt, and handled about three hundred thousand dollars in hard cash without having the bad luck to lose a cent.

The difficulty and expense of hiring craft to go out to the ship was so great that Swivel agreed to the purchase of a little boat for this purpose. We therefore bought a little twenty-six footer with a fifty horsepower engine, which took her along at fourteen knots. Steel rings were put in her fore and aft, so that she could be hoisted on the yacht's davits. I knew next to nothing about boats, but my brother, who was a sailor, showed me the ropes, and used to go with me until I learned something of the rudiments of seamanship.

# CHAPTER XIII

## A SHAKE-DOWN

DURING the next few months many things happened; there is no space here to relate them all, but there is one incident which is worth telling.

The lawyer, Finnigan, sent me a message asking me to call to see him, so I went to his office scenting trouble.

"We are both busy men, Mr. Barbican, so I will go straight to the point," he began, leaning back in his chair, closing his eyes, and putting the tips of his fingers together in true professional style. "Your partner, Hoppit, has got into difficulties which may involve you seriously.

"I heard of this quite accidentally, and as you came to me some time ago and asked me to look after your interests in case anything went wrong, I invited you to meet me to review the situation and see whether, by timely action, we may be able to avert what may develop into a very awkward position. It is said that you and Hoppit unloaded the *Mermaid* twice, and the *Oldtown Cape* once; this means a turnover of about two million dollars, and consequently very large profits to you and him. Further, it is alleged that your introduction to Hoppit came through Mr. Mossard, who is a politician in good favour with the very highest authorities.

"I hope, Mr. Barbican, that you are not vain enough to think that you have done this immense business unknown to the authorities. Every move you have made must have been watched by them, but apparently you have been working under protection, the very highest protection, I may say, which Mr. Mossard says was arranged by him for you both on certain terms.

"Mr. Mossard, who is a close personal friend of a certain very eminent person, says that he has fulfilled his part of the contract, and now Hoppit, having made a large sum of money, refuses to pay for the protection he has received.

"Mr. Mossard is very angry indeed about it, and I fear that he regards you, being Hoppit's principal, as responsible for these debts of honour. It was a lucky chance which brought this situation, to my notice, as otherwise Mr. Mossard would have taken action already and 'blown the whole works,' as he expresses it.

"But I have succeeded in holding him back for a time until we see if it is not possible to safeguard your interests and liberty."

He sat there serene and detached gazing through his window at the wonderful panorama of houses, church spires, and skyscrapers stretched out below us like a map, and spoke so quietly and convincingly that it made me think the good Hoppit must have been playing a double game. The number of cases and the amounts of money were, of course, enormously exaggerated: Hoppit did not even know about the *Oldtown Cape*, and I had never even heard of Mossard, but there seemed to be a nut loose somewhere in our machinery.

"I know nothing of Mr. Mossard," I said, "and have never made him any promises. If Hoppit makes any promises, that is his affair and has nothing to do with me; if he did make them, it is up to him to keep them. Since I came to this country I have made very few promises, but what I have made I have kept."

"No doubt, Mr. Barbican, no doubt," he replied, "and if I had thought you were the type a man to go back on your word, I would not have consented to act for you. But unfortunately Mr. Mossard does not see it in that light, and at present he has the wish, and I may add the power, to upset your whole organisation, and we have to consider how to avert this."

"Well, if he has a grievance against me, why doesn't he come and meet me face to face?" I argued impatiently. "I'll tell him that if Hoppit made him any promises, it is a matter between the two of them, and I have no desire to be mixed up in it."

"Perhaps I might get him to meet you," answered Finnigan.

He put through a telephone call, and after a brief conversation with someone turned to me and said, "He will meet you here at three o'clock, if that suits you?"

At three o'clock I returned, and found Finnigan talking to Mossard, a short stoutish man of about sixty; as they turned at my entrance they were talking to one another about their friend X., who was the Lord High Vendor of Justice in the city, a man so prominent that his name is well-known even to the British public.

It was fairly obvious that this was done to impress me, but at the same time it was no bluff, for since seeing Finnigan in the morning I had found out that they were both intimate friends of the man in question, and that the lawyer, as I had been told before, was an influence in one of the most powerful political organisations that the world has ever seen.

Finnigan, assuming a pontifical air, made a brief resumé of what he had said to me in the morning.

"Now I want to see you two gentlemen get together and fix up things to your mutual satisfaction. As you both know, I have no interests to serve, but want merely to save you both great deal of trouble, which there certainly will be unless this matter is cleared up."

Mossard had maintained a stolid silence up till now, but after Finnigan had finished speaking he strode up and down the room a few times, and then exploded like a sixteen-inch shell.

"Hoppit promised to pay for the protection. How much have you lost up to the present? Nothing! and why? Because I gave you 100 percent protection. And now that he has cleaned up a fortune he refuses me my share. The people who gave you the protection have come to me for the brass, and I haven't got it. That crook Hoppit has stalled me time and again, and now it can't be put off any longer. It's a case of pay or take the consequences."

"I told Mr. Finnigan this morning," I replied meekly, "that I have authorised nobody to make any promises on my behalf, and that if Hoppit had made you any, it is a matter between the two of you and no concern of mine. What do you want to drag me in for? Why not see him yourself and have it out with him?"

"I wouldn't demean myself by being in the same room as that goddarned crook, far less speak to him. He's a liar and a swindler, and he's going to have a sharp lesson. He can't fool about with men like——, but I won't mention names. If he tries his monkey tricks on them he will soon find himself behind the bars for ten years. They will put a cheap little bootlegger like him away where he can't do any harm. I have no feeling against you personally, but you are in with a real bad actor. If you don't pay at once you'll be put away with him."

He halted out of breath and purple in the face.

"How much do you reckon he owes you?" I inquired.

"I am going to have five dollars a case on the two loads of the *Mermaid*, and the one load of the *Oldtown Cape*. That comes to two hundred thousand dollars. If you can't pay it all down in a lump sum, you can pay half now and the rest over the next month or two. The money's not for me, it's for others—men whose names can't be mentioned,—but you will soon know what sort they are if you don't come across with the dough pretty damn quick."

The demand, of course, was perfectly preposterous, and showed that he had not much knowledge of the financial end of the rum running business, so I thought the best thing was to play for time in order to talk to Hoppit and find out how the land lay.

"I'll see Hoppit, and hear what he has to say about it," I answered.

Mossard strode out of the room, slamming the door behind him. Finnigan remained seated at his desk drumming on a book with his long fingers; his face was expressionless, and he was looking at me intently with his steady grey eyes.

"We had better get it fixed up pretty soon, Mr. Barbican.

"There is all the makings of a nasty mess here if Mr. Mossard is not satisfied. Fortunately I have persuaded him to hold his horses until you have had an opportunity to get things straightened out. But he is so angry that there is no saying what he will do if you don't get a move on. Once he speaks the word he will put in motion machinery which neither he, nor you, nor I could stop."

I went out of his office and returned to my rooms to smoke a pipe and think the matter over.

It seemed as though Hoppit had certainly fallen foul of the powers that were, and that having failed to get at him direct they were trying to get at him through me.

It was impossible to leave the city with the *Mermaid* only half unloaded and many large debts to be collected; equally impossible to pay him a tenth of what he demanded, even were we willing to do so, but on the other hand, the cool capable Finnigan seemed to take a serious view of the matter, and unless he was a marvellous actor, the old fellow was really labouring under some grievance, and was liable to do almost anything unless he was appeased in some way.

The first thing to do was to see Hoppit, for there are two sides to every story, so I telephoned to him to come round to see me, and I told him what had happened.

He listened without making a remark until the story was finished, but by the aggressive way his jaw stuck out it was not difficult to see what line he was going to take.

"You go to work and tell that dirty old bum of a cheap politician that I'll see him in hell before I give him a dime. I meant to tell you the other day how he tried to shake me down in the same way. He's just a lousy ten-cent four-flusher out to make some easy money, and he thinks he will shake it out of you easier than he will out of me.

"When he tried it on me I gave the crazy old swine a proper earful, told him just where he got off at—and that's why he won't see me again. He's so crooked he could hide behind a corkscrew, and couldn't fall down a well.

"I am surprised at Terrence Finnigan having a hand in it, but they are probably in on the deal together and have agreed to split on what they get out of you. If he tries to get at you again, tell him to see me; I'll go to work and fix him good and proper."

It was rather an embarrassing situation, each party thirsting for battle, with myself as the proposed battle-ground.

One or other of them was bluffing, and the question was which?

It looked as though it might be Hoppit, so I pressed him hard to find out what it was that gave him such supreme confidence, as he was apparently keeping something back.

"Well, Barby, if you must know, here's what happened, but you must promise not to tell a living soul.

"About four years ago I went to work and fixed up..."

Then followed a long story of lying and graft in which Hoppit had not been dishonest according to his standards, but the old fellow Mossard had acted as go-between and had swindled both parties.

In the United States there is a profession known as that of the "fixer," who is the exact counterpart of the "intermediary Jew" in Roumania. A man wants some favour from a politician or other authority; the politician or official is willing to give it to him for a consideration, but each is too cautious to approach the other directly. So the buyer of favours goes to the fixer, who is often a minor politician, tells him the story and says how much he is willing to pay; the fixer goes to the official, gets the concession, and after collecting the money from the buyer, pays the official either in cash or in some round-about way, so that it will not be possible to trace it afterwards should there be any inquiries made. Some of the coin, of course, clings *en route* to the fingers of the fixer.

Thus the seller and the buyer never have any direct dealings with one another.

Old Mossard, besides various other occupations, numbered that of "fixer" among his activities.

"So you see if that mangy old buzzard dares to interfere with me, I'll go to work and fix him good and proper the moment he opens his darned mouth, and he knows it. Just you keep right out of it, Barby, and if he ever does anything, that crooked old bum will wish he was at his own funeral before I have finished with him."

If Hoppit's story was true, it certainly looked as though he had a strangle-hold on the old man; the good Hoppit, of course, was himself a skilled liar, but from his entire confidence it looked as though he was telling the truth on this occasion, so I decided to stand by him.

But it felt rather like walking through a tiger-infested jungle with a gun which might go off and might not.

I saw old Mossard again, and after a long haggle he agreed that fifty thousand dollars down in cash, and a hundred thousand dollars paid in installments, would stave off the authorities.

Every once in a while I would see him and put him off with hopes of future payments, but I never gave him a dime. Once he was particularly exasperated about the delay, and was base enough to suggest that I was playing with him.

"We have found out all about you, who your family are, and where they live. It would make a nice little article for the London Sunday papers, wouldn't it? '——'s son turns rum-runner,' and photographs of you and your family. That is what will happen if you do not hurry up and hand over the dough."

This really touched me on the raw, but did not help him at all. Normally I am a rather timid person, but on this occasion I kept a stiff back, and never regretted it. However, I had to be courageous, because there was nothing else to do, but if the old fellow had demanded five hundred or a thousand dollars he might have made something.

He is still trying to squeeze me, although he has come down to twenty-five thousand dollars, with five thousand on account.

But the old man is not in the strong position he was a short time ago, as the Lord High Vendor has been deposed and another sells in his stead. I have taken the trouble (and gone to some expense too) to dig up the past of Mr. Mossard, and if he should try to make more trouble for my friends or myself, he will find that there are occasions when villainy can be met successfully with villainy.

This affair had many ramifications and wasted much time that might have been better spent, but these little things cannot be avoided in a game like this. I often wondered whether Hoppit was right when he said that the whole scheme was evolved by the suave Finnigan, who kept his own paws out of the mud by appearing in the role of a lawyer looking after the interests of his client.

He never sent me in a bill for these interviews, but, on the other hand, never said one word which could be construed into a threat, or that could not be brought up in public.

# CHAPTER XIV

## AEROPLANES AND SMUGGLING

ABOUT the same time a rum-runner that I knew and liked happened to meet me in the street.

"Hello, there, Barby! I've been looking for you for some time. Come along and have a drink. Where shall we go?" He looked round to get his bearing. "Gosh, it's two blocks to the nearest speakeasy, leastwise to the nearest one I know, for there ain't one block in the city without at least one hooch-hole in it." He piloted me to an office building, up two flights of stairs, and into a bar with every sort of liquor ranged on a shelf.

"Four hundred simoleons a week these fellows pay for protection," he remarked as he ordered drinks, a Scotch for himself and a sherry for me, for which he paid a dollar and a half, and gave a quarter to the waiter. "Four hundred iron men a week and even that isn't a 100 percent protection, for only last week they were shook down for five hundred by a stray fellow from the Department. Still it pays them hundreds a week profit, and beats rum running any day.

"What I want to ask you is this: did you enter the United States on the 20th of. . . . and come by. . . . and is your full name. . . . and did you open a banking account at the bank of. . . .?"

He gave me information about myself of which I thought not a soul was aware.

"It's like this," he continued, "a friend of mine was having a glass of beer in that German place on Broadway, and at the next table there were two fellows talking about you, and him being a friend of mine, and knowing that you are a friend of mine, he changed his wave-length and listened in. It was two fellows in the booze business themselves, and they were saying that something you were doing was interfering with them, and they were going to put one over you. My friend heard them planning the frame-up. They said that the son of the . . . was a friend of theirs, and they were going to work it through him. They had traced you back through the immigration offices and are going to get you on some immigration charge, and also something to do with the income tax. Anyway, whether they have anything on you or not, it will mean inquiries and investigations which won't help you any."

I had no knowledge of any enemies, except old Mossard and perhaps Finnigan, and wondered who it could be.

"What sort of fellows were they?" I asked him. "As I didn't see them myself I can't say exactly, but my friend said that one of them was a tall fellow all slicked up like a parlour snake. And there was something else about him too, but I have forgotten what it is—let me think—yes, I remember, he goes about with a high-stepping cutie who's ace-high on the face and figure; she's known as Y."

Immediately I knew; it was the elder Currant.

I thanked my friend, who had gone to a lot of trouble about the matter, and began to make inquiries, from which it seemed that his story was true enough. I went round to see the two genteel brothers, and found them in a well-furnished flat, where they were entertaining two young women of surpassing beauty. They hailed me cordially by my Christian name, or rather what they thought it was, and pressed a drink on me.

Pretending to have heard nothing of their plans, I was equally cordial, and thinking it no shame to meet guile with guile I put up to them a scheme whereby I was going to ship over for them on very favourable terms some special Scotch, which they would be able to sell at a large profit. I kept them stringing along for some time on this story, and that was the last I heard of them.

Meanwhile the *Mermaid* was not being unloaded nearly as fast as we had hoped. At first the ice prevented the boats from coming out; when that broke up, two coastguard pickets were stationed to guard the port from which most of our buyers used to come; there were other ships anchored nearby which sold at a lower price than we did, and gave more extended credit, while on a falling market Swivel refused to drop his prices.

The big Americans in the business were now bringing out their own ships, and where formerly there was ten dollars profit to the ship, ten dollars profit to the man who bought from the ship and took the goods to the beach to sell them, and ten dollars profit to the man who bought on the beach and took the goods to the city, now there was only one profit of twenty dollars made by the one concern.

The big operators brought the goods direct from Europe and themselves had a complete ozganisation which took them as far as their city warehouse, and made one profit of the whole thing where before there had been three profits; they cut the price, and thus made it hard going for the men who bought from the independent ships.

Hoppit used to buy a good deal of Scotch from the *Mermaid*, beside the Cheviot, and was rapidly rising in the world and making money. He sometimes had on credit goods to the value of twenty-five thousand dollars, but I always arranged things so that I owed him at least as much as he owed me, for my men used to collect the money for the Cheviot which he delivered.

About this time Swivel began to get very irritated about the slow progress we were making. The expenses were very heavy, sales were slow, and altogether he became discontented. As a business man he had two outstanding failings: one was that he thought he could out-bluff the Americans, who were nearly always too smart for him; the other was that he could not be made to see that quick certain profits are better than larger profits uncertain and delayed.

Another thing happened which I did not hear about until some time afterwards. Once when business was very slack, and the *Mermaid* used to lie rolling on the swell for days at a time without seeing a boat, a rum-runner came out to buy. Swivel quoted him a price.

"But Barbican's schooner is selling two dollars a case cheaper than that!" protested the man.

"What's that?" asked Swivel, "has Barbican a schooner out here?"

"Sure thing," answered the rum-runner, "and he is selling goods cheaper than you are, and unloading fast."

This gave poor Swivel furiously to think, and he came to the conclusion that I had a schooner there and was diverting his buyers to my boat by offering goods to them cheaper than he did. He checked up this information by inquiring cautiously from other boatmen, and it seemed correct, for several of them knew "Barbican's schooner."

So Swivel made arrangements with certain rum-runners who came to the ship, whereby they were to sell the whole cargo and cut me out, and occasionally I used to wonder when I was out on the ship why his behaviour was so frigid. It was not until some time later that he found out that the boatmen had told the truth, and that it was another man named Barbican, whom I knew well, who owned the ship.

Sometimes when it was not possible to get out to the ship by boat I used to hire an aeroplane and drop him a message from the air. The letter used to be put in a golden syrup tin, and vaseline smeared round the edge to make it water-tight; the tin was tied on the inflated inner tube of an old motor tyre, and after sighting the ship I would make a sign to the pilot, who would fly low over the ship from stern to bow. When just over the stern the tube was thrown overboard, and sometimes fell in the water and sometimes on the deck. Once the aim was too good, for it nearly fell down the funnel, but luckily missed it by a foot. When bomb-dropping in France, I had never thought that the art would come in so usefully many years afterwards in piping times of peace.

The letters that were dropped from the air would usually be somewhat as follows: —

"(1) Market better off Pinuckle Point. Will you move there at once to a point 10 miles N.-W. from the lighthouse?
Yes . . . Wave red tablecloth in bow.
No . . . Wave red tablecloth in stern.

"(2) Will you lower the price of Scotch one dollar, sell as the market is falling and it is impossible to sell at the present price?
Yes . . . Wave white tablecloth in bow.
No . . . Wave white tablecloth in stern.

"(3) Do you need fresh meat?
Yes . . . Hoist flag on foremast.
No . . . Hoist flag on mainmast.
Enclosed is mail for you and crew.
Will come out by boat at first opportunity.
Last remittance wired home O.K.
Don't give Hoppit further credit until I have seen you."

After dropping the message, we would circle round until the replies had been signalled and then fly back again.

On one occasion after failing to reach the ship by water several times, an aeroplane was hired at an aerodrome about a hundred miles away from where the ship lay at anchor. There were no sea-planes available, so an ordinary single-engined land machine was used, the pilot being a game little fellow with a perpetual grin who went by the name of Dandy.

On this trip, when we were about half-way there and out of sight of land owing to the mist, I shouted back to him, "What course are we on?"

"Don't know; haven't got a compass," he replied. "It's up to you to show me where to go."

If we had run into thick weather it might have been awkward, as the ocean is no place for a compassless land machine, but fortunately the sun was shining, and there was no great difficulty in guiding him to the right spot.

When we got back, Dandy said that he had not discovered the lack of a compass until we were well on our journey, and preferred to go on rather than turn back.

Sometimes on these excursions there would be as many as thirty or thirty-five rum-ships visible within a hundred miles of the city.

If thirty ships averaged a sale of three thousand cases a week each, it made ninety thousand cases a week coming into the district; putting the retail selling price as low as sixty dollars a case this would mean a turnover for the trade of $5,400,000 a week, or approximately $300,000,000 a year, and I consider this a low estimate. Of course, this sum was widely distributed between shipowners, distillers, banks, financiers, boatmen, drivers, rum-runners, bootleggers, police, prohibition officials, politicians, and the hosts of others interested in the business one way or another.

The graft market varied widely, for the more stringently the law was enforced the higher was the amount paid in graft, which thus probably varied between 6 and 12 percent of the turnover. To put it at the lower figure, it would mean an annual payment of $18,000,000, and this is tribute paid by the rum-runners and operators only; it does not include the much larger sums paid by the speakeasies, restaurants, cabarets, hotels, and other places which sell drink by the bottle and the glass at prices very much higher than sixty dollars; nor does it allow for the imports by rail and road, which are considerable; nor for the sale of the homemade liquor; nor for the graft paid by secret stills, breweries, and distilleries; nor for a host of other smaller sources. At this time I would put down the annual graft paid in cash to officials in this area of, say, a hundred miles square at a minimum of $25,000,000, but probably it was double this amount.

There has been much talk about rum running by air, but the amount brought in by aeroplanes is negligible. On several occasions I went into the question very fully with seaplane pilots, both British and American, but came to the conclusion that it was not worth doing unless the price of Scotch went up to the neighbourhood of ninety dollars a case, which it is unlikely to do.

A seaplane can only be loaded on a calm day, and can only take forty-five cases per ton of lifting-power. The pilot requires very high wages, and the overhead expenses are heavy. To make the scheme pay the plane would have to make frequent trips between the ship and the landing-place and unload in daylight, so that it would not be long before it attracted attention.

I know several men who have done it both succesfully and unsuccessfully, but as far as smuggling liquor into the United States is concerned, the flying machine is unlikely to do more than provide sensational copy for journalists, and possibly a pretext for spending more millions of the nation's money in the formation of a flying revenue service.

Things were so bad at Ozone that Hoppit, my brother, and I went out in the little boat and suggested to Swivel that he should move to Hawkes Point, to which he agreed.

On arriving at the new position our little boat was lowered into the water again, and the three of us went ashore.

# CHAPTER XV

## TAKING OUT THE MAIL

I always carried the mail to and from the ship in a canvas bag which the ship's carpenter had made for the purpose, with pieces of lead inside so that it would sink when thrown overboard. Luckily this only had to be done once.

I was in the little boat by myself on the way back from the ship; it was about midnight, and pitch dark. There were several prohibition boats about, and I was keeping a sharp look-out for them, as they had a nasty habit of stopping their engines and drifting about listening for the sound of the rum-runners' motors, and that is how they caught me.

A large boat suddenly appeared beside me out of the darkness, with the white spray dashing up from her bows, and visible because of the phosphorescence in the water.

"Stop your engine and tie up alongside us!" hailed a gruff voice.

The other boat travelled two to my one, so there was no other alternative. She came close up, and the faint glow from their compass-light showed several men and the glint of revolvers, so picking up the mail-bag I dropped it into the sea with many feelings of regret for all the wives and sweethearts who would never get the letters which had been so laboriously penned for them on the *Mermaid*.

The other boat ran alongside, and a dark figure with a silver shield on his coat and a revolver in his hand jumped down into my little craft.

"All right; there's only one man here; you stand by while I search him," he called back to the crew.

He slipped down on to the seat and sat beside me.

"Hello, Barby, I thought it was you by the sound of your exhaust," he exclaimed; "I've got to put up a bluff because there's a new guy on the boat that I don't know yet. You haven't got a bottle of Scotch with you, I suppose?" he continued, with a note of eagerness in his voice.

"Sorry, Jack, I haven't," I answered, "I wouldn't dare even to have my breath smell of booze with a dangerous Government agent like you about. But there's a load on its way in now, so if you will look round to see me tomorrow I'll give you a case for yourself and the crew."

"We've just caught one fellow," he remarked, "poor little chap. He only had fifty cases on board, but they probably meant a lot to him. He tried to get away but couldn't, so beached his boat and ran off in the dark. We pinched the boat and the booze, and have just come back from turning it over to Hank."

"Well, one is enough for tonight," said I; "I have a boat with two hundred and fifty on its way in now. John will be coming along by here, keeping inshore close by the fish-traps; you had better stay well out so as not to see him. Tom will see you in the morning to settle with you."

"All right, old man, I'll be round for that case tomorrow after-noon." With that he called up his boat and went dashing away into the darkness, well satisfied with the encounter, which would mean a certain five hundred dollars in his pocket the next day after he had seen Tom.

Thus the letters had been thrown overboard unnecessarily, and I was sorry, but perhaps it was just as well, for Jack was a treacherous fellow, and if he had found them and thought that he would have gained more by giving me away, he would willingly have done so without a moment's hesitation. Not long afterwards he was out on the yacht talking to Swivel, whom he knew had a grievance against me. He offered to get me arrested and put in gaol on some trumped-up charge—an offer which Swivel, being an Englishman, promptly refused.

There was one difficulty which rather complicated life, for it was the recognised thing in the trade that people seldom told the truth.

When a boat-load of three hundred cases was coming in, Tom Hoppit would always ask me to tell the prohibition men that there were two hundred and fifty, and thereby save two dollars a case on fifty cases; or if we sent six cars into the city, to say that only four had gone, so that if the Government men on the road took Tom's word, they would receive their dues on only two-thirds of what had gone in.

The junior Government man who collected a thousand dollars from a rum-runner would tell his superior officer, to whom he was supposed to hand over the loot, that he had only received six hundred, and so it went on all through the game everyone trying to swindle everyone else.

Personally I think there are few things worth lying about—money-making is certainly not among them,—so I did not fall in with the "custom of the trade," beyond a vague "I don't know" when people asked leading questions I did not wish to answer.

It was not so much the fact of being caught oneself that mattered, but the possible consequences to the ship. At that time the law was that ships of nationality other than American could not be molested outside the three-mile limit unless they had been in contact with the shore.

This "contact with the shore" was rather a shadowy thing, and as we did not wish our ship to provide the test case over which the question was to be fought, we used to be very careful.

Everyone agreed that sending one of a ship's own boats ashore would come under this heading, but it was an open question whether sending a man in from the ship in a shore boat, or sending in mail, could be included. In the early days of rum running, when the ships used to lie only four miles out, the captains, and often some of the crew would come ashore for a few days' spree, and, as they were then making money faster than they could spend it, they used to have some pretty good times.

There was also an old law, which I believe was enacted during the war between the North and the South, whereby a vessel with contraband found "hovering" within a twelve-mile limit could be captured. There was considerable doubt as to whether this "Hovering Act" could be enforced now, but we always bore it in mind.

American boats with liquor on board could be confiscated by the U.S. authorities in any part of the world, and that is why rum running ships had to be under a foreign flag.

Once it happened that more than two months had elapsed since the crew of the *Mermaid* had received any letters from home, and although they were the best of good fellows they were getting a little restive, and Swivel was having difficulties with some of them.

The mail had been sent to me long ago, but had been delayed *en route*, and everytime I went to the ship the men used to crowd to the rail and ask anxiously, "Have you got the mail this time, sir?"

"No luck today, but it is on its way," I had to reply.

After several weeks of this they were getting worried and discontented, and used to come to me with cables to send to their wives and families, and asked if their letters might come direct to me so that they should not get lost on the way.

At last I received a cable from a certain foreign port to say that the mail had arrived there, and would be sent on to me in the city.

To make sure that everything would be right I went to the post-office to inquire about the arrival of parcels from that place, and was told that all parcels arriving from there were kept until called for, and had to be opened in the presence of the Customs officer and be examined by him.

Now the letters would all be addressed with the name of the ship, and as every Customs man in the place knew all about her, it was more than probable that they would be stopped, the contents read, and the person who went to claim them kept for inquiries, so it seemed prudent to act with some care.

I made efforts to establish what the Americans call "connections" with the post-office department concerned, but the time was too short. I cabled in cipher to the port to stop the letters being mailed, and explained what the difficulties were.

A reply came saying that they had been given to the purser of a passenger steamer which was sailing that day, and that he had promised to mail them when he arrived at the American port where I was.

This seemed a simple solution of the difficulty, but the steamer came in, and after two days had gone by without the packet turning up, I began to get a little anxious, for, if they had been stopped by the authorities, it would probably lead to inquiries being made for me.

So going down to the docks I went aboard the ship, and finding the purser, asked him if he had received the letters and had posted them.

"Yes, sir," he replied, "the parcel is down in my cabin addressed to you and already stamped. I have taken it with me several times to post it, but each time I have been stopped by the Customs men, who say they can't let it go ashore until they have examined it, and as I gathered from the lady who gave it to me that it was something confidential, I did not like to let them do this, so brought it back again, and here it is."

He took me down to the cabin and showed me the bundle, which was too large to conceal under my coat.

"You had better be careful," he said. "They caught a man bringing something ashore a few days ago, and at the moment they are rather sharp on everyone."

Telling the obliging purser that I would be back soon for my parcel, I walked off the ship to see what sort of scrutiny the Customs men made of people going ashore, and was glad that I had not got it with me, as it would have been impossible to get by.

In about half an hour I was back again with my friend Marion, and we went down to the purser's cabin. On opening the parcel we found about two hundred letters and a number of packets of newspapers.

"Do you think you can manage them?" I asked her.

She eyed the heap.

"Well, no, there is too much of it," she answered. "We'll throw away the newspapers," I remarked, and tearing off the names and addresses, we threw a lot of them into the purser's wastepaper basket.

"All right, I'll do my darndest," said Marion, and turning one of her forty-horse-power smiles on the purser, she added, "You two can go outside for a minute."

We obediently went out, and in a few minutes the door opened and Marion stood there. The heap of letters was reduced to a few dozen.

"I couldn't quite manage the lot," she said apologetically. "Something would have busted if I had taken any more. Does my figure look all right?" she added a trifle anxiously.

"Beautiful!" answered the purser with almost unnecessary enthusiasm. The remainder of the letters I slipped into my pockets, and they were not enough to make me bulge uncomfortably.

"We'll just walk once or twice round the deck to make sure that everything is all right," she said.

So we took a little promenade, and nobody who did not know her well would have noticed that she was a trifle stouter than usual, and walked perhaps a little stiffly.

"I'm all right here," she murmured, patting herself gently about the place where girls used to keep their waists once upon a time. "And I'm all right here," she added, patting herself gently about the place where they keep them now, "and my garters will hold. It's the elastic round my plus-fours that worries me; if they give way those pop-eyed old pug-dogs down below will have the paper-chase of their lives. But what the hell! We'll take a chance on it! Come along, Barby; let's get out of this. That good-looking purser is working up quite a palpitation about me, and if we don't get a move on quick, he will be after me again to get my telephone number. He's made a date with me as it is, but if he waits for me he'll die waiting."

We walked boldly down the gangway, under the eye of the Customs man who was standing there. All went well, and after passing some more Customs men, with a sigh of relief Marion climbed cautiously and stiffly into the taxi that had been waiting for us.

"You look out of the window," she ordered.

I obediently gazed out at the passing shops, and after a time was allowed to bring my eyes back to the taxi and rest them on the pile of letters, which we put into an empty suitcase I had brought.

I took them a hundred and fifty miles to the port near which the *Mermaid* was lying, and then there arose the question of how to get them out to the ship without having to run the risk of throwing them overboard if I was stopped and searched by one of the Government boats, of which there were several cruising about in the neighbourhood. I was on friendly terms with most of them, but one never knows what is going to turn up in this business; there might be a strange man on one of them, or a boat might come butting in from some other district, and it was just as well to be careful.

When they search a boat at sea, they usually make a pretty thorough job of it, and a little boat like mine did not have much room for hiding things. I thought of several schemes, including that of nailing the letters underneath the keel in a waterproof cover, and of putting them in a tin can with a sinker, line, and float attached, in case they had to be thrown overboard.

Finally, I got a four-gallon oil can, opened it with a tin-opener, put the letters inside, and soldered it up again; then I cut the bottom out of a much larger tin, put the first one inside it, and soldered it up again with such care that there were no signs of it having been touched. The big can was then filled with engine oil, the idea being that if any one screwed off the stopper to look inside, they would only see the oil.

"It will sure take some slick guy to guess there's anything inside," remarked the boy who was helping me, with a chuckle, as he poured the oil in. When he had finished filling it, I peeped inside, and there was the bright surface of the smaller tin, which, being lighter than the oil, had floated to the top

However, with some pieces of wood we jammed the small tin at the bottom of the big one so that the oil completely covered it, and the whole thing went out to the *Mermaid* in my little boat, and reached safety without any mishaps on the way.

The six hours spent in sealing up the tins had been wasted; but not altogether, for the careful person who takes a hundred precautions, of which ninety-nine are unnecessary, lasts longer than the bolder man who may take ninety-nine risks and get away with them, but gets caught out the hundredth time.

# CHAPTER XVI

## HANK'S OFFENSIVE

Now about this time the enterprising Hank obtained permission to emulate Admiral van Tromp and sweep the rum-runners off the sea; he was going to make the biggest "drive" that there ever had been, and "clean up" the ocean of those pestiferous smugglers.

American officialdom is not free from the national habit of doing things by violent spasms, and seems curiously incapable of sustained effort; they have "liquor drives," "gambling drives," "dope drives," "modest bathing-dress drives," and many other sorts of drives.

The authorities have a victory as brilliant as Hannibal, and point with pride to their city, empty, swept, and garnished—not a bootlegger, a crapshooter, a dope-peddler, or a white thigh to be seen.

But the enemy, with Fabian astuteness, has retired in good order before ever the howdahs of the official elephants appear on the horizon; they lie low for a week or two before drifting back to their former hunting grounds, and soon everything has resumed its normal course.

The strategy of Hank was simple and effective, but he fell down on tactics. Owing to the position of the various harbours and channels, there were only about five places where contraband could be run into that particular district on any large scale. His plan was to blockade four of these with prohibition agents and boats, and to guard the fifth himself. He argued that cutting off the supply would raise the price and leave a sufficient margin of profit to allow certain privileged rum-runners to pay him two or three dollars a case for bringing in their supplies through his own pitch. This would bring in a rich harvest for him, which would, of course, have to be divided with the high officials who had given him the job, and the low officials whom he employed, but the money would roll in so fast that there would be enough for all.

His first action was to close all the ports of entry, which was quite easy to do for one who knew the game as well as he did, for it was not so very long since he had been a rum-runner himself. We were now feeling the pinch, and ships lay for weeks outside unable to get rid of their cargoes; overhead expenses piled up, and the agents on shore began selling at very low prices just to get rid of their goods without making a loss. Small lots of a few hundred at a time were sneaked in, but there was very little big business.

My idea now was to try to turn this new situation to our advantage, so I had a talk with Hank on the subject.

At first he was cautious and distant, but later on we became quite good friends, although we both understood, without saying it in so many words, that our affection for each other was based chiefly on the money we hoped to make by a little prudent cooperation.

He allowed me to bring in the Cheviot in small quantities, and received, to the best of my belief, two dollars a case for this. I was no direct party to the proceeding, for personally I have never paid a cent in graft, hush-money, or blackmail. When there was work of this sort to be done, I preferred to pay a little more and put it on one of the natives to deal with his own countrymen, and so keep myself clear of the business.

Hank had a gang of three other ruffians—temporarily hired by the Government,—who lived with him in the places where he went.

They had a fast boat which made thirty-five knots, and in this they used to visit the gangs which he had posted at different places along the shore. He knew perfectly well that the moment his assistants got the chance they would let the rum-runners through if they paid well enough, and he was anxious to avoid this, as it was part of his plan to make things really "tight" for a while.

These men wore no sort of uniform, and outwardly there was nothing to distinguish them from any other crew of rum-runners or hijackers, except that very often their six-shooters were worn in sight instead of being concealed. They also bore the usual little blue-and-silver badges on their waistcoat pockets, but these were not visible. These badges gave them authority to do pretty much as they pleased in the way of holding up people on the road, searching outbuildings, stopping and searching boats and motor-cars, and generally making themselves a nuisance to peaceful citizens and rum-runners alike, with revolvers well to the fore and the dim shadow of the law behind them.

One day we were talking about some shooting affair, when Hank turned to me and said good humouredly, but with a note of underlying menace, "If you shoot me, Barby, it's murder; if I shoot you, it's self-defence." And this was very true. It is a spirit which is not uncommon in the American Police, and is one of the reasons why so many American policemen are murdered.

When there is rough work afoot, the lawbreaker knows that if the police get him, they are liable to maltreat him whether he surrenders peaceably or not, so he prefers to attempt to knock out the policeman in the hopes of escaping, rather than run the risk of being knocked about without putting up a fight. This may sound exaggerated to European ears, but a first-hand knowledge of American police methods would convince anyone who might be sceptical.

The danger of allowing the police to use firearms indiscriminately was once brought home to me very forcibly when watching a Canadian fisherman making preparations to start on a smuggling trip in his little schooner. He was a mild capable little fellow of about thirty, one of nature's gentlemen, and as honourable as men are made, as I have good cause to know, having trusted him with eleven thousand dollars in cash because he had an honest face, and without even knowing where he lived. I was surprised to see him slip a six-shooter into his pocket as he left his house.

"What are you taking that for, Luke?" I asked him. "This isn't a cinema show or the States. There is none of that sort of stuff round here."

"Well, it's like this, Mr. Barbican," he answered, "I ain't never carried no gun before, but last time I was landing some rum that temperance inspector Nacey bobbed up with some of the mounties just as I was loading the kegs on to a truck. The truck driver had squealed on us. There wasn't no chance for us to get away, but that Nacey began firing his gun at us and the bullets went ping-ping right past my head. We was none of us armed neither.

"There ain't no man going to shoot at me like that again. Next time he pulls his gun I'll pull mine, and the best man will win.

"If I'm caught running booze, I'm caught, and ready to take my medicine, and that's all there is to it, but I'm damned if I'll stand being a target for a liquor inspector without a chance to shoot back."

I had several confidential talks to Hank, and suggested that he should direct the rum-runners to the *Mermaid*, and get a dollar or two from us as well as the two or three dollars he collected from the boats that came in.

For weeks I nursed him and the idea, and told Swivel all about it.

Finally, when Hank had put the fear of death into the rum-runners, and very little liquor was coming in, I worked him up to the point of saying that be would consider it. This plan, if carried out, would mean that we would sell the cargo of the *Mermaid* in a week or two, and turn an unsuccessful voyage into a very fair one. But as this would involve paying the honest Hank some fifteen or twenty thousand dollars of Swivel's money, it was necessary to get the latter's approval before arranging it. I therefore persuaded Hank to promise me he would pay a visit to the ship, on condition that if any rum-runners came there while he was on board, or on his way there or back, he would turn a blind eye on them.

One fine spring morning I wandered down the dock to where the Government boat was tied up, and waiting until nobody was looking, I slipped on board and down into the cabin without being noticed.

After a while Hank, his engineer, and his Government gun-man (who was my friend Jack) came aboard, and as these three limbs of the law prepared themselves for the fray, it was amusing to think that it was not so long since all three of them had been rum-runners themselves.

Telling me to lie low, they started up the engine, and the boat was soon scudding across the water. When we had been going about half an hour, Hank suddenly shouted an order to the engineer, the boat shot forward faster than ever, while the man at the wheel altered the course. Through a crack in the cabin door, Hank could be seen gazing ahead through his glasses, and pointing out something to the other two men; they all pulled out their revolvers to examine them, while Hank, coming down into the cabin, took out a couple of Winchesters and pushed cartridges into each of them. He went out again and stood with the others, his hand shading his eyes, and his great hawk-like nose and stringy neck thrust forward as he gazed after his quarry.

Glancing through a porthole, I saw that we were making for a little fishing boat which was bobbing on the waves about half a mile away.

"Eagles chasing a tom-tit," I thought to myself.

The engine slowed down, and Hank made a sign to me to keep still; the little porthole was suddenly obscured as we ran alongside of the other boat, so that it was not possible to see anything from the cabin.

Above the hum of the engine Hank's voice rang out—

"Where are you going to?" he shouted harshly.

"Out fishing," was the sullen reply.

"Where are your nets?" he demanded.

"We left them at G——. We are on our way to get them now."

"None of your lies to me, you goddarned lousy smugglers! Show me your papers, and look quick about it, or I will sink you."

There was a pause while Hank evidently examined the boat's papers and found them in order.

"I know well enough where you are going, you dirty sons of

dogs," he roared at them. "You are going out for a load of booze. If I catch you within ten miles of a rum-ship, I'll shoot your rotten old scow so full of holes that the fishes will swim in and out. Get to hell out of here, and remember I warned you."

Hank jumped back on our craft, bursting with righteous indignation, and we proceeded on our way. I caught a glimpse of the boat as she turned back, and recognised the two men, whom I knew were out for a load, but they were so cowed that they put back home again.

In another twenty minutes we were out at sea.

"Come along out, Barby, and show us the way; you ought to know it better than we do," Hank called out.

So I climbed up on deck and found that we were about five miles from the shore, and making some twenty-five knots. The boat had been built by a rum-runner specially for his business, and had been caught, or at any rate confiscated, by the prohibition men and was now used by them for chasing the rum-runners.

I took the wheel and steered her on the course for the *Mermaid*. To manage a really fast boat is no easy job until a man has caught the knack of it, for if there is anything of a sea running they are hard to steer and pound very heavily.

"Do you see that steamer over there?" inquired Hank, pointing to a funnel just visible on the horizon. "Have you heard anything about her having dope aboard?"

"Yes," I answered. "And if she has, I hope you will pull her in and send them all to prison. But people say that out of spite about every ship in the rum fleet. They say it about us. It is reported that she has a lot of Chinamen on board too, but I don't believe it. Nobody would be such a fool as to run Chinamen and booze together."

"I may be a bit easy-going about the liquor, Barby, but I always say to my boys, 'If ever I catch one of you bastards letting in an ounce of coke, I'll sure make the lousy grafter wish he had never been born. I'll thrash him within an inch of his life; I'll fine him out of every dollar he has in the world and gaol him for ten years.' That's one thing I won't stand for."

"I quite agree, Hank," I replied. "We are bringing in good whiskey, which merely saves people from poisoning themselves with bad. You and I are public benefactors, and deserve the thanks of the American nation.

"But dope is a different thing. A man ought to go to the chair for that, and if ever I can help you to land a dope-merchant in your net, I will gladly do so."

But all the time I was in America I never came across any authentic trace of the drug traffic, although there was a lot of talk about it.

No decent rum-runner will touch dope, however large the profits.

Only once did I hear anything definite about running in Chinamen. A rum-runner told me he had seventy Chinks hidden in Cuba, and had been offered a thousand dollars a head to put them on the beach in the United States, where covered motor-trucks would be waiting to receive them. The money was to be held by a famous "Tong" leader in the big city, whose word was said to be as good as the Bank of England, and I was invited to take a half-share in the venture.

But there was not a very large profit in it after paying all the expenses, and in any case I had no desire to be mixed up in that sort of thing, so declined with thanks.

On reaching the yacht we all went aboard, and as they were a tough-looking trio, with no official badges in sight, I had to take Swivel aside and explain who they were, and suggest what line he should take.

He was usually hail-fellow-well-met with the rum-runners, and made himself very popular with them, but on this occasion he failed to hit it off with these three men, and did not handle Hank in the right way. However, they were given food and cigars and drinks, and after an hour or so, left the ship. We gave them a few cases for them-selves, so the engineer and Government gunman were contented enough with the trip, but Hank was disgusted at Swivel's failure to come to terms with him.

While we were on board a fisherman had come alongside for a load; Hank had seen him coming, but walked into the cabin pre-tending not to have noticed anything, while I went to the side of the ship and shouted to the man to go away and come back in two hours.

On the way shorewards we saw a speedboat loading alongside a schooner, and had he wished to do so, Hank could easily have cap-tured her and brought her in, but he remembered his promise to me, and we did not alter our course.

"There's that son-of-a-gun of a Dick out again," he grumbled; "I've been lying up for him for weeks past. However, I'll let him get away with it this time and get him next trip. That's a dandy boat of his, too, and will do for me fine when this one has knocked herself to pieces."

We reached Hawkes Bay after dark, and slipping ashore without being seen, I went back to John's house. After this Hank did nothing to help the *Mermaid*, and had only caustic remarks to make about Swivel, but he allowed me personally to come and go unmolested and to take off the rest of the Cheviot.

It had taken months of work and planning to bring about this situation, and now that Swivel had been given the opportunity of a lifetime, he had refused to use it. From this moment I decided to sever my connection with him as soon as the rest of the Cheviot was taken from the yacht; also I knew that behind my back he was arranging with some other people to handle the rest of the cargo in my place. Our ideas about the right way to carry on business were very different, and there were other points on which we disagreed, so we arranged to cease working together.

In many ways I was sorry, for he was an able, courageous fellow, and in matters relating to the sea was the last word in proficiency; his ship will go down in the history of rum running as the most picturesque and the most efficient that ever rode at anchor in "Rum Row." Had he been as good a business man as he was sailor, he and his partners at home would have made their fortunes; as it was he did only fairly well, and his partners moderately well.

It had always been part of the policy of the worthy Hoppit to drive a wedge of disagreement between myself and Swivel, or anyone else with whom I was working, hoping thereby to strengthen his own position.

Seeing that relations between Swivel and myself were somewhat strained, he lost no time in turning the situation to his own benefit. After I had been out to the *Mermaid* for the last time and settled up accounts with Swivel, Hoppit went out himself. Apparently he first flattered his host by telling him that he was entirely at one with him in his estimate of my character, and then after a few stories to show Swivel how I was trying to cheat him, he enticed goods from him to the value of $6400, for which he promised to pay when he had sold them.

When I met Swivel later he asked me to collect the money from Hoppit on his behalf; I told him that the business was no concern of mine, but that if I could get the money out of Hoppit, I would do so.

To cut a long story short, I extracted $1400 from Hoppit, and cabled it over to Swivel, but could get no more.

Some time later I asked Swivel to pay a debt of £100 which he had long delayed settling under one pretext or another, but he refused, alleging that he had proof that Hoppit had paid over to me the remaining $5000 which I had failed to pay over to him!

Poor Swivel, he must have spent his money even faster than most rum-runners to be forced to descend to such cheap tricks to evade his debts!

A fortnight later I was back in my home in England, walking to church with my old folk, who had no idea of my occupation, and as the bells chimed, the rooks cawed, and the farmers stood chatting in groups round the church porch, America and rum-running seemed to belong to another existence.

# CHAPTER XVII

## THE VOYAGE OF THE *HORSA*

THE portions of the Cheviot which had gone out on the *Mermaid* had now been sold, and with the proceeds everyone had been paid back the original cost of this part of the cargo, and 50 percent profit as well.

Now came the problem of how to ship to "Rum Row" the remaining two-thirds which Swivel had left behind in Europe.

There were then two rum running ships which were loading on the Continent, and would, I knew, be willing to carry my Cheviot as freight.

The first was a fine well-appointed steamer named the *Arrow* belonging to a large American concern of good repute, which worked in the same neighbourhood as I did; the other was the *Horsa*, a battered old tub, whose sea-going days were nearly finished. She had been chartered by some Jews who had barely enough capital to put the deal through, and she was already freighting goods for three other groups of operators.

Naturally I tried to get the first ship to take my cargo, but she was going to sail a few days too soon for this to be possible, so I had to arrange with a little Jew, Addy Ackman, to take them across on the *Horsa* for a dollar and a half a case. More Cheviot was added to the amount already waiting, and my shipping agent suggested to several distillers that they should send a thousand or two cases apiece on consignment, which I could sell for them and send the money after it had been sold. This they did, bringing up my total cargo to some seven thousand cases.

Now to put good whiskey on a ship without an honest and stout-hearted man to look after it is to invite trouble; a man had to be found, and a good man too. Then I bethought me of a friend, somewhat senior to myself, with whom I had once served in a small campaign. He had been all over the world shooting, exploring, and adventuring, and had spent many years horse and cattle ranching.

I knew he would be an ideal man for the job if he could be persuaded to take it on, so I wired to him, and we met in London.

He seemed amused at the idea, and being one of those lucky foot-loose people who always keep their guns well oiled and their kit half-packed ready for their next adventure, he was able to start at once.

The idea of Teale as a rum-runner was humorous, for never did there walk in Hyde Park a more typical specimen of the English country gentleman.

He views the world like Zeus from the heights of Olympus, and many a time when worried or perplexed by the trials that beset a smuggler trying to earn an honest living in an alien land, his calm and detached way of viewing a situation has made me lean on his judgment.

I found that the other concerns were sending two supercargoes apiece to look after their interests; this was quite an unusual precaution, and made me think that they did not trust little Addy, fearing perhaps that he might try to make away with their whiskey. If there should be any rough play going, this would leave Teale in a minority, so it appeared to be good tactics to find him a staunch comrade. I knew him well enough to be sure that if any trouble arose, he would be astute enough to have one of the other combinations on his side, and so secure a two-to-one majority. And that is how Ryan took to the sea; a red-haired Irishman who had served through the war with the machine-guns; a man of few words, indomitable pluck and persistency, and a marvellous gift for handling men.

The steamer was loaded after the usual worries and difficulties which are inseparable from the despatch of a rum-runner. Teale and Ryan were installed in their little cabin with a regular armoury of revolvers, pistols, rifles, black-jacks, and other weapons of defence, and away they sailed.

I crossed the Atlantic in a liner, and arrived there before them to have all the arrangements ready on shore for lifting off the load.

But on getting there everything seemed to have gone wrong. A German Jew, who had been sent across to Europe by one of the concerns which had goods on board, had been talking too freely, with the result that there had been quite a flare-up in the press on both sides of the Atlantic, which had given the *Horsa* a lot of undesirable publicity.

Everyone who had goods on her became uneasy, for we heard from several sources that the Federal authorities intended to seize her as soon as she arrived, and there were some very anxious days of waiting until news came of her being sighted.

The war between the Government and the rum-runners is really a rather one-sided affair, with no justice for the smugglers, except what they can afford to buy at exorbitant prices. If the authorities take a dislike to a ship they just send out a cutter, and tow her in on the flimsiest of excuses. If the rum-runner fights the case in court and loses, he is ruined. If he fights the case and wins, the months of delay, the legal costs, the demurrage on the ship, the heavy pilferage of the cargo, the bribes that have to be distributed to various officials, and a hundred and one other expenses, usually cost more than the cargo is worth, so either way he is ruined.

The *Horsa* had orders to anchor a full twenty miles offshore, for the new treaty between the United States and certain European countries had now been signed, whereby a ship could be captured if it could be proved that she had sent liquor into the country when she was within an "hour's sail from the shore." There was nothing to worry about in this provision, but there was a clause added to the effect that if she loaded any boat which could make the shore in an hour, the vessel herself would be considered as being within an hour's sail, and therefore liable to seizure.

This left all sorts of loopholes for trickery, as was shown in the case of the *Arrow*, which had been seized by the coastguard as the result of a "frame-up" by the prohibition officials. Two Federal prohibition men, one of whom I knew well, as he was formerly a rum-runner and had then joined the prohibition forces to become one of Hank's men, went out to her in a speedboat, pretending that they were rum-runners, and persuaded the supercargo to sell them a few cases, although he had received orders from his owners to sell to no one. They then made a bee-line for the beach, and claimed that they did the distance in less than an hour, and as the ship was under the flag of a country which had signed the treaty with the U.S.A., a cutter was sent out and towed her in despite the protests of the captain.

Her cargo was unloaded, and she herself was kept tied up for over a year, while the lawyers fought the case, and the whiskey "leaked" from the Government bond at the rate of sometimes hundreds of cases a month. Whether she was released in the end I have never heard, but I was devoutly glad that she had sailed too soon to take the Cheviot.

As soon as the *Horsa* arrived, everyone who had goods on board made a rush to get off their part before a catastrophe occurred. Every evening there were more boats around her than the sailors could load, and the supercargoes contended with one another as to whose turn it was to have the use of the sailors to load the boats sent out by their people on shore; it was a case of grab who grab could.

Tom Hoppit and Ernest Sankey had split partnership now, for which I was sorry, since the plump Ernest was as honest as men are made. I would have thrown over Hoppit and worked with Ernest if it had not been for the fact that the wily Hoppit got himself appointed as head "fixer" for the district in which I worked, and he only allowed people who were in his good books to work, so I had perforce to continue with him.

He had not sufficient funds to buy the whole cargo at once, so I was between the devil and the deep blue sea. If it was taken off gradually, there was the risk of the ship being seized, and if it was all landed in a hurry, Hoppit could not pay for it and it would lie on shore at my risk, for though the canny Tom was ready enough to take his share of the profits as they came in, and even his share of small losses, there was no doubt that he would "leave me to carry the baby" if there was a big loss.

I made a compromise by telling him that I would take a third share of the risks and profits after the Cheviot left the ship, so we landed the cargo as quickly as we could, and took the chance of the cargo being seized or hijacked on shore.

The ordinary Scotch was sold at a low price for cash to various bootleggers, while the Cheviot was stored in houses, barns, cellars, cow-sheds, boathouses, and all kinds of hiding-places within seventy miles of our headquarters at Hawkes Bay.

It was an anxious time and took much planning and hard work; the most valuable cases had to be sent in the more trustworthy boats to the "drops" where they were least likely to be pilfered or stolen; the different brands had to be sent as far as possible to a storage near their final destination, and champagne had to be stored in places where the frost could not get at it.

Life was one constant effort to make smooth running in an organisation which I had made theoretically perfect, but which was continually breaking down owing to the failure of the human element; however, in a business of this sort, it is not possible to employ the services of "Admirable Crichtons." Not one in ten of the Americans I employed were honest beyond a certain point; the great thing was to find out what that point was!

One cold evening as I was climbing into bed I suddenly remembered that some Mumm champagne of 1911 vintage was stored in a barn seventy miles away; it was said to be frostproof, but I had not seen it myself, and my window-panes were covered with frost. I slipped on my clothes again, and inside of two hours pulled up in front of the house to find the barn full of holes and cracks, which would certainly let in the cold. The farmer and his son were routed out of bed, with many grumbles, and we piled straw over the cases until they were protected.

About this time I found myself being watched very closely by Hank and others in the Government service, and began to fear that for some reason they had taken a dislike to me, and were collecting evidence with a view to making things unpleasant.

One of them, who was showing considerable interest in me and my doings, one day asked me point blank if I was not connected with a certain Englishman whom I will call "B," whose name was then very prominent in the press as a self-avowed rum-runner. His barefaced way of raising money for his ventures was regarded by American officialdom as a direct challenge to their authority, and they were out for his blood if they could get it.

I told him that I had nothing whatsoever to do with "B." This man knew me and took my word for it, but said that there were other men working on the case who would not be so trusting, and advised me for my own safety to meet them and convince them myself about it.

I agreed to do this on condition that we meet in a friendly way, and that "anything I said would not be taken down in evidence against me." Next day I went downtown and met him and two other high officials from the Department, and they stood me an excellent lunch in a restaurant near police headquarters.

They were very decent fellows as American functionaries go, and were certainly out red-hot to catch "B." Having heard that he was in the country, they were as keen as a pack of hounds on a dewy November morning, for "B.'s" brush would have been a feather in the cap of any of them.

As both "B" and I hailed from London, England, they took it for granted that I knew him (and perhaps they were not very far wrong), and began eagerly questioning me about him.

They were very friendly, and the lunch they were standing me was very good, so I was loth to accept their hospitality under false pretences; besides that, if I scratched their backs now, perhaps they would scratch mine later on, so I gave them a fairly good description of the gentleman in question and what he was doing, and could almost hear their brains clicking as they registered every word I said.

In case they should have thought that I was ready to give away a fellow-countryman, they might as well know now that the description of him was taken from a Chicago paper I had seen a few days before, where an excellent photograph of him was printed. I happened to know that he was in England at the time, and the account of his doings was taken from a recent issue of the *New York Times*.

However, the result was that they went away pleased with me, I had a good lunch, and "B" was none the worse for what I had said.

A few days after this, "B" was lucky in not losing a load of some hundreds of cases. A man I knew named Gee had arranged to come in one night with a big load off one of "B.'s" schooners, and somebody in Hawkes Bay was talking about it too freely

Now Jack, the Government agent, was hanging about Hawkes Bay at a loose end; the Department of Justice had caught him out over something and had given him the sack, so he was prowling round like a jackal looking for pickings from either side.

He overheard the news, and hoping to ingratiate himself again with the Department, he went and telephoned the information to the nearest prohibition unit, who sent out boats to catch Gee.

But Gee somehow got wind of this, and in a furious rage collected some of his friends, armed them with black-jacks and jumped in his speedboat. They made a bee-line for Hawkes Bay, tied up at the pier, and looked around for Jack. As luck would have it, he was right there on the pier, so they set upon him and beat him up thoroughly until he howled for mercy.

Having given him what they thought he deserved, they jumped back into their boat and steered for home, having spent less than five minutes ashore, but they were five minutes that Jack will not forget in a hurry.

The last time I saw Jack he was looking bronzed and affluent.

"What are you doing now, Jack?" I asked him. "I'm a supercargo on a schooner outside," he replied with a grin; and so he was.

# CHAPTER XVIII

## MAISIE THE BOOTLEGGER

AMONG the most regular of our buyers was Maisie Manders. She was a damsel of some thirty summers, plump and determined, with brown eyes, dark hair, a rosy complexion, and a great gift for repartee, refined and otherwise. She played a very fair hand at poker, could put away half a bottle of Benedictine at a sitting and still behave like a perfect lady, and fearing neither God, man, or the weather, could keep her end up in any situation in which she found herself. Altogether, she was as tough a little twenty-minute egg as ever flattened out a Plymouth Rock under a balloon tyre.

Clad in a fur coat and a smart little hat with a veil coming down to her chin, she would jump in her great Packard coupé and cover the hundred and twenty miles from her home to Hawkes Bay inside of three hours. On reaching the village she would hunt up someone who had the brand of goods she wanted, and after beating him down at least a dollar a case below his lowest price, she would pay for thirty cases.

With the order in her pocket she would then drive off to the place where the whiskey was stored, usually some lonely farm or shack several miles away, and there load up her car. She always did this herself to make sure that it was well done.

It would give a respectable London wine merchant a headache to see a rum-runner opening a case of wet goods. If there are wires round the case, the edge of an axe is slipped underneath and a sharp jerk upwards snaps the wire with a crack like a pistol shot. The case is then put on end, and a deft blow of the axe in the right spot splits it in two and it falls apart.

The beginner breaks a few bottles learning how to do it, but with a little practice soon picks up the art. Given cases without wires, a good man can open ten cases a minute, while an expert can work even faster, very seldom making a false blow or breaking a bottle.

Opening the lid at the back of her coupé, Maisie would climb inside, and someone would hand her up the bottles two or three at a time. The bottom layers would usually be left in the straws to prevent any breakage or jingling, for the rattle of loose bottles, or whiskey running out of a broken one, has landed many an honest rum-runner in gaol.

She packed them neatly, neck to neck, and in three-quarters of an hour the back of the car would be full up to the top with twenty-eight or thirty dozen bottles; a layer of straws was then put on the top to pack everything down snugly, and the lid shut down and locked.

This being done, she would proceed to remove all traces of straw and work from herself and the car, then with an empty straw-case she carefully dusted over the running boards and mud-guards, until there was not a scrap of dust or paper left

"Now it's my turn, Barby," she would turn to me and say. "You brush me down while I touch up my dial," and while I did this with another empty straw-case, she would pull out her vanity bag and put on the war-paint which is used so freely by American women high and low. After she had put on her fur coat and toque, she looked as though she was turned out for a call at the White House, and jumping in the car, would pull up both windows and lock both doors from inside.

"It would take a can-opener to get me out of here once I am in," she used to say. "When I am locked in my coupé they would have to smash up the car to get at me, and it would take a real tough guy to do that to a good-looking young lady like me, and without any evidence too. Besides, I might not wait for them to try," she would add pensively as an after-thought.

The car now had on it an extra load of two-thirds of a ton, but an additional leaf in the springs, and large balloon tyres blown up very hard, prevented the casual observer from noticing how heavily loaded it was.

Day and night she would tear over those roads all alone, roads over which men used to prefer to travel in company after dark, and as often as not with a gun in their pockets.

Sometimes she would arrive in the village in the dead of night. I have seen her pull in at two o'clock in the morning when everyone was abed, and just curl up in the seat of her great car and sleep peacefully until aroused by the sound and smell of frizzling bacon; then she would rub her eyes, climb out of the car, and wander into the dining-room to join the half-dozen rum-runners breakfasting there. Rather frowzy and tumbled she looked when she came in, but after a couple of minutes in front of the looking glass with a pocket comb, a lip-stick and a powder puff, the sturdy little lady sat down looking as fresh as paint.

The bungalow where the rum-runners used to congregate was usually crowded, and one evening when Maisie arrived there, every room was full to over-flowing, so she had to sleep in the "sun-parlour"— the glass-covered porch in front of most American houses.

There were no goods for sale just then, and as I had some whiskey down there which had to go to a place a hundred and fifty miles away, I arranged with her to take as many cases as she could get into her car, and to pay her three dollars a case for the job. It seemed little enough, but it was the current price, and it did not do to pay more, as it would have made discontent among the other drivers.

However, it was work which was by no means unpopular with her, as on arrival at the stately mansions to which the goods were consigned, she was quite a heroine in the servants' hall, and I have my suspicions that many a bottle of choice champagne, intended for the millionaire owner, was opened in her honour by hospitable butlers, and recorded as "arrived broken."

Next morning before daylight I routed the drivers out of bed, and we made ourselves tea and toast in the kitchen.

Maisie had not appeared on the scene, so I took a cup of tea into the sun-parlour, and after much shaking, succeeded in waking her up. She looked at the tea and toast.

"Barby, you are a dear!" she said, raising herself on one elbow and sipping the tea.

"Come along, Maisie, I want you to be loaded and away by seven o'clock, as we have news that the Revenue men will be on the road at E—— about nine, and I want you to be through before then."

"All right, I'll be up to Sam's for that load before long."

Sad to relate, that cup of tea was wasted, for the deceitful young woman found someone with some Scotch to sell, and bought a load for herself. She never showed up at Sam's, and what was worse, the other two drivers spread about the story of the morning tea being taken in to her, and that cup of tea, with many colourful additions, sticks to me as closely as the axe does to George Washington. A tough little Yank she is, but I always liked her for her hardihood, and like her still, even though she made a hatful of trouble by her treachery; but her kind are all like that—it is born in them.

Talking of running whiskey in a coupé reminds me of a cunning gadget which Antler told me he had fitted to his Buick.

When the police catch a car with a load, they usually jump aboard and make the owner drive to the police station. Antler packed his bottles like Maisie in the back of the car, and there was a collapsible bottom worked by a wire running to the driver's seat. His scheme was that if ever he got caught and had to drive the policeman to the station, he would go forty miles an hour over the worst piece of road he could find, making all the noise possible with his Klaxon, and pull the cord. The bottles would fall out on the road and be broken, and on arrival at the police station his captor would find the evidence gone, and people are not supposed to be convicted without tangible and drinkable evidence.

I never heard whether it worked or not. I hope the cord jammed when he pulled it!

In return for what he had done for me one way and another, I gave him thirty cases "on the cuff"; he was to sell them and pay me after he had received the money, keeping a handsome commission for himself. The thirty cases were sent to his garage, and that is the last I ever saw or heard of them or him. Whenever I went to see him to get the money, he was out or away; several nights I went down there after dark and waited outside his house for hours with a "persuader" in my pocket; but he never showed up, and I still have to collect the money from him, and I probably will in the long-run.

But most bootleggers are unstable, and ready to become hijackers, Government spies, or to swindle their friends if they think it is going to put a few immediate dollars in their pockets.

Antler, after being friendly and hospitable, robbed me; Maisie later on turned hijacker and then informer; and it was the same with most of them.

I remember once going into John Blake's house after being away for a few days, and finding there a rum-runner named Roger with whom I had done business, and whom I knew quite well. There were several other people in the room drinking whiskey, and I joined them.

"It's a long time since I saw you, Roger! How's business with you now?" I asked.

"Oh, all right, Barby," he replied.

"Are you down here for some goods?" I inquired. "If so, the *Mermaid* is anchored offshore with the best of everything, and a low price for an old friend like you."

"Well, as a matter of fact, I am not buying anything just now, thanks; I suppose you haven't heard that I am on the other side of the fence now?" he remarked casually, holding aside the lapel of his coat and showing the Government badge pinned on his waistcoat.

He had been sent down there to catch the rum-runners, and there he was drinking with us and chatting about prices and ships. His old friends and the others who would pay the recognised tribute would be allowed to work, while outsiders would be "pinched" as fast as he could catch them.

Another typical example of this was Pip-squeak, a fair-haired lad with red rims to his pale blue eyes, and deep lines of vice cut into his pallid cheeks.

He lived amongst us in Hawkes Bay, and used to do a bit of boot-legging, mixing without question among the rum-runners, who were accustomed to discuss their plans freely in front of him. Nobody knew anything about his past, but he was accepted as a matter of course; personally I am given to judging people almost entirely by what I think is written on their faces, and I took such an intense dislike to Pip-squeak that I gave him the cold shoulder and never had anything to do with him.

One evening I was sitting at supper in the bootleggers' boarding-house, as it was called, when the door burst open and in rushed Pip-squeak; the tears were running down his pale face, his breath was coming in gasps, and he was trembling from head to foot.

"Gimme a gun! Gimme a gun!" he panted wildly, rushing up to his room.

He soon came clattering down with a double-barrelled shot-gun in his hand, into which he rammed a couple of cartridges as he made for the door.

"I'm goin' to bump off the dirty swine! I'm goin' to bump 'em off! I don't care if I go to the chair for it!" he muttered brokenly between great sobs which shook his whole body.

I sat still and watched him with equanimity, hoping that Pip-squeak's enemy, whoever it was, would get one in first, and thus rid the world of a being it could well do without.

"I don't care a darn if they are Government guys! Nobody is goin' to treat me like that and get away with it! I'll bump the b——s off, so help me God!" he added with his hand on the door-handle.

This put a very different aspect on affairs; I did not in the least want any of the local prohibition men shot. We were working togeth-er very happily, and a shooting affair would mean a descent by the police, followed by investigations and inquiries, so I stopped the demented fellow and took the gun from him.

He was not very loth to let it go, as his courage had already begun to ooze away, so hiding it away I left him to be looked after by one of the men who frequented the place.

The next day I heard the story from Hank and others.

It was said that Pip-squeak had previously been mixed up in

some dope-peddling affair, and had been caught by the police, who gave him the alternatives of a long spell in gaol, or of acting as a stool-pigeon among the rum-runners; he naturally chose the latter, and unbeknownst to us in Hawkes Bay or to Hank and his men, was in direct communication with police headquarters in the big city.

Hearing of a big load that was going to be landed nearby one night, he communicated with police headquarters, which telephoned down to Hank to ask him what he was doing to let such an important piece of news escape him, and telling him to go and make a seizure when the boat came in.

In the course of what they said, they let out that their informant was Pip-squeak, and that he was their stool-pigeon in Hawkes Bay.

The worthy Hank was not only annoyed at being hauled over the coals like this, but feared that if Pip-squeak was reporting direct to the city, he might find out more than he was meant to about what was going on. So that evening he went outside the village with two of his men, and sent a message in to Pip-squeak that someone wanted to speak to him on the road.

The unsuspecting stool-pigeon went out into the darkness, whereupon the Government men fell upon him with their blackjacks and banged him about until he was almost unconscious; they then warned him that if he was not out of the place within twelve hours, they would shoot him on sight. Sore, blubbering, and enraged, he rushed down to the house for a gun to shoot them, but cowardice and wiser counsels prevailed, so he left Hawkes Bay next day, a sorer and sadder pigeon after his fall between two stools.

# CHAPTER XIX

## THE *PRAIRIE SCHOONER*

WHEN there were only a few hundred cases left on the *Horsa* I went out with three boats to take it all off. Teale and Ryan were there safe and sound; their work had been done under great difficulties, what with the foreign crew, the impatient boatmen, and the other supercargoes wanting everything their own way. They had taken on board seven thousand cases, and as my boats had taken off seven thousand and fourteen, it was evident that the others had not been able to hoodwink them over the count.

We held a council of war about the future; Teale decided to come with me on John Blake's boat to have a look at America, and Ryan to go back home to escort over the next load.

As Teale was climbing on to John Blake's boat, a sudden lurch threw him into the sea between John's boat and another of about fifteen tons. They were grinding their sides together, and he was in imminent danger of being crushed between them. I leaned over from one boat and grabbed his right arm, while a brawny fisherman on the other boat seized his left.

Meanwhile, John, who had seen what had happened, with great presence of mind threw in his clutch and spun over his steering wheel to port in order to keep the two boats apart. Neither the fisherman nor I had time to notice this, and we each hung grimly on to the arm we had clutched, while poor Teale was being pulled asunder like a merry-thought between the two boats.

"You take him!" I called to the fisherman, letting go my arm, as there were two men in the other boat. They hoisted him aboard, and after circling round we came back and took over Teale, his baggage, and several gallons of the ocean.

"I might as well put on some dry clothes," he remarked as casually as though he were stepping out of the pool at the Bath Club, instead of having narrowly missed being squashed as flat as a piece of paper.

As we chugged landwards, he changed his clothes in the little cabin, and I kept plying him with Scotch lest he should take a chill. It took three and a half hours to get in, and by the time we tied up to the wharf the bottle was empty and Teale was full.

We climbed up the slippery piles in the dark, and for the first and last time I saw the dignified Teale three sheets in the wind. We piloted him to Joe's house and entered the warm brightly lighted sitting-room where Mrs. Blake was entertaining some of her friends; it looked very pleasant and cheerful after being out on the cold sea.

"In vino veritas" is a true saying, and never was its truth more apparent than now. On being introduced to Mrs. Blake, Teale gave her a courtly bow as though he were being presented to a grand duchess; "I am really extremely sorry," he remarked, "but the ocean round here is rather potent, and after swallowing several quarts of it, I am slightly indisposed. I shall be all right in the morning."

We sat him down in a chair, and although he was as drunk as a man can be without falling off his seat, he chatted wittily and amiably with the company, while Mrs Blake, with her usual hospitality prepared supper for us.

After supper we went to bed, and next morning Teale arose as fresh as a lark. Such was his landing in America.

After a day or two I decided to go up to the city.

"There's that case of high-powered booze in your bedroom, Barby," remarked Hoppit as I was leaving. "Mr. Wartenheimer is paying four hundred and sixty bucks for it, and I don't like to let any of the drivers handle it for fear they should lose it or break it. You will be passing right by his house, so perhaps you would drop it there? It must be a thousand proof to get all that money. Mind it don't blow the back off your auto if you break a bottle."

It was a case of 1875 liqueur brandy for which that most eminent city father was paying such an exorbitant price; it was placed in the back of my car with Teale's luggage, and in a few hours we drove into a park and pulled up in front of a sort of glorified Windsor Castle.

"A bootlegger like you ought to go round to the back door," remarked Teale severely.

A flock of English footmen appeared when the door was opened, and I told them to take the box out of the car and give it to Mr. Wartenheimer personally.

The next few days were spent in winding up affairs; the money was cabled to the distillers who had sent the whiskey on consignment. The cash received for the Cheviot was sent home too, the subscribers receiving back their original capital and with it a good profit, and besides this there were accounts for boats, storage, motors, drivers, and other things to be settled.

When everything had been paid and everyone satisfied, there was still a good profit for me, more, indeed, than I could have saved in many years' toil in some less speculative profession. However, it had been gained by months of hard work, risks, and worry, and was well earned.

Now came the question of the next move.

Several wires had come from London offering me goods on consignment, and my shipping agent cabled that the owners of a suitable steamer were willing to charter her at a reasonable rate.

I had made three successful trips, and by keeping myself well in the background had, up to the present, avoided any unfriendly notice by the authorities; also, though I was, to the best of my belief, the last Englishman left who was shipping goods out and selling them off the coast, I got on well with the other rum-runners. Everything on my little pitch was working smoothly, and I knew every rum-runner, boat, and drop within fifty miles. The demand for Cheviot was steadily increasing, and there seemed to be no reason why a fourth trip should not be equally successful as the previous ones.

The voice of caution said, "Be content with what you have gained, and get out of the business."

But the restless spirit of America was upon me.

"You can't give up now," it urged; "there is no cowardice like that of a man who is afraid of his own success. One trip more and you will be able to buy enough War Loan to bring you in a modest income for life.

So I decided to carry on, although now I wish I had decided to be a prudent coward.

There are certain formalities which have to be gone through before leaving the United States, including the answering of rather leading questions as to the amount and source of income received since arrival in the country. As I had received no assistance or protection from the State for my business, I did not think it necessary to pay any income tax, and a couple of bottles of Cheviot to the right official secured all the necessary documents for departure.

I left from one of the smaller ports of the country, whence Binny and his wife came to see me off. No one ever had a better friend than he had been; always ready to take more than his share of risks and dangers, always cheerful when things were going wrong, and vastly better than I at handling a situation which needed the mailed fist.

I recall how once I was summoned to appear in court in person on a charge of exceeding the speed limit; it was essential for me to be on the coast a hundred miles away to watch some cases being landed, and I was in a quandary.

"I'll go to court for you!" proffered Binny.

No proxies were allowed, but he said that he thought he could bluff it through.

He went to court and fell asleep while waiting for my case to come on. He was awakened by a loud voice calling "James Barbican; James Barbican."

"Here I am," he answered.

Standing next to him was the policeman who had stopped me two days ago and handed me the summons. However, he successfully pleaded guilty, paid the fine, and came away.

Few people ever have the chance of putting their friends to the test; a man goes broke or gets into trouble, and they melt away at an astonishing rate, but the joy of finding the few true ones more than makes up for the loss of the many.

On board the ship there was an elderly Jewish operator who had been in the business some time, and who had made and lost several fortunes. We became very friendly, and towards the end of the voyage he spent an evening giving me good advice.

He was not beautiful to look upon, being short and fat, with typically Jewish features and a pendulous under lip. But Jews do not carry their characters written in their faces like the Gentiles do; you have to look into their eyes in an unguarded moment to see the real man.

This old fellow had the wisdom of all the ages hidden in his dark gloomy orbs. In my imagination I took him out of his pepper-and-salt suit, and pictured him in flowing robes and a turban, sitting under a palm-tree gazing at the last rays of the setting sun over the Sinai desert.

"Well, my boy," he said, "I hear you cleaned up a hundred grand over the *Horsa*, and I'm glad to hear it."

"I wish I had!" I exclaimed.

"Well, anyways, you if did pretty well on it. Now you take my advice and turn legitimate right away. If you keep on at the game you are bound to take a knock sooner or later, and lose what you have made. You put your dough into Victory bonds, lock them in your safe deposit, throw away the key, and forget about them.

"You can make just as much legitimate as you can at this racket. You've been up against the slickest crooks in creation, and now you are on the way home with the bacon. You be content with what you've got and quit!"

He puffed away at his cigar for a few moments and then glanced at me mournfully.

"But you won't take my advice, any more than I would take it myself if I was you, and you'll be sorry later."

Once more I found myself home again, walking to church with my dear old folk, the bells ringing as before, the same rooks cawing, the same farmers chatting by the church porch, and the grimy old *Horsa*, speed-boats, and whiskey-cases seemed to belong to some far-away dream.

There were a few peaceful days spent at home. It was possible to forget my occupation for a while, except when sometimes I used to imagine that the sedate old portraits on the dining-room wall looked down on me with a frown of disapproval.

The various people who had speculated in the previous three ventures seemed pleased enough with the result, and were ready to have another flutter. Also several distillers offered me a whole shipload of whiskey and wines on consignment, and there was a suitable steamer available for charter, so I decided to go ahead.

It was a great responsibility to take over such a valuable cargo in addition to the Cheviot. In the event of anything going wrong, my friends would know that everything possible had been done, but most of these distillers were comparative strangers to me, and in a business where no accounts are kept, and no receipts given or received, it is awkward to have to meet people with the story of a loss.

However, "nothing venture, nothing win," and if all went well they stood to make a handsome profit, which would come before mine.

In a short time I had sent a naval officer out to France to inspect the *Prairie Schooner*, the ship I thought of chartering, and as he reported favourably, I chartered her and loaded her with twenty-six thousand cases, which included five thousand I was freighting across for a big concern on the other side.

Ryan and the retired naval officer went across on the steamer in charge, and after the usual alarums and excursions of loading, they left the Continent and headed for America.

Next to the *Mermaid*, the *Prairie Schooner* was the best equipped rum-ship that ever sailed to Rum Row.

She carried a crew of twenty-eight. There were wireless aboard and a loud speaker, so that the officers and crew could listen-in to music and concerts. There were nets, chutes, mooring ropes, winches, fenders, and other gear for unloading, all of the best, while the crew had ample supplies of their native wines, and plenty of beer, tobacco, and cigarettes. The supercargoes had everything arranged for sending cipher and code messages to me, both by wireless and other means, while Ryan had his machine-gun, as before. Also there were plenty of rifles, revolvers, and shot-guns to repel attack should the hijackers come out.

I went aboard a liner which was due to land me in America at least a week before the *Prairie Schooner* reached her position.

Two days out a big storm arose and gave us a good battering. I used to lie awake at night as the ship shivered from end to end with the blows of the waves, thinking that if it was bad for us, it must be ten times worse for the little tramp steamer, and fears for Ryan and the cargo added at least ten grey hairs to my head.

So severe was the storm that the liner was damaged, and had to put back to England for repairs, so I eventually landed in the United States a week late.

Although the passport and immigration regulations are supposed to be so severe, any fool who likes can get through them by saying he is "in transit" for Vancouver, Papua, the South Pole, or anywhere the other side of America.

# CHAPTER XX

## THE HIJACKERS SCORE

On arriving at the old hunting-ground things were very much altered from what they had been eight weeks before.

The much-talked-of prohibition fleet, after many false alarms, had sprung into being in the shape of a number of destroyers, which were supposed to make about thirty-three knots, and a host of seventy-five foot patrol boats each carrying a crew of from five to nine men, and armed with one-pounders and machine-guns. They were fitted with two engines apiece and made about eighteen knots.

The crews were specially recruited, and received about sixty-five dollars a month pay, and the boatswains who commanded them about a hundred and twenty dollars. Some of these men were quite decent fellows, but many of them were pretty tough citizens; they used to swagger along the streets of the seaside villages, carrying cut-lasses, revolvers, and occasionally rifles, and the women and girls, who had no fear of insult from the rum-runners were in the habit of being rather chary about going out after dark when these fellows were about.

For days I awaited news of the *Prairie Schooner*, and as she became seriously overdue I grew more and more worried about her, thinking of the terrible storm she had encountered.

However, at last the boats sent out to find her reported that she was anchored twenty miles offshore, but that there were so many of the new "seventy-five footers" about, that it was difficult to get into communication with her.

One trying aspect of the situation was that the ship had come out with the intention of "selling over the side," which meant that the buyers either paid on shore and received an order on the supercar-go, or else went direct to the ship and paid him for what they took,

But now these men could not buy because they could not get out to the ship; the small men, who had been my mainstay, were

141

practically eliminated, and the only people who were able to work were those with large funds or influence behind them. But as concerns of this sort always had their own goods and their own ships, they did not need to buy from me.

So I set to work to make an alliance with some other rum-runners and form a group strong enough to buy large quantities and dispose of them quickly when landed. They would thus be in a position to find the cash for the "protection" money which the new Government forces would demand as soon as they had settled down and found their feet.

The head prohibition officials must have possessed a simple and touching faith in the integrity of their fellow-citizens. They signed on temporary men for a strenuous and hazardous job, paid them low wages and expected them to remain honest, when by closing their eyes for a few hours they could make as much as by six months' conscientious work. The large majority of these men used to admit openly that they had entered the Government service for what they could make out of it, and the taking of bribes from the rum-runners was as much a part of their routine as receiving their monthly pittance from the Government.

Day after day the ship lay there and we were unable to get to her; it cost over two pounds an hour to keep her there, and in bed each night I used to think— "There's another fifty pounds gone west."

Day after day Hoppit used to assure me that he was hard at work making arrangements, and that we would soon be unloading the ship as fast as the men could put the cases over the side.

Most of this subterranean scheming and plotting I left to him, having no special desire to be mixed up in it, so for a time there was nothing to do but watch and wait.

We managed, however, to take off two small loads.

There was a rum-runner named Will, a tall broad-shouldered fellow, lean and powerfully built. When a youngster he had left Denmark to seek his fortune in the New World, and still spoke with a slight foreign accent. He had a strongly-featured face, a straight nose, a firm mouth, and a mass of brown curly hair which he seldom covered with a hat. He had the far-seeing eye of the sailor, and spoke but little, but when he did, it was to the point.

As a daring navigator and astute rum-runner he had no equal on the Atlantic coast, and in addition to this the luck of the very devil, and was as straight and honest as they make 'em.

When things were hard it was always to him that we turned, and although nobody else would go out now, he agreed to try. We started out in the middle of the afternoon, and after dodging several prohibition boats we reached the *Prairie Schooner*, and took on two hundred and sixty-eight cases. Leaving the ship after dark, all went well until we got off Hawkes Point, when the propeller hit something in the water, probably a piece of floating wood or a lobster-pot buoy, and was bent so badly that the whole boat vibrated from end to end and the speed was cut down to about half.

At two o'clock in the morning it was obvious that we could not make the landing-place where the men and trucks were waiting for us, as with the reduced speed dawn would be upon us before we got there.

There was a dense fog, and it looked as though daylight would find us at sea in plain view of the prohibition boats, which were unpleasantly thick on the water just then.

"Shall we try for Pawson's?" I suggested. "It is nearer, and we might wake him up and make him rout out some men. It seems to be our only chance."

"All right," he replied, changing the course of the boat, and in an hour some fish-traps loomed up ahead of us, showing that we were almost on the beach. Will tied up the boat to one of the stakes, while I rowed ashore in the dory to see where we were.

Stumbling along the beach in the dark, it seemed that Will, with his unerring instinct, had hit the bull's eye even in the dense fog, for we were only a few yards away from Pawson's. I made my way to the house, and to my surprise found people moving about, although there were no lights visible.

I found the fisherman himself, who said that he and his men were waiting for a boat which had not turned up, probably having been lost in the fog. I told him what had happened to us, and he agreed to take our load, so I rowed back to the boat, gave Will our exact position, and he nosed the boat cautiously along the beach until he came to Pawson's little jetty.

We all worked desperately hard to get the cargo ashore before daylight, but dawn broke while we were still only half unloaded; Will's luck, however, held as usual, and the dense fog covered our movement as well as the darkness had done. The whole lot were safely housed in Pawson's garage, the boat slipped away silently into the fog, and Will went home to bed after another night's adventure and another streak of luck, having earned $1608 between supper and breakfast.

Six days later he again went out and returned safely with two hundred and forty-two cases. Knowing every current and rock as he did, he managed to elude the seventy-five footers which were naturally rather chary of getting too near the beach, especially when there was any sea running.

This boatload was sold, but owing to the vigilance of the Revenue men nothing more was done for some days, for new brooms sweep clean until they get acquainted with the floor and learn in which corners the gold dust accumulates.

We got in two more small lots safely, but at this rate there was not even enough profit to pay the overhead expenses.

Arrangements were now concluded with Hoppit and the two other chief rum-runners in the district that the four of us would run together, each taking a 25 percent share of the risks and profits. They were to pay me a low price on the ship, and I took a 25 percent share in this, and also in the profits made by selling on shore. If the whiskey was lost after it had left the ship, the 75 percent paid by the other three would still be sufficient to cover the cost price, so it was a case of "heads I win, tails I don't lose."

One morning at eleven o'clock the other two men came up in their motors in a great hurry with the news that everything was arranged for us to work for that one night only. I wanted to bring in a few hundred cases, not wishing to take the risk on a very large quantity, but conditions were such that if we were to work at all, it had to be on a big scale.

So the boats were sent out with their orders on the ship.

Most of them were to unload at one place, and soon after dark I was down there waiting for them with four dories, four waggons, and about twenty men, most of whom were local fishermen.

It was a lonely bay with stretches of sandhills all round, and not a house or a road within miles.

The men huddled together in a little wooden shanty to keep warm, while one or two of them patrolled the beach with me to watch for the arrival of the boats.

Shortly before midnight there was a small dark patch visible on the water; it remained motionless, so pointing my electric torch downwards on the sand, I gave three quick flashes. This was answered by three tiny sparks of light from the boat, which began to move silently inwards.

When she was a hundred yards from the beach there was the faint rattle of an anchor-chain being let out cautiously, and the boat was again motionless.

By this time the men had come out of the shack and had put off in the dories. The motor-boat handed the cases down to the dories, which plied between the boat and the shore until the whole cargo was unloaded.

The waggons were driven right down to the water's edge, and the cases were lifted from the dories straight into them. When there were about thirty cases in a waggon, the driver whipped up his horses and took them three hundred yards to a dump behind the sandhills, where they were stacked under the supervision of a trusted young fellow named Dub Prince, who kept tally of every case that arrived.

Soon another loaded boat arrived, and then another and another until there were more than could be unloaded. There was no moon and it was very dark, but in spite of this, the work went on methodically and smoothly; no talking or smoking was allowed, no lights were shown, and the soft sand entirely swallowed up the noises of the waggons and tramping feet.

Hour after hour the boatmen, team-drivers, and other men toiled away without rest for food or drink; we watched the sky anxiously, and when dawn arrived there was still one boat only half-unloaded, and another one on which we had not even started work, with an indignant crew asking what they were to do.

This was all due to Hoppit's stupidity in failing to send the largest boat to be unloaded at another place where men and teams were waiting for it.

I stationed the oldest man on the top of a sand-hill, telling him to keep his eyes fixed on the sea and give warning if any Government boat came into sight; having done this, I went back to the beach and urged on the men to work even faster. They were almost dead beat now, and each case seemed to weigh a hundredweight, but they responded as gamely as Americans usually do in an emergency, and the boat was soon unloaded and chugging back to Hawkes Bay.

There were now left one deeply laden boat with three hundred cases on board, two dories, two teams, a dozen men, and the huge dump of two thousand cases behind the sandhills, which it would take half a day to cart off to the various places where it was to be stored.

The look-out man came running towards me.

"Cutter coming up!" he shouted breathlessly.

I ran to the top of the nearest sandhill, and there coming slowly along the coast was a seventy-five footer, with the revenue flag flying from her stern. In five minutes she would round the headland and see everything in the bay.

I tore down to the water, and passing the two teams, ordered them to hide behind the sandhills, and then told the men to leave the dory on the beach and get away out of sight.

There was a dory half loaded alongside the motor boat, so I yelled to the men, "Cutter coming! Row ashore!"

They pushed off, the two men from the boat leaping aboard too as they left, and pulled for the beach as hard as they could. They dragged the dory on the beach, and as they did this I saw the masts of the cutter sticking above the headland. In one minute she would be round it.

Telling the men to lie on the beach behind the dory, I threw a piece of tarpaulin over the light-coloured cases which lay in the bottom of the boat and then ran into the sandhills, rounding one of them just in time to stop a team from driving into the open.

At this moment the cutter came round the point, and I could read the big black letters on the bow, C.G. XOOX. They were not looking for gold dust in the corners, and the crew were all out to catch anything they could.

I thought the game was up; there was a boat and loaded to the gunwale, anchored in a spot where no boat ever did anchor; there were two dories at the water's edge, one of them half full of whiskey cases with four men hiding behind her; and worst of all, the whole beach was scored with waggon tracks leading from the waves to the sandhill behind which there was a stack of cases worth $100,000. It was the sort of capture which coastguard officers would dream about, but think too good to be true. To the best of my belief a seizure of this size had never been made by the coastguard before.

I peered from cover, a stunted bush, and watched the cutter slowly emerging from behind the point. She carried a larger crew than usual, and I could see some of them examining the coast with their glasses.

There was not one chance in a thousand that they could miss seeing what was going on.

She crawled along at about four knots; we all kept still as death, the only sounds being the chirping of some little birds and the occasional champing of the horses' bits.

It seemed bitterly hard to have such a big success actually within our grasp, and then have it torn from us by the carelessness of Hoppit, who, by the way, had gone home to bed.

It took the cutter fifteen minutes to get opposite the rum-boat— which was only four or five hundred yards from her,—the longest fifteen minutes I have ever known; then every moment that she continued on her way my hopes rose, until half an hour after the alarm having been given, she slowly disappeared round the other headland.

Hardly able to believe our good luck, I wiped the sweat from my forehead and breathed a prayer of thankfulness that a hundred and twenty dollars a month in the United States could not hire intelligence as well as honesty.

"Come on, boys," I called to the men, as soon as the cutter's masts were out of sight, "let's clean up the job."

In broad daylight, with that cutter only two miles away round the corner, we unloaded that three hundred cases and piled them on the dump.

Two thousand, nine hundred and seventy-one cases were landed altogether; it was one of the biggest coups that had been pulled off in that neighbourhood, and about noon we fell on our beds too tired even to undress or eat.

The telephone wires were now kept busy telling the various bootleggers within a hundred miles that there were goods for sale, and they began coming down in their cars to purchase them.

Early one morning while Hoppit and I were still abed, we were awakened by a big burly man dressed in a green chequered shirt and thigh-boots. It was Pawson, who lived on a lonely spot on the shore, with the sea on one side of him and the forest on the other.

"I've been hijacked!" he announced glumly.

Hoppit sat up like a shot rabbit.

"What's that?" he exclaimed. "Go to work and spit it out!"

"They got about fifty cases," said Pawson, and proceeded to tell his story. About midnight he had been awakened by someone tapping at his window; be opened it and put out his head to see who it was. There were three men there who said they were Federal officers come to search the place for liquor which they had heard was stored there. One of them was wearing the uniform of a State trooper.

Now Pawson ought to have known that no police or Government official has the right to search a place between sunset and sunrise, but he foolishly went outside the house to talk to them in the hope of being able to buy them off.

But as soon as he came out they prodded him in the stomach with revolvers, and made him go with them to his garage and then demanded the keys from him; he refused to give them up, so they burst open the doors with a crowbar they had brought with them, and loaded up their two cars, one of which was an "Essex," Pawson said.

Having done this they relieved him of the loose cash which he had in his pocket, about fourteen dollars, and drove off through the woods threatening to shoot him if he followed.

"Didn't you get a chance to have a shot at them, Pawson?" I asked. "You have a scatter-gun there in your house."

"Well," he answered, "to tell you the truth, I didn't like to take a chance on shooting a trooper."

"You ought to have gone to work and plugged the whole goddarned lot of them," said Hoppit savagely.

"Why didn't you come and tell us right away so that we could have followed them?" I asked.

He had no very good answer to give to this, but I gathered that they had him pretty well scared.

I jumped into some clothes, and he led the way in his car, while I followed in mine. His wife gave me some breakfast, and a few casual questions dropped between bites of bread drew replies from her which seemed to tally with her husband's story.

I found the lock wrenched off the garage, as he had said, and the tracks of two cars to and from it; on checking up the remaining cases it seemed that they had stolen sixty-eight cases of ours, and ten cases of champagne belonging to another man, their booty having a market value of $2812, not a bad haul for one night's work.

We got on the trail of the hijackers' cars, and followed them half a dozen miles through woodland paths, and another ten miles along the main road, but lost the tracks near the neighbouring town. The only reward for our trouble was one case of "Rob Roy" whiskey, which we picked up in the middle of the road some two miles from the house. It had evidently fallen off the hijackers' car without their having noticed it.

One of the cars had an odd pair of tyres on the back wheels, so I made a drawing of them and motored round the district trying to pick up the trail again, but the ground was dry and no sign of them could be found.

Then I went to the houses of two men whom I suspected of being in the hijacking business, but there were no traces of cars having been in or out of their houses recently.

Hoppit thought that it was a fake hold-up and that Pawson had been in with the robbers, but I thought that it was genuine. We put various people on to try to find out where the whiskey was so that we could go and recover it *vi et armis*, but that was the last we ever heard of it.

"What about Maisie?" I asked Hoppit. "Do you think she would be behind a thing like that? She's so tough you couldn't cut her with a knife."

"Well, she might go to work and do it," he answered, "but I doubt it."

That afternoon I went to our chief storehouse, which was a farmhouse in a lonely spot not far from the sea, and I told the farmer what had happened.

"You mark my words, Sam," I warned him, "they found a soft thing at Pawson's, and having tasted blood they will put up a bigger show next time. They will give it a few days' rest and then have a try at this place. Get a good fellow to live here with you, one who will shoot first and ask questions afterwards. Buy a couple of savage dogs and turn them loose at night. Put up extra wooden shutters on all the windows, and never come out of your house in the dark to load any cars until you are sure the people are O.K."

Next day I went up to see him again and found that he had got a man, ordered the dogs, and put up the shutters. He showed me his armoury, which consisted of a couple of shot-guns and a revolver, and assured me that no robbers should take anything out of the house save over his gory body.

As long as he kept indoors he could not help being safe, for all he had to do was to loose off his blunderbuss at any one who tried to break open windows and doors, and, as the house had wings and projecting windows, he would be able without exposing himself to put a charge of duck-shot into anybody who was monkeying about.

The stock was being sold gradually, and I spent some time in looking round the country trying to get a clue to the hijackers, or any doubtful characters who might be masquerading as policemen. As a result I got on to the tracks of two men who were reputed to have State troopers' uniforms in their possession, and one of them was a friend of a policeman I knew well; a pleasant jovial fellow never above accepting a couple of bottles of whiskey and minding his own business, and who was probably quite capable of doing a hold-up job if he saw a good chance of pulling it off. He was not himself, however, one of the three men that Pawson saw, for he would have been recognised.

In the village we had an office with a book-keeper and three or four trusted men who used to receive the buyers on their arrival; after having paid the money and received a written order, the boot-legger would be escorted by one of these men to the "drop," where the car would be loaded and the buyer sent on his way.

At some drops it was only possible to load at night because of inquisitive neighbours or passers-by, and new customers or those who were not trusted overmuch were taken to places where only small quantities were stored, so that if they gave the place away, or tried to hijack it, there would not be a heavy loss.

One morning, a week after the hijacking episode, I went down to the office and found Dub Prince very much put out—as I was when I heard his story. He said that at two o'clock that morning he had been returning to the office from Sam's after loading up a bootleg-ger's car; on taking the goods the man had paid him eighteen hun-dred dollars, which he had put in his breeches' pocket to bring back to the office safe. It was dark and raining, and he was going slowly round a bend in the road when he was held up by five men with guns, one of them dressed as a State trooper. They dragged him out of the car and searched him; they did not take the trouble to put their hands in his breeches' pocket, but ripped them open, tearing them right down from waist to knee; they then jumped in his car and drove away, leaving him to trudge home in the rain. The car he found next day behind an empty house in a lonely spot, but the eighteen hundred dollars were never heard of again.

This brought the hijackers' profits up to four thousand six hundred and twelve dollars in a week, all easy money without a blow being struck or a shot fired.

On occasions of this sort, men have to depend on their own right arm to secure justice, for it is obviously impossible to call in the police. Many of the murders which take place in America are merely rough-and-ready justice dealt out to men who have swindled their partners over some deal which will not bear the investigation of the police or press; or else the summary execution of a murderer by avenging friends, who know that the murderer is too rich or too influential for the law to give him his desserts.

"They will go on doing this until someone stops them," I said to the boys in the shack, "and it is up to you to show them that we are not all boobs down here," I added, looking at Dub.

They got out a collection of rifles, shot-guns, and revolvers, and began industriously oiling and cleaning them.

"We had ought to have done this before," remarked Dub, "but when I get a sight on one of them fellows I'll fill him as full of holes as a piece of chicken-netting."

So I left them polishing and furbishing their weapons now that the horse was stolen, and thought of the excellent words of Benjamin Franklin—

"Twice armed is he whose cause is just,
Thrice armed is he who gets his blow in first."

# CHAPTER XXI

## THE BATTLE WITH THE HIJACKERS

THAT same evening I was sitting in the parlour talking to a man named Richardson, a man I had run across in the city. He was rather a mysterious little fellow and I did not know in the least what he was doing in America, but we found out that we had several mutual acquaintances in England, so we became quite friendly. Some days before, when I was leaving the city to come down to Hawkes Bay, he said that he would like to come with me in the hope of seeing some excitement, as he was at a loose end, and would be glad of an excuse to go anywhere or do anything. I told him that there was seldom any excitement, and that it was mostly a question of hard work and sleepless nights, but if he liked to come along and see how the business was carried on, he would be welcome.

So he went down with me in my car, and helped me a good deal in one way and another.

As we were chatting, the door opened, and there entered a fat young Jew who said that he wanted to buy some champagne. I did not know him, and was careful at first, for it is a favourite trick of the Federal Prohibition men to pose as bootleggers, make a purchase, and then arrest the man who has sold to them. The affair with little Bayne had made me cautious.

I asked the Jew some questions, and he seemed all right, so I gave him an order for fifteen cases of champagne in exchange for seven hundred and thirty-five dollars, and not happening to have the regular order-book on me, I wrote a note to Sam, telling him to give the bearer fifteen cases of Heidsick Monopole, for which I had received the money. The Jew motored off to Sam's to get his champagne. I remained there chatting with Richardson, and we were joined by Pettit, one of the members of our little syndicate.

About midnight the door burst open, letting in a blast of wind and rain, and in stamped the young Jew, accompanied by a satellite of his, both of them soaked to the skin and covered with mud up to their knees.

They began to shower curses on everyone and everything, but a stiff drink and a cigar apiece calmed them sufficiently to enable them to tell their story intelligently.

"We went down to Sam's," said the Jew. "He poked his head out of a window, and we told him we had an order for some booze. He read it, and said it was a phoney order, and told us to beat it. As we went away he began shooting at us out of the window, and we heard the bullets whizzing by our heads, so we beat it quick, and didn't dare go back for our auto, which was stuck in the mud just opposite his door. We've walked all the way back, seven miles in the pouring rain, wet to the skin. That's a nice way to treat a fellow— take his money, give him a phoney order, and then try to kill him."

Being the sort of man who had probably never been shot at in his life, he was all of a dither, and seemed quite peeved, but a couple more drinks and a bit of blarney made him feel better, and I promised to go back with him to put things right.

Richardson went up to bed, and I persuaded the reluctant Pettit to run the three of us in his car up to Sam's to see what the trouble was about.

When we arrived near Sam's house, the others seemed somewhat reluctant to approach, so leaving them in the car, I went up to the front door, and shouted up to Sam's bedroom window. He popped his head out, and seemed a trifle hostile until he understood that it was I.

"There's been some hijackers here with a phoney order, so I shot at them, and they ran away and left their car here."

"That's all right, Sam," I answered. "Those fellows are O.K.; I've brought them with me, and we want to get the stuff out, so come down and let us in."

"All right, Mr Barbican, I'll be with you in a minute," he said, closing the window.

I turned round and could see the dim shadow of Pettit's car, which he had driven up closer while I had been talking. The lights, of course, were not on, as we always turned them out when approaching the farm, so as not to attract the attention of any passers-by. There were several dark figures moving about, and one of them came to meet me.

When he got close he suddenly pushed out his arm, and thrusting a revolver against my ribs, said harshly, "Hands up, you son of a b—; quick, or I'll shoot you through the belly."

He gave me a push, and I found myself standing with Pettit, the

Jew, and the other man, all of them with their hands in the air, surrounded by five men with guns, one of them dressed with the wideawake hat and khaki uniform of a State trooper.

The gentleman behind the gun was so insistent that I should raise my hands that there seemed to be nothing else to do, so they reluctantly went up.

Never in my life had I felt quite so mad with myself. Pawson and Dub Prince had each been caught napping, and I had cursed them for it, and here was I, already forewarned, caught as badly as either of them.

The first thought was that Sam would come out and leave the door open for the hold-up men to enter and steal all our goods, so I shouted out as loud as I could, "Don't come out, Sam! Hijackers!"

This seemed to annoy the dark-featured gentleman who was taking such a special interest in me; he hit me on the jaw with his revolver, and said that if I opened my mouth again he would "bump me off," and spoke as though he meant it.

"Who the hell are you, anyways?" he demanded, peering into my face.

"And who the hell may you be?" I retorted.

"You'll soon find out before we are through with you. You'll wish you'd never been born, you dirty lousy son of a b——."

They then ran their hands over us to see if we carried firearms; they found nothing, luckily missing the little .320 which was in the outside pocket of my jacket, a gift to me from a friendly policeman.

"Get up on the porch there!" ordered the dark man, and with much foul language and many threats they herded us up on to the verandah, and made us stand in a row with our backs to the wall.

As we walked, I had crowded up against one of the others, and dropping my hand into my pocket got hold of my revolver; very comforting it felt, too, nestling in the palm of my right hand. But the dark fellow was keeping too close a watch on me, and even if one or two of them had been knocked over, the others would have got in their shots before there would have been time to deal with them. So I decided to bide my time.

"Now they are going to search us, as they did Dub Prince," I thought. So I dropped the revolver into a doll's perambulator at my feet.

"Where's them other seven guys?" asked the dark man of the State trooper, looking round and counting his men.

"Round behind loading up the trucks," was the answer.

"You stay here with me to guard these men, and the rest of you go round behind and help the others load the cars," he ordered.

By this time Sam had appeared, and had been forced to join the rest of us.

The dark man and the trooper remained guarding us, and the others disappeared behind the house. Now that there were only two I tried to parley with them, but all the reply from the dark man was, "Shut your goddarned mouth!"

The seven hundred and thirty-five dollars I had just received were in my pocket, together with several thousand more besides, and I wondered how long it would be before our captors went through our clothes. Pettit had a good deal of cash on him too, and if they had been content with taking the money alone they would have made over five thousand dollars that night. But they made no move to do this, and merely busied themselves with keeping their guns waving from one to another of us about the waist-line.

The odds were now rather better, so very gradually lowering my right arm, I picked up the revolver from the perambulator and covered the dark man to hit him about the middle waistcoat button. With luck there would be just time to get him, and then drop the other with a quick snapshot before he had time to swing his revolver round. But it would have to put them right out of action, for I am not a good enough shot to drill a hole through two arms in the dark without any risk of missing. If one of them was merely wounded, he would have time to shoot before he was knocked out by a second shot.

The trigger began to go back, and never was a man nearer to the happy hunting grounds than was that black-haired hijacker; but it is wonderful how quickly a man is forced to think when he is in a bit of a fix, and three thoughts flashed across my mind before the revolver went off.

First, being rather timid, I did not much care to shoot a man in a policeman's uniform for fear of subsequent complications; secondly, it hardly seemed quite the thing to drop the two men when they did not even know they were going to be shot; and thirdly, there were so many people about that someone would be sure to talk, the police would come down and find our store and we would lose everything.

This last thought decided me, and I resolved to make a bolt for the bushes and scare the hijackers away by potting at them from the darkness. The verandah on which we were standing ran the whole length of the house, with a waist-high railing on the outside; the end at which we were standing was nearly flush with the ground, but as the house was built on the side of a hill, there was a ten-foot drop at the other end on to a pile of stones.

Waiting until the dark man's gun was pointing at someone else, I suddenly turned and bolted like a rabbit down the verandah, with my revolver in my hand, expecting every moment to hear one of the guns go off behind me.

I vaulted over the railing at the end, and not being one of those cool brave people whose step is unhurried by the thought of a bullet in the back, I took off with such haste that my foot slipped on the wet planks, and although I got over the railing, instead of dropping on my feet, I landed all in a heap on the stones below, and saw a thousand stars and stripes as my head banged against something.

The next thing I knew I was legging it down the hill as hard as I could go, with the dark man in full pursuit. My revolver was gone, having probably dropped out of my hand as I fell; it was no good trying to tackle the gang armed only with my little blackjack, so I made a detour through the bushes, and hit the road about a mile below Sam's place in case they followed along the highway.

Afterwards I learned that, failing to catch me, he had returned to consult with the others as to their next step.

"Who was that guy?" they asked their prisoners.

"A crazy Dago," answered Pettit. 'He's not acquainted round here, and he'll surely get lost in the hills."

I padded down the road as hard as I could go, after filling my pockets with biggish stones to throw at their wind-screens if they came up behind me in their cars.

After running five miles I came to the house where Richardson was sleeping, and by this time I was pretty well blown.

"Come on, Richardson, hijackers!" I panted.

He jumped out of bed like a sleeping terrier who has heard the word "rats," and slipped on boots and an overcoat over his pyjamas, while I loaded the little .25 pistol which was lying on his dressing-table.

There was an old car of mine standing outside in the rain, and in a couple of minutes we were slithering along the muddy road at forty miles an hour back towards Sam's place.

After a mile the road divided, one fork leading back the way I had just run from Sam's, and the other to the village.

"Go to the village in the car; wake up the boys in the shack, and bring them along to Sam's; there are anything from five to a dozen hijackers there cleaning out the place. And for the love of Mike, drive carefully," I added, for Richardson was a skillful but reckless driver, and only a few days before had wrecked a new car of mine at this very spot. "Remember that if you take a toss before you get to the village, I am properly in the cart."

He went off in the car, while I walked back towards the farm in the rain and darkness, all the time looking ahead for signs of the hijackers' cars, and behind for signs of Richardson with reinforcements.

Half a mile farther on there was a cutting on a curve in the road, and a big tin advertisement lay derelict by the side of the ditch. I propped it up across the road, making a barrier upon which the hijackers would come suddenly; they would be forced to pull up and swerve violently to avoid it, and on the bank above I collected a pile of stones for ammunition.

After firing the pistol once to make sure that it was working, I sat down on the stones and waited for what seemed an age with nothing but the pattering of the rain to keep me company.

After a while it seemed as though Richardson must have had more than enough time to reach the spot where I was, and I imagined him skidding into the water at one of the sharp turns he had to take; then I began to wonder whether the hold-up men had some back way I knew nothing about by which to get away from Sam's and avoid returning by the only road which led to it.

Unable to bear the inactivity any longer, I left the barricade and walked onwards. Having the little pistol, my blackjack, a pocket full of stones, and the prospect of help coming up from behind, I felt more secure than I had when running down the same road an hour and a half ago.

At last the lights of two cars appeared coming up from behind me. I stood out in the middle of the road and held up my hand; it was Richardson with three men from the shack armed with the weapons they had been cleaning so industriously not many hours before. It was disappointing that he had not brought more men, but he said that some others he had asked to accompany him had shown a decided preference for their beds when they heard what was afoot.

My plan of action was hurriedly sketched out to them. On approaching the farm, all the lights were to be turned out, and the two cars placed across the road in a cutting so that there would be no room to pass on either side. Richardson was to remain there with his little revolver to form a sort of Hindenburg line in case the enemy broke through, while the remaining four of us were to surround the house and hold up the hold-up men.

"Whatever happens, don't shoot unless you are absolutely obliged," I warned them, "and if you have to shoot, aim at legs and tyres, and don't forget there may be a dozen of them."

We climbed aboard the cars and went on at breakneck speed through the rain until we reached the bend in the road just before the farm. The two cars were drawn across the road, completely blocking it, and Richardson remained there standing in his pyjamas in the mud, shivering with the cold. I left him because I knew he would stick to his post, and would not fail if it came to a pinch, and also because I did not want him to get damaged in a scrap in which he really had no interest, but as it turned out, he had the most risky job of all.

The three boys I sent round to the other side of the house to take the hijackers in the flank, and they disappeared into the darkness at a run, with their guns and rifles held forward, eager but cool, with Dub in the van, keen to avenge himself for what had happened to him only twenty-four hours ago. Nobody could wish for a gamer trio of comrades in a rough-and-tumble than these three young rum-runners.

I went round the house on the near side, and as I approached a dark shadow flitted round from the front where we had been held prisoner to the back, where the cars were probably being loaded. The hijackers could be heard running about and starting up the engines of their cars.

"We are here by my car!" shouted Pettit's voice; he probably anticipated a little firing, and being in a line between the two parties, wished to avoid being shot by both.

By this time I was only a few yards away from the hijackers,

"Put your hands up! You are surrounded!" I shouted.

A couple of shots from a heavy calibre revolver sang by my head. In reply someone fired at the flash with a left and right from a shotgun, and this seemed to cool the ardour of the gunman.

There was more noise of self-starters grinding; men were running about and shouting; there was more firing from both sides, and the headlights of a car were turned on with a blinding flash, but another left and right put out the lights and stopped the motor.

Farther away another car was started up, and with headlights blazing went round the other side of the house. Two more barrels of duck-shot went after it, but apparently with no effect.

Running round to the front of the house, I saw the tail-light of the escaping car bouncing down the steep hill over the grass, spurts of flame showing that the hijackers were firing as they went, while answering flashes from the hillside showed that my three boys were not idle.

Someone handed me an automatic pistol, but it jammed, and I threw it after the car, swearing never to touch another again, for they are always liable to let you down just when you want them most. The car, with all its lights on, lurched crazily over the grass, and gained the road.

For the first time that night I was really worried, for there was nothing between that car-load of gunmen and liberty but one little man in his pyjamas with his pocket pistol, and he could hardly be expected to be a match for them.

I yelled at the top of my voice to warn him.

"Gone away! Gone away! Mark over! Mark over!"

With the three boys at my heels I ran as hard as I could pelt down the road towards the barricade in the hopes of reaching it before Richardson was wiped out.

We arrived, puffing and blowing, to find him completely master of the situation. The escaping car had been obliged, of course, to pull up, whereupon Richardson had stepped out of the shadow in which he had prudently been standing, and ripping away the side curtains from the car, had waved his tiny pistol in their faces. Making up for his lack of arms and numbers by a torrent of good army cusswords, he had attained what Sir John French once described as a "moral ascendancy" over the enemy.

Wrenching open the door on his side of the car, he made them get out one by one, promising them the most horrible death if they raised a finger against him, while I opened the door on my side and dragged out two of them, holding my blackjack poised over their heads ready to give them a rap if they became aggressive.

With no gentle hands they were marshalled into the glare of the headlights and deprived of their arms. The trooper's bandolier with a number of .455 cartridges was taken from him, and a stout truncheon with a lump of lead protruding from the end was found hidden in the back of the car.

There were five of them, and a sorry-looking bunch they were; one seemed to have his eye shot out, and the blood was running down his face; the dark man and the trooper collapsed on the ground and said that they were dying. The latter at any rate was not shamming, to judge from the way he jumped when his back was touched to see where he was hit.

"Where are the rest of you?" I demanded.

"Don't shoot! Don't shoot! We are all here," was the reply.

The dark man, who had been the leader so full of ferocity when he had the upper hand, now raised himself to his knees in the muddy road, and lifting his hands as though in prayer, whined for mercy. We were quite a little annoyed with them, and they seemed fully to expect they were going to be killed on the spot.

"Don't kill us! Don't kill us! Have mercy on us!"

"We are beaten! We are beaten! We give in!"

He literally grovelled, in the mud, and snatched at our hands to try to shake them. Never have I seen such a disgusting exhibition of cowardice, and the trooper was nearly as bad. I could not help thinking of five Russians I once saw standing under telegraph posts with ropes round their necks for exactly a similar offence as these men had committed—robbery with violence. They went a little pale, it is true, but not one of them uttered a word or moved a muscle until their toes were well off the ground, when, I suppose, they could not help it.

The fair-haired man with the wound in the head was being supported by another man very much like him, evidently a brother, while the fifth man stood with his hands in his pockets edging away towards the darkness.

I went up to the fair-haired man to see how badly he was hurt, and to my amazement found that it was Maisie's brother. Only the day before I had given him and Maisie lunch in the local eating-house, and wasted a perfectly good cigar on him.

It was difficult at first to see if the boy's wounds were serious, as there was so much blood on his face, but it looked as though some shot had gone into his eye, and he had a scalp wound as well. The other two men on the ground kept groaning and saying that they were dying, but they got very little sympathy, as they were probably making the most of their injuries.

"Looks like a movie play!" remarked Pettit, who had driven up in his car now that the scrapping was over.

The first signs of dawn began to show in the east, and it was high time for this collection of bloodstained men, motors, guns, and wine bottles to be cleared off the road.

I felt that I had done my part of the job, and that it was up to Pettit, as the leading man there and a native of the country, to take the lead, so I took him aside.

'We can do one of two things,' I said to him: "take them to the house and keep them prisoner for a few days until we move the booze to a safe place, or we can let them go.

"If we keep them, one of them may go and die on us, and as so many people are in the know about this show, somebody is bound to talk. If the police come down here and find a corpse, there might be a bit of a fuss.

"On the other hand, if we let them go, they will probably keep quiet for their own sakes, for it is gaol for them if they are caught. They can't afford to talk, but if they do, it will be awkward.

"What do you think about it?"

We walked over to look at our prisoners.

"Shall we hand them over to the sheriff?" asked Pettit, winking at me.

"Yes, for God's sake hand us over to the sheriff. Do what you like with us. We are friends now; we've had enough!" groaned the dark man from the mud.

"Well, we've got to do something," remarked Pettit, glancing at the sky. "Better let them go; they won't come down here again in hurry."

The Essex car in which they had tried to escape was filled to overflowing with our choicest liqueurs and wines, carefully packed in their straws, and it would take a long time to unpack them, so I started up my old car, which was worth less than theirs, and told them to get in.

"Beat it, boys, and get yourselves patched up. You are lucky to be alive, and if you come fooling round here again, you won't get off so easily. Bring the car back to me tomorrow—you know where to find me."

The Manders boy, with his hand to his bleeding head, groaned out pathetically, "I ain't got no money to pay the doctor."

I thrust my hand into my pocket to find a few dollars, but before I could get at it, the last hijacker had been thrust inside, aided by a lusty kick on his posterior, and the car began moving down the hill, with the other Manders boy at the wheel.

With a few choice parting words from Richardson warning them to keep their mouths shut, they disappeared down the hill, a humble carful of humanity, all except the driver Manders, who muttered as the car moved away, "Someone is going to pay for this."

The hijackers' car, with its load of liquor, was started up, and one of the boys put aboard to take it to a safe place. The engine, however soon seized up, as the duck-shot had pierced the radiator, so one of the other cars took it in tow.

In the grey dawn we walked back to the farm, feeling quite pleased with ourselves for having rid the countryside of such a gang.

A motor truck was standing behind the buildings, filled with our choicest champagne; knowing the run of the place, they had taken only the very best. The wind-screen, head-lamps, and radiator were all shattered with shot, so another car and the other two boys were told off to tow it away.

"We may as well get everything we can away from here, in case those fellows talk," I remarked to Pettit.

We found the fat Jew, his chauffeur, and Sam having a drink in the parlour, and we did not need much persuasion to join them. Nobody on our side had been hurt, although a good many shots had been fired by the hijackers, to judge from the number of .455 cartridges which were picked up afterwards. The chief subject of interest was whether the trooper really was a trooper, or only a hold-up man dressed in a trooper's uniform.

To a foreigner it seemed almost incredible that a real policeman would be foolhardy enough to come on an expedition like this in full uniform, though the others seemed to think it was quite possible. I had kept his coat, hat, and belt, in which there were various official marks, in the hopes of being able to identify him should the need arise. His revolver we sought for everywhere, but it had disappeared in the mêlée.

"Well, I suppose we had better be getting on with the job," remarked Sam, going out to mend the shutters, which had been torn down to gain an entrance into the house.

The other men were told to fill up Sam's truck and take it away to some safer place, but it was found that the distributors had been taken off both the truck and Sam's car, presumably a precaution taken by the gang to prevent Sam from following them to give the alarm.

The rest of us motored down to the village to get some breakfast, and to send up more trucks to Sam's to move as much as possible of the whiskey.

The Jew, with a presence of mind typical of his race, went nosing round until he found where one of the hijackers' cars had been towed, and having run it to earth, I saw him leisurely loading his own car with the champagne for which he had paid me the previous night. Dub, unmoved by the battle, was standing by counting each bottle to make sure that he did not take advantage of the general confusion to take more than he had paid for.

About six in the morning it struck me suddenly that my old car had not much petrol in it, and that there was the possibility of the hijackers being stuck on the road miles from anywhere, which was the last thing we wanted, for the sooner they got under cover the better for everyone concerned.

So filling several cans with petrol, I got a fisherman to take me seventeen miles along the road in his Ford truck, until we were within sight of the next village, where they could have obtained more supplies had they needed them.

Their tracks were plain to see all the way, and in one place there were marks in the wet soil showing that within the last few hours a large car had been backed from the road to a spot where it would not be visible to passers-by. Very likely it was Maisie in her Packard, who had been waiting there to relieve one of the overladen hijacking cars of some of their plunder.

She should have gone all the way to boss the foray herself, for if she had, there would have been a more favourable ending for her family. She would have been worth any three of those men put together.

At the end of the journey I asked the fisherman what I owed him for the thirty-four mile run.

"Nothing, Mr. Barby, nothing," he answered; "I'm always glad to help out anyone who is in a bit of a jam."

The Americans are a great people in an emergency. They are always ready to help one another, and do not expect to get anything for it. Probably this trait is a survival of the spirit of the old frontier days when everyone had to hang together for mutual protection.

We next began to arrange to move everything from Sam's, even though it hardly seemed likely that the hijackers would be such fools as to talk themselves into gaol.

About noon I went to the place where I was staying, and there was a long-distance telephone call for me. It was Maisie.

"Is that you, Barby? I've been trying to get you for the last two hours. Those fellows who got shot are in a bad way, and one of them is going to die. My brother will lose his eye, and they think he has some shot in his head. The whole goddarned thing was a frame-up, and I sure am sore about it. One of them has gone and split the whole story to the cops, and there are twenty troopers on the way down to pinch you and the booze."

"When will they get here?" I asked.

"They left about two hours ago, so will be down to your place in an hour or so. They are coming in autos."

"Thanks, Maisie; it was very nice of you to telephone."

She was going to say some more, but I rang off, as it was a party line, and the prohibition agents have a way of listening-in at an inter-mediate town.

It was really pretty decent of her to ring up like this, for she must have been quite vexed at the failure of the scheme, to say nothing of her brother being hurt.

Vengeance in the shape of twenty stalwart policemen was now bowling towards us at thirty miles an hour without any effort on her part, and yet she took the trouble to ring me up and give a warning.

What queer things women are!

By now several hundred cases had been moved from Sam's, and it seemed a good time to be moving myself, for I was the only one whom the hijackers knew by name, and it would be me for whom the troopers would be looking. A man was sent to Sam's to tell them to go on working as hard as they could to get everything away, and that we would give them half an hour's notice before the troopers arrived. Richardson, who was as game a fellow as any one could wish to have with him in a tight corner, was to remain by the tele-phone, and, on receipt of a message, to jump into a car and give warning to the men.

Pettit was to drive to a place some fifteen miles along the road in the direction from which the troopers were coming, and wait by a telephone booth until he saw them pass, when he was to call up Richardson, who would be waiting for the message.

I went with Pettit in his car, and he dropped me at a railway station whence trains ran up to the city. Everyone advised me to make myself scarce, as if the man dressed as a trooper really was one, his comrades would not be very kindly disposed towards me. Exactly what they might do could only be appreciated by one who has been up against the American police, or seen them man-handling a prisoner against whom they have a grudge.

There was an hour to wait at the station for the train, and as the troopers would be sure to know my name, appearance, and whereabouts, I did not make myself over-conspicuous. The obvious thing for them to do was to telephone down to the local police to watch the one road and the one railway by which it was possible to escape from this district.

I stood behind a pile of lumber keeping a bright look-out for anyone arriving who might be a local sheriff or policeman. At last the train came in, and I climbed aboard with a feeling of relief, having worried myself unnecessarily (not for the first time) by overestimating the intelligence of the police.

Some hours later I stepped off the train and mingled with the crowd in the city, the safest place for anyone who desires privacy.

Afterwards I heard that everything had gone according to plan. Pettit had remained for several hours beside the telephone until he saw the troopers go by; he telephoned to Richardson, who motored to Sam's and gave the tip to the men working there. By this time a large proportion of the cases had been taken away to other places for storage, or hidden in a neighbouring swamp.

I went back to my rooms in the city, and left it to one of the principal natives concerned to straighten things out; he assured me that it would only be a matter of a few days before we were back at work again.

Meanwhile, word came up from Hawkes Bay that there were "process-servers" looking for me down there. I did not know exactly what a "process-server" was, but it sounded unpleasant, so I decided not to make their closer acquaintance, and to lie low for the time being.

Next day I was sitting in my room feeling rather worried, and counting up how many cents a second the steamer cost lying there doing nothing, when Richardson blew in.

"That fellow really was a trooper, and he's dying," he announced cheerfully. My heart sank into my boots as visions of packed juries and Sing-Sing floated into my mind. "But I don't think it will matter much if he does," he went on. "When the troopers came down they were out for blood, but when they heard the truth they were furious with their own man, and said it was a pity that whoever bowled him over didn't make a proper job of it."

He handed me a bundle of newspapers, and under all sorts of startling headings the papers had given a highly coloured and inaccurate account of the whole affair, written up from such scraps of information as could be picked up.

Here was a pretty mess!

The obvious thing to do was to make myself scarce, but with the ship lying off the coast, quantities of liquor stored on shore, and money owing from various people, there was nothing to do but to hang on as long as possible and salvage everything I could before retreating.

There was already a heavy loss to face, for the troopers had found what was left in Sam's house and had destroyed it, and one of them, while wandering aimlessly about the countryside, had stumbled on the pile of cases hidden in the swamp, and these also were destroyed.

Sam's place was remote; there was only one road leading to it, and the whole countryside was agog with curiosity, so as far as I knew the troopers did not have the chance to cart away any of the loot to sell on their own account. They had to be contented with what they could get under their skins, and from all accounts that was no small quantity.

# CHAPTER XXII

## ESCAPING THE POLICE

FOR some days there were extensive intrigues and subterranean plottings, and it seemed that it would be possible to hush up the affair so that we could set to work again very shortly; the story of this time would in itself fill a book, but there is honour among rum-runners, or at any rate some honour among some rum-runners, and it must remain untold.

I changed my name to "Jack Burns," moved to other quarters, and spent most of my time planning moves for the future in case the situation did not right itself.

The trooper did not die, Maisie's brother got better, and the dark fellow disappeared, leaving no address to which we could send flowers or inquiries. To this day I have heard nothing about him beyond a vague rumour that someone had found him lying wounded in a hut some miles away from Sam's place.

He was an ex-policeman, but was no longer connected with the force like the trooper. So now the police had in their hands four out of the five men concerned, for the trooper turning informer, had landed himself and three of the others in gaol.

At their trial they told a fairly good story, making out that we were the aggressors, and that I had made a murderous and unprovoked attack on them, and as there was nobody there to contradict them, three of the men got off scot-free; but the informer himself, besides losing his job in the police force, received a sentence of eight months' imprisonment. It would have been better for him if he had kept his mouth shut, as he had been advised to do.

The more sensational newspapers, with their usual ingenuity, found a number of choice words to describe us honest merchants, who were but attempting to defend our lives and property against, the attack of armed robbers: "Bootleggers' bump-off men," "City gunmen," "Plug-uglies," "Rummers," and other kindly epithets.

Besides our own little troubles, the whole industry was in a state of upset on account of the campaign launched by the prohibition officials with their fleets of small cutters, which were sent to anchor alongside the rum-ships and prevent the shore-boats from communicating with them. For years past everyone had wondered why the Government had not done this, and now that they had actually woken up to the only way of competing with the difficulty, it threw everyone's arrangements into disorder.

Since the only thing to do was to retreat and try some fresh scheme, I sent wireless messages to the ship to tell her to meet me at a certain British port, but the American stations stopped the messages, even though I had them sent off from Canada in a code which made them appear to be harmless inquiries about someone's health.

Boats were sent out with messages to Ryan, but they were either caught by the coastguard before they reached the shore, and fined for some real or imaginary technical offence, or else were unable to get near the ship on account of the four Government craft which were anchored round her. For a week I tried to get into touch with her, but could not go myself on account of the process-servers who were looking for me at the seaside places.

One evening, some two weeks after the beginning of the trouble, things came to a head. The evening newspapers came out with a great flaring headline saying that several men, including myself, had been "indicted" by a jury, and this meant that we could be arrested on sight and deposited in the lock-up.

I looked in to see Hoppit, and went up in the lift to his luxurious apartment, where he had so often wined and dined me. On these occasions I had admired his eighteen pairs of new shoes at fifty-five dollars the pair, his dozen new suits averaging a hundred and sixty dollars the suit, his stacks of silk shirts at fourteen dollars each, and carpets, ties, chairs, handkerchiefs, and cigars all on the same scale.

I rang the bell, and the door was opened by a tall man with a handsome face and a pleasant smile.

"Hallo! Barby. Come along in," he said hospitably.

I entered not feeling altogether at ease, for this was Tim, one of the chief prohibition agents for the part of the country where I worked, and although he was a guest in my friend's apartment, I did not know what his attitude would be now that our fortunes were so unstable and it was unlikely there would be any *pourboires* coming his way. But of all the prohibition agents I knew, he had always seemed far and away the best, and I had a genuine liking for him, apart from any business reasons.

Pettit and half a dozen other men were there, and I joined them in drinking to a speedy end to our present anxieties.

Tim handed me a glass of Sauterne, for which he had a special liking.

"Well, Barby, here's success to crime!" he said cheerfully, raising his glass to his lips. "I am sorry to hear about your difficulties; if only I had known earlier, I could have straightened everything for you, but by the time that I heard about it, things had gone too far to be stopped. Anyhow, here's luck to you, and if I were you I would try a change of air just now."

Being an alien, my plight would have been much worse than that of the others if the authorities had roped me in, so at their urgent insistence I jumped into my car and steered north for Canada. My plan was to get there as quickly as possible, and try to get into touch with the ship direct from a Canadian wireless station and order her to a British port; failing that, to get hold of some Canadian fishing-boat and go down the five hundred miles to her by water.

While I was in the city Teale had taken out fresh registration plates for my car, giving my new name and address as Jack Burns of 46A East 51-1/2 Street, as the number of my old identification plates would be known by those who wished to have the pleasure of making my closer acquaintance.

Whenever I had occasion to change my name I always chose a new one with my own initials, so that I should not be traced by those nasty little red cotton signs with which the laundry people insist on decorating the articles entrusted to them by their victims.

I drove for some hours heading north, and I must confess that I was looking lot forward with relief to finding myself on Canadian soil, for being a quiet law-abiding person both by nature and upbringing, this little difference of opinion with the authorities was rather trying. As I drove along through the night I could not help thinking of the one and only time I had fallen foul of the law.

It was when I was riding my bicycle home late one night through the country village where my parents live: the lamp went out but it was only a short distance to our front gates, so feeling in a reckless mood, I decided to take a chance and rode on.

All went well until I was within fifty yards of home, when the village constable stepped out from the shadow of a tree and stopped me.

"It has only just gone out," I pleaded humbly.

"But it is quite cold," he replied grimly, placing his large hands on the top of the lamp.

The result was a five shilling fine, and a mild remark from my father—

"The family has lived here for several generations and never broken the law before."

I believe that he took it quite seriously to heart, and so did I for his sake. What would he have said if he could have seen me now?

All went well until midnight, when I was passing through a little town some hundred miles away from the city. Several roads ran into a square, and not knowing which to take, I stopped to ask a motor-cycle policeman who was on point duty.

"Which is the road to Binton?"

He jerked his thumb towards the opposite corner of the square.

"Thank you," I said, forgetting that I was in the United States, and slipped in my gear to go on.

"Hey!" he suddenly said, "why did you come the wrong side of that red light down there?"

"I'm sorry," I answered meekly, "I am a stranger here; I'll be more careful next time." As a matter of fact I did not see a red light and doubt if there was one. He probably was so surprised at the "thank you" that he grew suspicious, and invented the light in order to have an excuse for holding me up.

"Show me your licence," he ordered.

I looked round to see if there was any chance of getting away from him, but he held the handles of a powerful Indian motor-cycle, while there were two other motor-cycle policemen close by. They all carry revolvers, so the only course was to try a bluff.

The licence was in my pocket, but if he had read the evening papers he could not help recognising my name, and would know that I was "wanted."

*Que faire?* Nothing, except once more to hope that police intelligence would be on a par with police manners.

I handed him the little blue ticket, and watched his face closely; it showed no sign of interest as he read the name. I gave a sigh of relief as he handed it back to me without a word, hoping that my troubles were over for the moment.

"Show me your car registration," he said.

Here was a poser. My driver's licence was the original one in the name of James Barbican, with the address of a big hotel in the city, while Teale had got the registration plates under my new name of Jack Burns, with the address 46A East 51-1/2 Street, and owing to my hasty departure I had not asked him for the new car registration certificate. It was necessary to think out a story without much delay.

"Haven't got it with me," I answered.

"Is it your car?" he asked suspiciously.

"No, it was lent to me by a friend."

"You come along with me to the police station," he said.

He piloted the way on his motor-cycle, while the other two policemen looked on. Again I glanced round to see what chances there were of escape, but my Dodge would have had as much chance of getting away from three motor-cycle policemen as a pug dog from a trio of greyhounds, for these Indian cycles will overtake a car doing sixty miles an hour.

To try to escape was certain trouble, while there was one chance in ten of pulling off a bluff if the local police were of the same calibre as the others with whom I had so far come into contact, or to be more accurate, avoided coming into contact.

The car was left outside the police station and the policeman escorted me in. A burly red-faced sergeant sat behind a desk and glared at me with hollow shrewdness from a pair of round horn spectacles while my captor said his say.

"Where are you from?" asked the sergeant, with a great show of ferocity.

"The St Francis Hotel," I replied, giving the address which was on my licence, and which I had left ten months ago.

"Whose auto is that?"

"It belongs to a friend of mine named Burns, and he lent it to me."

"Where does he live?"

"46A West 51-1/2 Street," I answered, giving the address of the house in which I had been living as Burns.

"How long have you known him?"

"A good many years," I replied quite truthfully.

"Where are you going?"

"Binton."

"Why are you going there?"

"To meet a friend."

"Where will you stay?"

Fortunately I knew the name of a hotel in Binton, so replied instantaneously, "The Ritz-Carlton."

"What is the name of your friend?" he suddenly shouted at me.

This was a bit of a poser, for he might telephone to find out if this imaginary person really existed; there seemed to be only one way out of this.

"It's a lady, and I couldn't mention her name without compromising her," I answered gallantly.

"Frisk him," ordered the sergeant.

The policeman stepped forward and ran through my pockets, feeling me down to see if there were any papers or a revolver hidden on me. I thanked my lucky stars that a few hours before I had destroyed every scrap of paper and hidden away my revolver.

When going where there was any risk of being picked up by

police, coastguard, or prohibition men, I had always taken care to run through my pockets to make sure that there was nothing in them to identify or incriminate me. Five hundred times I had done this unnecessarily, and now the five hundred and first time it saved the situation.

"Search the auto!" snapped the sergeant, and the policeman went out, to return in a few minutes saying that there was nothing in it but a suitcase containing some clothes. If the mutton-headed fellow had looked a little more carefully, he would have found a spare set of number-plates which would have given them something to talk about.

"Now then, come clean!" shouted the policeman, seizing me from behind and shaking me roughly. "Tell us all about it and it will be best for you in the end."

"We are keeping you until the man Burns comes to identify you and the auto," remarked the sergeant.

Here was a pretty kettle of fish! As long as they held me, they would have to look a long time before they found Jack Burns, and in a few hours' time the morning papers would arrive, and then they could not avoid seeing my name. I already saw myself peering at the blue sky through the bars of Sing-Sing.

Things seemed about as bad as they could be, so there could be no harm in trying the effect of a little blarney.

Looking the sergeant straight in the face, I said angrily, "What in hell do you think you are doing? Do I look like an auto thief? I've got to get on with my journey, and can't spend the night here to amuse you! Telephone to any friend of mine in the city, and if they don't curse you for waking them up in the middle of the night, they will tell you that I am not the sort to steal autos."

I gave him the names of several people I knew who had nothing to do with the rum-running business, and told him to telephone to them.

"Nothing doing. You say this auto belongs to Burns, and we've got to check up on it that you are O.K. What's his telephone number, and I'll get the city police to call him up."

"Pertater II, III," I said, giving the number of the house where I had been living as Burns up to a few hours ago, "but he is a gay bird who is out at cabarets every night, and won't be back for hours yet.

The sergeant made no reply, but taking up the telephone, called up police headquarters in the city. After some delay he was put through.

"We've got a man here who says his name is James Barbican, he's driving a Dodge coupé, registration number O.O. xxx., and engine number zzzxyy. He says the auto was lent to him by Jack Burns 46A East 51-1/2 Street, telephone Pertater II, III. He gives the names of Z.

.. and Y ... and B ... as references. His story don't sound too good.

"Check up on it. I'll hold him here until you ring me back."

Here was my last chance gone! The local police might have missed the local papers, but there was no chance of police headquarters in the city not knowing that I was wanted.

Bulldog Drummond would have walked up and down the police station whistling a merry little roundelay, and finally have walked out of the place in a policeman's uniform and ridden away on one of the Indian motor-cycles.

But there were no spare uniforms about, and my mouth was so dry that I could not whistle; all I could do in the way of bravado being to smoke Camels and hum the tune of "Through the Night of Doubt and Sorrow."

As I walked up and down the knotted board floor of that police station, casting round for some means of escape, I wished with all my heart that I could put in my place that ingenious and versatile gentleman "Sapper." I have the most profound admiration for him and all his works, but I would wager him a case of champagne to a bottle of beer that he would not have been able to extricate himself or me from that position except with the aid of sheer blind luck.

The car was standing outside the door, so near and yet so far. The key had been left in the ignition, and the petrol tap turned on; I measured with my eye the distance between the door and the car, and the time it would take to hop across the road, start the car, and be off; but with three burly policemen in the room and several motor-cycle men within call it was hopeless.

Strategy seemed to be the only thing now.

"If you don't want to starve me as well as keep me waiting here all night, I am going out to get some supper," I remarked to the sergeant.

He nodded, and I walked out of the place, but the policeman who had brought me there dogged my steps. My idea was to try to slip away on foot; it would be a pity to lose the car, but it would cost me the price of many cars if they caught me and I had to pay the lawyers to keep me out of gaol, like poor Jim League.

"There's an all-night eating-place round the corner in the square," remarked the policeman.

So I entered, but he remained standing all the time watching me through the glass door. The restaurant seemed to be one of those useless places where everything comes and goes through the front door, and there is no back door.

After a small meal, which I did not enjoy very much, I returned to the police station with my satellite, who had not given me a dog's chance of a break away.

171

"Is everything O.K. now? I want to be getting on," I said jauntily to the sergeant.

He shook his head, but condescended to make no further reply.

For another hour I paced up and down that bare room, waiting for the telephone call which it seemed a hundred to one would put me under lock and key.

At last the telephone bell tinkled; with an impassive face the sergeant repeated what was being said to him from the other end of the wire.

My name, height, the colour of my eyes, weight, shape of nose, colour of hair, and other things he jotted down on a pad as he said them aloud.

He looked up at me several times to compare notes.

"Yes, that's him all right," he answered.

My heart sank into my boots.

"Guess we'll have to chase you," said the sergeant, glaring at me over the top of his horn goggles.

What did the word "chase" mean? It did not sound very hopeful. To hide my uncertainty I began lighting a cigarette slowly and deliberately, looking at the man without any expression on my face.

"You can go," he said reluctantly, jerking towards the door with his thumb. Hardly able to believe my ears, I lingered to make inquiries about the road to Binton, stepped into my car, and drove away.

For the first five miles I drove quietly, looking behind frequently to make sure that I was not being followed; then I stepped on the accelerator and did the next twenty-five miles in half an hour.

I often wondered how it was they let me go, but I know no more about it than the reader, for everything happened just as I have related. Possibly it was due to faulty liaison between the motor licence department and the "wanted men" department in the city.

Knowing that when they discovered their mistake they would telephone up the road to have me stopped, I turned off at right angles to my course and made for a town which lies in a different direction to Binton. Seeing a woodland track leading off the main road, I turned off my lights and went down it. In twenty minutes the number-plates were removed and hidden down a rabbit-hole, and a fresh set put up in their place.

About dawn I ran into a small town, placed the car in a public garage, took train to a seaside place a hundred miles away, and put up at the hotel under the name of Johnnie Bust.

It was some weeks before I heard the sequel to the night's proceedings. Not many hours after the sergeant had allowed me to "chase," there appeared at the door of 46A East 51-1/2 Street some workmen who said they had been sent by the electric light company to locate a defective wire. In the course of looking for it, they searched the house from top to bottom for signs of Mr. Jack Burns, and more especially for any papers he might have there. But they had no luck, for Mr. Jack Burns, alias Mr. James Barbican, was staying at a seaside hotel several hundred miles away as Mr. Johnnie Bust, while his papers and accounts were in a safe deposit box rented by Mr. Jeremiah Broke at the C . . . Bank in Fifth Avenue.

A few days later they came again, but with the same result.

I always wish I could have been a fly on the wall of that police station next morning to see the old sergeant's face when he heard what a fat juicy blue bottle he had let slip through his web.

The next few days I spent by the sea trying to get into communication with the ship by means of wireless, but the American stations again blocked the messages.

So I decided to go up to Canada, and either wireless to them direct from there, or, failing that, to take a Canadian boat and go down myself.

I therefore took train from the seaside to a small town in the United States on the Canadian frontier; on arriving at the station I put my suitcase in the cloakroom and took a walk round to reconnoitre the position, for, though I have crossed many frontiers, I had never been over the American-Canadian one, except by train, and did not know what the formalities were.

There was a river running through the town; on this side it was the United States, on the other, Canada. It would have been child's play to swim across after dark, as I had once crossed a frontier before, but there was a bridge with American officials at one end and Canadians at the other.

It was pouring rain, and although motors and people carrying parcels were stopped, ordinary foot passengers did not seem to be molested, so, turning up my coat-collar, I walked across and heaved a sigh of relief on finding myself once more on British soil.

This is an abrupt ending, but I cannot finish the story because I do not know myself how it is going to end.

Teale and Ryan are enduring hardships and having adventures beside which mine are but milk and water. Would that I could be sharing them!

Also there is more to say about Jalleno, Pettit, Hoppit, and Richardson, from whom my emissaries are at the moment collecting some money they owe me. Whether it will ever be told Heaven only knows!

# NOTE

As the contents of the following chapters do not conveniently fit into any particular part of my narrative, I have placed them at the end of it. I can vouch for the truth of everything set down as having happened to myself; the rest is hearsay, but is also true as far as I know.

AUTHOR

# PART II

# CHAPTER XXIII

## TALES OF A SUPERCARGO

My friend Barney was in port and came up to see me. He was a tough citizen of about thirty-five, who in his time had played many parts: most of them had been hard parts, but he had the greatest of all gifts, that of being able to laugh at his own misfortunes. I prepared for him with my own hands a supper of buttered toast, onion omelette, and Lawson's whiskey, and having filled himself to the full, he sat back in his chair, lighted his cigar, and began amiably meandering about some of his experiences of life as a supercargo.

"We were lying off the coast on the old *Nimrod*, when a seventy-five foot cutter came up alongside and the bosun hollered out to know if he could come aboard.

"'Sure thing, come along up, Buddy,' I says.

"So up comes the coastguard guy and we have a drink together, and he tells me a long story of how he had promised to run in a load from the *Phyllis Firefly* and had everything fixed to land it that night; he said he couldn't find the *Phyllis* and wanted me to give him five hundred cases on credit for the parties he was working for.

"Not knowing nothing about him nor them, I says, 'Like hell, I will! You have as much charnst of getting a load of booze off of this old scow as a woodpecker of boring a hole in a safe-deposit vault.'

"I thought he was trying to bull me, but he was so darned sure about the whole thing that I began to ask him a few questions. He told me the landing place and the names of the people he had fixed up with, and it seemed that it was my crowd. They must have been pulling in goods from the other schooner as well, without me knowing it.

"I asked him a lot more questions, and there seemed to be no doubt he was working with my folks, so I thought to myself: 'Oh, hell! This is too good to miss. I'll take a charnst on him being on the level and give him a load.'

"So I did, and he landed the five hundred with only one shy, which he and the crew had probably drunk on the way in; and my boss gives him his five bucks a case. After that, him and three of the other seventy-five footers used to pull regular from us.

"Of course, they take a bit of a charnst, but they nearly always get away with it. A seventy-five footer will take about seven hundred cases of Scotch, but it is best to give them only five hundred, and then they float so they hardly show they have anything on board. Even if they do get pinched, they always have some heifer dust ready about laying a trap for a ship, and trying to make the shore in an hour to get evidence against her to have her pulled in.

"You remember about that seventy-five footer with a full load that got taken in by one of the big cutters?

"That was a dirty double-crossing son-of-a-dog of a coastguard man who handed us a rotten deal; one of our boys had arranged with him to take in a load off a schooner on his seventy-five footer, and after agreeing to do it, he got the wind up and went and squealed on the whole works to an officer. They sent him out with a crew of picked men, and took the cases from off of the schooner, but things went wrong and the whole shooting match ended up at a coastguard base.

"Ever since then that dirty son-of-a-gun has been a stool-pigeon for the coastguard, and whenever he sees me coming along he shoves his hand in his jacket pocket and keeps me covered until I am out of sight; but I ain't going to bump him off. No, sir, the lousy squealing rat ain't worth the trouble, but somebody else is very liable to do something to him one day soon, and a darned good job too.

"Last time I sees him I says to him quite pleasant like 'There'll be flowers in your house soon, but you won't smell them, you rotten little cross-eyed snooper.'

"Yes, Barby, them men on the seventy-five footers have great opportunities, and those that haven't neglected them have made quite a pile of dough. All the same it's quite a risky job, and they are entitled to their money as long as they play straight with you, for them little cutters is mighty poor sea-boats.

"Did I ever tell you how I nearly slipped in through the pearly gates on one of those goddarned rotten rat-traps? It happened like this.

"The old *Nimrod* was lying thirty miles offshore, and we had been there for three weeks without getting word from our folks on the beach. There was a seventy-five footer lying alongside us all the time and one day I saw them pulling up their mud-hook in an almighty hurry.

"'You sure are not going to leave us all alone?' I shouted to them.

"'We've got a storm warning by radio, and we're going to beat it while the beating's good,' they answered.

"I asked them if they would take me ashore with them, as I wanted to see my crowd to find out what was wrong that they didn't come out to get the stuff off. They said they would put me on the beach and they wanted five hundred bucks, which was out of the question, but in the end I squeezed them down to a hundred, so I put off in a dory and went aboard them.

"Before we got half-way to the shore it was blowing a living gale, and the little boat had a pretty rough time in the big seas; for twenty-four hours it was touch and go, and we expected to go to the bottom any minute. At last we got in sight of Pinkerton Harbour, and, as you know, there is a real son-of-a-gun of a bar to cross there. Waves as big as houses were crashing over it, so that it looked impossible for any boat to get over it right side up; but we'd got to get in somehow, as our gas was nearly gone and our anchor would never hold her off the beach.

"The bosun of the cutter turned on a switch in the cabin wall and said, 'Hello, there! we are Coastguard Cutter XOOX, and we are outside the bar at Pinkerton. We have only two hours' gas left, and it is too rough to cross the bar. Can you help us?"

"A voice came back from the wall. 'We'll send out a cutter to help you. She won't cross the bar, but will wait about inside, and if you turn over she will probably be able to pick some of you up.'

"It was the wireless telephone working, and the voice came twenty miles from some guy sitting in an easy-chair in an office, and I would have given the hundred cases of my own Scotch I had on the *Nimrod* to change places with him right there.

"We were close to the town, and every time we came to the top of a wave we could see the faces of the people standing on the promenade having a free show of us drowning; it went to my heart to think of all the wasted gate-money there was there.

"After a while another seventy-five footer came inside the bar, and we hoped they would come out and pick us off, but they were too cagey for that, and waved to us to come on in.

"So there being nothing else to do, we headed for the breakers and went in on the top of a big wave. By some accident we stayed right side up, and we went shooting past the other boat like the Knickerbocker express going through a local station. They turned to follow us, and as they were broad side on, a big wave caught them and washed one of the crew overboard. They spent quite a while looking for him, and didn't find him, but we had no time to waste on dead Revenue men, having been so mighty near dead ourselves, and we went right on in to the coastguard base and tied up alongside a lot of other cutters.

"They hid me in one of the men's bunks and covered me over with a blanket.

"You lie there till I give you three taps on the back and then hop out and beat it pronto,' says the bosun to me.

"Then I heard a strange voice outside say: 'I am coming on board to inspect this boat,' and I sure thought I was on the way to the hoosegow. But the bosun said all the boys was sleeping below nearly dead, and the voice went away.

"In about an hour someone came down and tapped me three times, and I jumped out of the bunk. It was the bosun, and he said it was all clear and I could beat it. I peeled off five twenty-spots from my roll, and gave them to him. He had wanted me to pay when I came aboard from the *Nimrod*, but I wasn't giving him his century until be put me safe on the beach. Think what a sucker I would have been if I had paid them in advance and the boat had sunk on us, as it nearly did!

"I just walked ashore, right over the decks of several other cutters as though they all belonged to me, and took the train up to the city.

"What was I doing before I took to rum running, Barby? Well, I guess there wasn't nothing I hadn't tried out. I remember how once me and my friend Rubenstein was clean on our uppers, and there wasn't more than two dimes making their home in my pants pocket; we sure was hungry for the dough, for it was weeks since we had roped in our three squares a day. Seeing nothing else in sight, we decided on a hold-up.

"To do a hold-up in good style you want a gun, but we hadn't enough jack to buy one, so we went to a plumber, and with our last few cents we bought an elegant piece of lead pipe, which I figured would do just as well as a blackjack.

"Then we went to a classy location, just outside Holywood, and waited round in a darkish street for a likely guy to come along.

"'When you bean your bird,' says Ruby to me, 'don't dent in his dome; just give him a crack on the nut what will make him kiss the kerb for half an hour while we makes our get-away.'

"I was all shaking with excitement, never having tried the stick-up business before; I was afraid to hit too hard for fear of bumping the guy off, and more afraid to hit too soft for fear he might have a gun and bump us off.

"At last a wealthy-looking guy comes along wearing a hard hat. 'That's our meat!' says Ruby, 'he's sure a bank director, and his pocket-book is bursting with yellow-boys. Sock him one on the back of his neck, or you will only shove his lid down over his ears.'

"We walked up behind him, and it seemed to me that there was a cop looking at me from behind every gate-post, and my dogs was barking like a pack of hounds, but really there wasn't nobody in sight, and my shoes was rubber-soled and didn't make no more noise than a cat.

"But all that was on account of me being a bit nervous like, you see, being new to the game.

"I got right up behind him and lifted the lead pipe and socked him good and plenty on the back of the neck; hit him hard enough to kill an elephant, I did.

"Well, me being an amateur at the business, I hit him wrong, or the pipe was too soft, or something wasn't right. Anyways, I'll be hornswoggled if that goddarned pipe didn't go and wind itself round that old buzzard's gullet just like a snake.

"He let out a holler and bolted up the street, tearing at the pipe with his fingers and screeching like a dame what's got a rat run up her plus-fours. There not being no music in the noise he was making, we went the other way to what he had done, and Ruby says to me, 'I don't know which is the softest, you or that darned pipe.'

"There isn't nothing to this story really, but it just goes to prove what I was saying just now, that there ain't no room for amateurs in a business like that. A real hold-up guy would have known better and gotten him a stiffer pipe; all the same if that pipe had been stiff, the old guy would have been a stiff too, and I might have been up the river on my way to the chair, instead of sitting here drinking your Lawson.

"Anyways, after that it was the straight and narrow for yours truly, so I went into the rum running game."

"Well, Barney," I remarked, as he poured himself out another drink, "it won't ruin you socially to be connected with something honest."

# CHAPTER XXIV

## A TOUGH GUY

ABOUT midnight on New Year's Eve I was entering my hotel bedroom when the door opposite opened, and I was hailed by a dapper little Italian.

"The compliments of the season to you, Barby; come along in for a drink with my buddy, Ted O'Hara. He's the world's toughest guy, and I want you to meet him."

He dragged me into the room, where we found his friend standing on the hearth-rug handing out drinks to two men who were introduced as his skipper, Captain O'Leary, and his supercargo, Mr. Milligan.

O'Hara stood about five feet nine in height, measured about the same round the chest, and rather more round the belt; his hair was fair, his face heavy-jowled, his eyes blue and prominent, and he bore the unmistakable stamp of the successful Irish-American politician.

I had never met him before, but many were the tales I had heard of his great strength and his wild doings. Last summer he had reduced two motor-cars to scrap-iron by knocking down telegraph-poles when travelling at sixty miles an hour.

On another occasion he was driving a large car with thirty dozen of Scotch concealed in it, and left it standing in the street while he went into a restaurant for a meal. On coming out, he found standing by it a nigger policeman, who informed him that he had offended some trifling parking regulation.

"Yo' mus' come 'long to de police station wit' me," said the nigger, reaching out his hand to open the door and get inside the car.

"Sure I'll come," answered O'Hara amiably, pushing in front of the policeman, jumping into the driver's seat, and slamming the door behind him. "You stand right there on the step and show me the way."

The policeman obediently did as he was told, and holding on to the door with one hand, pointed down the street with the other.

The roadway was wide, and suddenly O'Hara stepped on the accelerator, and wrenched the wheel round, so that the car gave a violent swerve; at the same moment he gave the nigger a mighty punch in the solar plexus. The unfortunate man went head over heels into the gutter with all the wind knocked out of him, and O'Hara made for the State border at seventy miles an hour. That was the last he ever heard of parking regulations in the town of C—— for he always avoided it after that.

"It's bad enough to be run in by a white cop," he had remarked, "but it sure would get my goat to be pinched by a nigger."

While we were talking some business the door opened, and in walked a slight scholarly-looking man with grey hair, who was introduced as the "doctor."

"He's just come with us for a pleasure trip," said O'Hara to me in an undertone. "He's a retired gentleman with an income. No, sir. He hasn't nothing to do with us in a business way; he's just a friend of ours."

After staying a few minutes, the doctor went down to his room to bed, and as he was bidding us a courteous good-night, I could not help wondering what might be the ties between this quiet little man and the rough company in which he was found.

We discussed coastguards, speedboats, prohibition agents, and the hundred and one other things which go to make the life of the rum-runner interesting. About three o'clock the skipper yawned loudly. "Well, boys, what about a broiled lobster at Dader's?" he asked. Everyone agreed, and we put on our hats and coats, and made for the door.

"Where's your coat, boss?" asked Milligan of O'Hara.

"I don't need no coat," answered the tough Irishman casually.

"But it's zero outside, and you'll be getting the pneumonia if you go out of this hot room without one."

"That's all right—I'll take no harm," protested O'Hara.

"Where is the coat?" someone asked.

"Down in the doctor's room, and him asleep by now."

Then followed a long discussion as to what was to be done.

It appeared that the doctor did not approve of them gallivanting about late at night, and that none of these tough smugglers cared to brave his disapproval by going in to get the coat. Finally, like four mice on their way to bell the cat, we tip-toed to the doctor's room, and stood nervously in a group outside the door.

One of the others gently turned the handle and opened the door; the doctor was sitting on the side of his bed, his hands engaged in pedicultural operations, and his eyes in reading a book which lay open on the coverlet beside him, 'The Life and Letters of St Paul.'

"Where are you boys off to at this time of night?" he asked

"Just going to get a bite to eat before we hit the hay," one of them answered apologetically.

The hat and the coat were retrieved, and we all trooped out.

"He didn't seem to mind much," said Milligan with an audible sigh of relief.

The restaurant was full to the doors, and was a noisy disorderly place, although there were several sober people there besides myself.

O'Hara produced a bottle from his trouser pocket, but it did not last long, for what is a solitary bottle of Scotch among four gentlemen who have already whetted their appetites by putting away a couple in the last two hours?

"Where's them other two bottles?" he asked.

"In your bedroom," answered Milligan.

A hanger-on of the restaurant was given the key of the room and told to get the two bottles, but he returned in a few minutes saying that he could not find them; however, he produced from his pocket a bottle of bootlegged "Dewar's," which he sold them for six dollars.

I had a good look at it; the bottle, the non-refillable stopper, and the label, were all irreproachable, but the pungent fumes which ascended when the bottle was opened showed that it was phoney goods, so I refused the proffered drink.

"Don't blame you either," remarked O'Hara, taking a five-finger shot for himself; "the man who drinks that sort of stuff is sure taking a chance; but what the hell—? Here's luck! Pat, go and see if you can't find those two bottles of 'Ambassador' I left in my room; Mr. Barbican won't risk this stuff."

In a few minutes Pat returned, and triumphantly produced the two bottles from under his coat.

"No wonder that bootlegging bum couldn't find them. The doctor had hidden them under his pillow, but he was fast asleep, and I got them away without waking him. I knew him to do that once before."

About four o'clock, after we had eaten our lobsters, things began to get a bit slow, so I looked round to see what could be done to liven them up a little.

A Swede was playing "Sweet Rosie O'Grady" on an accordion, the Irishmen were roaring the chorus, and a good-looking young prizefighter, who had been engaged in a contest at the arena that evening, was dancing between the tables with a tall handsome blonde with a dark parting—the only woman in the place.

Now if there is one thing which is sure to start a rough-house, it is to take a man's girl away from him in public; so I remarked to O'Hara, "I'd like to dance with that girl; will you take care of her beau for me?"

Without a word O'Hara, with an agility amazing for one of his size, jumped up from his seat and slipped his great bulk between the bruiser and his partner; with a flick of the wrist he heaved her into my arms, and began talking to the bereaved man. The Swede had seen what had happened, and the accordion crashed out with redoubled noise; the lady took me firmly in charge and steered me skillfully between the tables, while I watched for the fun to begin between the Irishman and the pug.

But the latter took a look at the colossal form of O'Hara and walked away with a rather forced smile to another corner of the room. This tame ending spoiled everything.

"I don't want to take you away from your partner—better go back and join him," I remarked to the lady.

"No," she answered. "You'll do just as well."

Seeing an empty seat at our table, I steered her into it, and as the absent owner had left his drink behind, she was nothing loth, and put it away without more ado.

She was a clever amusing girl, and kept the whole table in roars of laughter with her humour and gift of repartee. She would by now have been a brilliant debutante had she been born in Park Lane or Park Avenue, but having first seen the light of day in a street down by the docks, she was entertaining a tableful of tough bootleggers in an all-night restaurant.

I wondered what would have happened to our own womenfolk if they had been born in the same environment?

"That little frail's quite easy to the eye," remarked O'Hara with an appraising glance at the young woman, "but I don't set much store by the girls myself. My old woman's good enough for me. She's well trained she is, for I started with her from the very beginning. Sometimes we has a row, and she reads the riot act, but then I only goes out and has one.

"Here's the tip for a peaceful life, Barbican: when you get married, the first time your wife starts to give you any backchat, sock her one in the kisser, and show her right at the start where she gets off at."

It was now five o'clock, and as I was sleepy I bade them all goodnight.

"See you again soon, Mr Barby," said O'Hara, crushing my hand with his gorilla-like grip. "And if you want a happy life, remember what I told you."

# CHAPTER XXV

## THE BOOTLEGGERS' BALL

SOON after my arrival in America there befell me a rather trying experience, which is not likely to be repeated, for once bitten, twice shy.

Some cheery rum-runners asked me to a party to celebrate the birthday of one of their wives, and it was to be an occasion of wine, music, and song.

"Will you bring your own sweetie along, Barby, or shall we find you one?" inquired my kindly host.

Being a little doubtful as to what sort of partner would be provided, I hastily said that I would bring my own.

Then came the question of whom to take.

The only girl I knew who would appreciate that sort of party was an art student named Marion —— her last name does not matter. She appeared to be the same type of girl who goes to the art schools in London, and is probably her American contemporary.

"Would you like to come to a bootleggers' ball?" I asked her on the telephone.

"You bet I'll come," was the reply, so on the appointed night, I called for her, and very nice she looked in a simple white frock with her dark coppery hair done in a low loop down on her neck in the way affected by artistic people in all countries.

She was a Bohemian sort of young person, and soon made herself at home. We sat down to a table groaning with good food, and I am sure that there was not a senator in Washington who had a better choice of drinks that night—and I ought to know, having replenished the cellars of so many of them.

First, for those who liked a drink so lacking in kick, there was 1917 Château Panillac, straight off the ice; then there was 1911 Mumm Cordon Rouge, served in tumblers, with young icebergs floating in each. Later on there was a fine old vintage port, also off the ice, but this was not very popular among the men, being regarded as rather a feminine drink; the ladies, however, found it go down quite smoothly when mixed with ginger ale, and the men added a little 1848 liqueur brandy to give it more pep. At the end of the repast there was Benedictine, Cherry Brandy, Crème de Menthe, and Grand Marnier, which were drunk either neat or mixed with soda water or ginger ale, while there was always a bottle of Scotch on tap for those who preferred it to the fancy drinks.

After dinner there was dancing, and the fun became fast and furious. It is to be feared that I rather deserted my partner in order to listen to the men, for with a few drinks aboard, the American rum-runner is the most amusing raconteur in the world; besides the racy language and dry humour of the Yankee, he has had endless adventures on which to base his yarns.

After a while I found Marion. "Enjoying yourself?" I asked her.

"Fine!" she answered. "This surely is the dandiest riot I have been to in a long time. Come and dance? If you won't there's plenty will. A glass of champagne and I'm anybody's!"

There was a sparkle in her eye and an abandonment in her dancing that had not been there at the beginning of the evening, and after the dance she insisted on having a drink, tossing off a tumbler full of champagne as though it had been lemonade.

"Go easy on the booze, sister!" I cautioned her.

"All right, Mr Volstead, I guess I can drink two to your one and still toe the line," she answered.

About midnight I came across her again, and by that time everyone was more or less lit, and she was no exception to the rule.

Of all the hateful things in the world a tipsy woman is the worst, and not relishing the idea of having her on my hands if she got that way, I picked out the other sober member of the party, and got him to bring his car round to the back door. I tried to persuade the lady to come home, but she was enjoying herself too much to want to leave. So on the pretence of looking for a drink she was beguiled into the hall, and once out of sight of the others, there was no difficulty in popping her into the car and driving off.

We drew up in front of her house. I fished the latch-key out of her bag, opened the door, escorted her in and fondly imagined that my troubles were over. But no such luck, for the stairs were too steep for her and she declined to be left alone in the hall.

"Which is your room?" I asked.

"Up the stairs on the right," she answered.

So with the "fireman's lift" I hoisted her on my shoulders, carried her upstairs, and seeing an empty bedroom, entered, dumped her on a little white bed.

I took off her shoes, put the water-bottle on a chair by her bed, switched off the light, and shut the door.

I had reached the top of the staircase when the landing was flooded with light, and a girl stood in an open door, with red hair all tumbled over her shoulders, and eyes blinking with sleep.

She stood there silently looking at me, and I looked at her.

"Where's Marion?" she asked at length.

"She was tired, so I brought her home," I answered. She stepped inside the bedroom, and saw her sister sleeping peacefully, with her hands crossed on her chest.

"Some jazz baby that," she remarked. "This is four times in a week she has passed right out. I'm always warning the silly simp about mixing her drinks, but she will do it. I hope she hasn't drunk any phoney hooch?" she added anxiously.

"No, I am sure she hasn't done that," I answered, knowing the name of every ship from which the drinks had come.

"That's good. She'll be all right in the morning; she always is; thanks so much for looking after her. I'll tell her how artistically you laid her out. Shut the door quietly as you leave; mother is a bit old-fashioned, and might be fractious if she saw Marion like this again. But these things will happen in the best regulated families, won't they? Good-night!"

As I came out the man in the car murmured suspiciously, "You've been the hell of a long time putting that dame in through the door."

That was the last time that I ever took a girl to a party. The responsibility is too great, and it is much simpler to go and take a chance on what you find there.

# CHAPTER XXVI

## AN UNLUCKY LOAD

My friend Rex Sherbourne was once waiting in a foreign port for a ship of his to start southwards with her load of whiskey. One evening as we were smoking together in his hotel bedroom, he told me the story of a strenuous two days he had spent when rum running was in its infancy. As it is typical of what is going on daily in the United States it may be worth telling.

"I and two other fellows once had a thousand cases stored in a fish-house away in the woods by the sea, and with Scotch getting eighty dollars in the city as it was then, that represented a tidy bit of money.

"Well, I and my partner stayed in a loft above the fish-house to look after the stuff while the other two fellows went off to bring the trucks. After a few hours I heard a holler from outside, and peeping out through a crack in the roof, I saw the sheriff from E—— and a motor-cycle cop and another man standing round the house.

"The sheriff came and banged at the door, while the other two men kept the place covered with their guns.

"'Come on out of it!' he shouted, 'we know what you've got in there.'

"We didn't move, but he kept on knocking, and said he would start firing through the wooden walls if we didn't come out, so the only thing to do was to go out and try to fix him.

"He was a nice soft-spoken fellow; you'd think butter wouldn't melt in his mouth if you stood him on his head on the cook-stove. But he was a hard-boiled guy when it came to talking turkey.

"We argued with that son-of-a-gun for half an hour, and nothing would satisfy him but to get ten thousand bucks, or hand us and the booze over to the police.

"'That's not a fair deal at all,' says I.

"'It's letting you off light,' says he, 'but to show how fair I am, we'll get in an arbitrator and we'll agree to go by what he says. Who would you like?' he asks.

"Not being much acquainted down there, I didn't know what to say; but the fish-house belonged to Peter Wright, my wife's cousin, and I hoped the sheriff wouldn't know this.

"'What about the guy this fish-house belongs to?' I said.

"'All right,' says the sheriff, 'I'll go and fetch him; his name is Peter Wright.'

"So he went away to find Peter, leaving the cop and the other man to see we didn't get away with the booze while he was gone.

"In a few hours the sheriff came back with Peter, who took me aside and told me that he had been able to fix the sheriff. He had the gall to pull a piece of typewritten paper out of his pocket, and on it he had written what each of them wanted to get out of us.

| | |
|---|---|
| Sheriff . . . . . . . . | . $3000 |
| Cop . . . . . . . . . | 1500 |
| Other man . . . . . . . | 500 |
| Peter . . . . . . . . . . | 500 |
| | ———— |
| | $5500 |

"'The five hundred bucks is for me for fixing the business,' he said. 'If it wasn't for me the sheriff would pinch the whole shooting match and send you boys to the pen, but I have talked him round, and just to oblige me he is being very reasonable. As I am doing you a good turn, worth a hundred thousand, I guess you won't grudge my five-hundred. It's only 5 percent after all,' he added apologetic-like.

'We argued and fought with that sheriff some more, but he said it was a case of pay or be pinched; luckily we had quite a bit of money with us, so we paid up and looked as pleasant as we could.

"'Now you boys has treated us handsome,' said the sheriff, putting all that good sugar of ours into his pants pocket, 'and that being so, we will make it our business to look after you and see you get the stuff away safe. Now listen! The Federal men is working the road, and if you move now, the stuff will be knocked off sure as God made little apples. You sit tight here, and when the roads are clear we will give you the highsign so as you will know it's safe to move.'

"Then they went away and left us.

"After all that excitement I fell asleep in the loft, and was woken up by a banging at the door.

I hoped it was Johnnie come back with the trucks, and looked out through the crack in the roof again to see if it was. But it wasn't. It was the deputy sheriff from L—— and another guy, and he hammered away and said he would shoot up the place if we didn't come out, so out we came again.

"'We've got orders to seize this place and run you two boys to the hoosegow,' he said.

"So I talked to them, and found them much more reasonable than the others had been. At first they wanted two grand apiece, but I explained the situation to them, and being pretty decent guys, they agreed to be satisfied with one grand each. By this time I hadn't enough dough left to pay them off, but the sheriff agreed to take a cheque; mighty nice of him, too, to trust us like that, wasn't it?

"'There are some strange motor-cycle cops on the road, and you had better not move the stuff until we give you the O.K.' they said as they left.

"Thanks, buddy,' I said, and thought to myself, 'like hell, we will. This darned fish-house costs more than the Ritz-Carlton to stay in!'

"After a while Johnnie came along with the two trucks and we didn't wait for no highsigns nor O.K.'s, but just piled the stuff on the trucks as quick as we darned well could.

"They wouldn't hold quite the lot, so Johnnie drove one truck and I drove the other, leaving the other two fellows behind to shift the cases that were left to some safer place.

"We each went a different way, so that if one of us was picked up, the other would not be caught too.

"There was a false end to the trucks, with a lot of pieces of timber stuck to them, so that they looked as though they were a load of lumber from the yards, and a very neat job it was.

"When I turned out of the woods into the main road, there was a small truck with two men in it waiting at the corner, and when I came out they started up their engine and came after me.

I stepped on the gas and tried to get away from them, but I was too heavily loaded, and they pushed in front of me, and when I reached a lonely part they pulled across the road and made me stop.

"They said they wanted fifty cases, or they would phone up the police and have me pinched. They had guns, and I was alone, so there wasn't much else to do but take off the false back and let them have what they wanted. While they were taking these a chauffeur came along in a private car and said he wanted seven cases, but by this time I was so goddarned mad that I socked him one on the dial and tipped him into the ditch.

"Just then the other two fellows saw a machine coming along in the distance, so they got the wind up, and beat it with only thirty cases, and I beat it too without wasting any time.

"All went well for a bit, and in another two hours I would have had the whole blamed outfit inside our garage in the city, when a motor-cycle cop shoots up alongside with his gun drawn and shouts out, 'Turn off up the next side road!'

"He seemed to mean business with his iron, so I turned down the next little road which led into the woods.

"Two grand or the cooler was his good-evening to me.

"I told him I had been shaken down three times and hadn't a dime left to buy me a cup of coffee, but he was an unsympathetic hard-hearted sort of guy, and seeing that there wasn't nothing to be made out of me, was going to take me to the police station.

"And he would have done it too, if I hadn't thought of the plan of paying him in kind what you in England call tithe. But the dirty son-of-a-gun wasn't content with a tenth.

"'I'll give you ten cases,' I says, 'and they are worth all of eight hundred dollars.'

"All right,' he says, 'chuck off seventy-five into the bushes there.'

"So down came the false back again, and he threw off seventy-five cases behind some thick bushes where they wouldn't be seen by anyone on the road. He followed me for some distance afterwards to see that I did not go back to pick them up, and then disappeared down a side road probably to get a truck to take his cases away.

"Soon after that I passed a telephone booth, and phoned back to a friend of mine who lived near-by. I told him to go to the place where the seventy-five cases were behind the bushes, and take them away in his Ford truck, and to look slippy about it so as to get there before the cop came back.

"By this time I was ready to drive the whole darned works into the sea and call it a day, but I just kept a-going and thought that there wasn't much left that could happen to me now; since the morning I was more than seven thousand dollars out, and a hundred and five cases shy.

"I kept to the side roads, and thought my bad streak was over. However, I was crossing a wooden bridge near P—— when there was a crash and a jolt, and the goddarned truck, stopped dead.

"I thought the axle was broke, but it wasn't. The weight of the truck had busted the bridge, and it was resting on its back axle with the rear wheels sunk through the broken planks.

"It was a lonely road with nobody in sight to help me out. My luck sure was clean out that day:

I had everything wrong except the toothache.

"I climbed down to go for help, and walked a full mile along that goddarned road before there was a house with a telephone in it; I called up the garage which owned the truck—luckily it happened to be not far away—and told them to send a breakdown car with plenty of big jacks.

"When I got back near the bridge, that lonely road was as crowded as Columbus Circle; the sheriff was there, a motor-cycle cop, and a whole lot of other folks who had sprung up from nowhere.

"I thought that it was all up this time, and strolled along as though that darned truck had nothing on earth to do with me.

"But when I got up close it seemed they hadn't spotted the booze, so I walked up bold as you please.

"'You will have to unload that lumber and jack her up,' says the sheriff. 'Come on, boys, and give him a hand.'

"'You needn't do that,' I said, 'there's a breakdown gang on the way here, and they will look after it.'

"'I never met fellows so anxious to help as those boys were, and it took me all my time to stop them from unloading that truck.

"When I walked round behind to see how deep the wheels had sunk, I found that a piece of lumber had fallen off, and a case of 'Holt's' was left in view. I couldn't fix it with the crowd there, so I took off my coat and stuffed it over the place.

"At last the fellows from the garage arrived, and as they knew what was inside the truck, they said there wasn't no need to unload her. They jacked up the rear axle, put some planks underneath, and I drove right into the city without being stopped anymore.

"Since the stuff had been landed it had cost a pile of money. When I got home that night I added it all up, and it was something like this:—

| | |
|---|---:|
| 1000 cases from the ship | $30,000 |
| Boatmen | 6,000 |
| Landing and carting to fish-house | 1,000 |
| Storage in fish-house | 1,000 |
| First shake-down | 5,500 |
| Second shake-down | 2,000 |
| Third shake-down at 50 dollars a case | 1,500 |
| Fourth shake-down at 50 dollars a case | 3,750 |
| Truck hire | 250 |
| Breakdown gang | 250 |
| | $51,250 |

"But Johnnie got in safe with the other truck, and the next day my friend with the flivver phoned me to say he had got to the place before the cop, and had saved seventy-five of the cases, all except three that were missing (which he had probably pinched himself), so we still made money on the deal.

"But what fairly got my goat was Peter: may I never pull another cork if that double-crossing yellow serpent hadn't been in with the sheriff and the deputy-sheriff and the hijackers and the motor-cycle cop and the whole darned bunch of them. Fifty-fifty he got on every-thing they made, and now he's asking a political friend of his to have the motor-cycle cop jailed for hijacking, because he says the cop is doing him out of his half-share of the seventy-five cases.

"Next time I meet Peter he's going to get his half-share in what the chauffeur got, damn his dirty hide!"

# CHAPTER XXVII

## BOOTLEGGERS I HAVE KNOWN

JUST as the army, the navy, the civil service, the church, and the ranch each produce their own type of men whose calling is written on their faces, so has the rum running been in existence long enough to develop not only a type, but also clearly defined varieties of this type.

Jews and Italians provide most of the red-tabs of the profession; I call it a profession on the authority of Izzy, a manufacturer of, dealer in, retailer of, and specialist in "Johnnie Walker."

Izzy was once buying from me some "Block's Ambassador" for flavouring his "Johnnie Walker Black Label."

"Yes sir," he said, "I reckon bootlegging's a profession all right; grocers and dry goods stores and shop-keepers and such like all has fixed prices for their goods, and them is businesses.

"Attorneys and dentists and doctors and them sort of guys, they don't have no printed menu so to speak, and they just sizes you up and sticks you for as much as they think they can shake out of you. Them's professional guys. I reckon, bootlegging's a profession all right."

It would be interesting to introduce Sir Alexander Walker to Izzy some day, and I say introduce Sir Alexander to Izzy as one would introduce a pupil to a master, for there is much that Izzy could teach him about making whiskey; how to fill non-refillable bottles without showing they have been refilled; the minute difference in the amount of creosote used to flavour "Red Label" and "Black Label;" that while denatured industrial alcohol redistilled in the cellar is good enough for the "Red Label," it is worthwhile to get genuine smuggled grain alcohol for the manufacture of the "Black Label" owing to the fastidious palates of the people who pay the extra fifteen dollars a case to get it; and a hundred other points which enable the enterprising Italian to accomplish in one day what nature and Sir Alexander take a dozen years to do.

But I am wandering from the subject, as Izzy has no more to do with the big operators than a latrine digger has to do with a Lieutenant-General.

The big men are mostly a pretty decent lot of fellows; there are crooks and swindlers among them, as there are in every business, but in a trade where nothing is put in writing and a man's word is everything, the bad ones tend to be eliminated because people do not trust them.

Looking at them as a class, and taking them by and large, they compare quite favourably with, say, the average American lawyer, although, in general, they are very considerably below the general run of businessmen.

The pick of the profession is the boatman; he must have pluck, and he must be honest, for many a man has ten or twenty thousand dollars handed to him in hard cash for buying goods at sea and should he come back with a tale of having been robbed of the money or hijacked of the goods, the operator has no redress, whether the story be true or untrue. In no occupation in the world is it more necessary to be able to sum up a man's nature at first glance.

After the boatmen come the automobile drivers, who need more nerve probably than anyone else, for they are the lawful prey of the police, the prohibition men, the hijackers, the State troopers, the motor-cycle police, and everyone who sees a chance of fleecing them of money or goods, while if there is no plunder to be squeezed out of them, their enemies are ready to tip them off to the authorities.

They need considerable tact, too. The driver who slips a policeman two hundred dollars to get by, when fifty would have fixed that particular limb of the law, finds himself unpopular with his employer, and equally so the driver who offers the policeman fifty dollars and gets arrested, when two hundred would have done the trick. The cheery diplomat who can get through the enemy lines with the aid of a bottle, a smile and a liberal amount of blarney is a man to be kept on the permanent pay-roll.

"Yes, sir, I guess I fooled that cop all right," said a driver to me; "he stopped me right in the town. I had thirty-eight cases in my coupé and the springs was down something terrible. A kid of ten would have known she was loaded. The traffic was stopped at a level crossing. There was a darned great Irish cop who watched the way my auto sagged when she hit a bump as I was slowing down and he comes over to me.

"'Guess you are loaded all right, Buddy,' he says, 'you had better come along with me to headquarters,' and he starts to open the door to get in with me.

"Then I spills him some sob stuff about my wife and sick kiddy, all the time pulling out of my pants some bills I kept there on purpose. He keeps his eye on it and sees a fat roll of yellow-backs; I kept him there talking until the traffic starts again and then shoves that wad in his hand. 'Here, brother, be a sport and let me go on,' says I.

"So he slips the bills in his pocket and lets me move along.

"I put one over him all right; there was nineteen one-dollar bills and one twenty yellow-back outside the roll, kept in place by a rubber band. The poor sucker thought he had made at least a four centuries tunes, but when he counts them he finds he has only thirty-nine bucks.

"I kept away from that road after that, and had an extra leaf put in my springs to stiffen them up."

There is a true story of a clergyman who was walking home one wet dark night when he saw the lights of a motor coming up behind him. He stood out in the middle of the road and raised his hand to ask for a lift, a thing which is very commonly done in the United States. The truck pulled up, the driver leaned out, and pressing something into the clergyman's hand, with feverish haste threw in his clutch and sped onwards. The surprised cleric struck a match to see what it was and found himself holding a fifty-dollar bill. A nervous rum-runner had mistaken him for a revenue man, and had not taken the time to verify his suspicions before endeavouring to placate him and pass on his way.

A driver on Long Island once had a remarkable escape.

He was speeding up the Merrick Road towards New York in a coupé well loaded down with Scotch. On the journey he broached cargo and drank himself as blind as an owl. In due course he ran foul of a traffic policeman and found himself in the lock-up.

Next morning when he had sobered up they allowed him to telephone to his boss to come down to bail him out. So the bootlegger came along, mighty glum at the prospect of losing his car and the whiskey, and having to pay the heavy bail and fines and lawyers' fees which fall to the lot of captured rum-runners. To his amazement they only fined the man twenty dollars and let him go. The rum-runner walked out of the police station and saw his car standing where it had been left the night before. He climbed in and drove away with his load intact, as for some reason they had failed to open the lid at the back and look inside.

One of the greatest enemies of the road rum-runner is the hijacker. These men usually work four or five together in a large open touring car, and with the greatest effrontery hold up trucks and cars containing liquor.

To give the devil his due, the police get after them and sometimes catch and even punish them, but the rum-runners, as a rule, have to depend upon their own strategy or quick shooting to cope with these gentlemen of the road.

There was once a man running a load of my Cheviot in a fast light motor-van on a windy rainy afternoon. In a lonely spot on the high road he passed an inn where two men were standing on the top step; as he went by one of them raised a revolver and took a couple of pot shots at him, both of which went through his windscreen, but missed him.

"Who were they, and what did they want, Harry?" I asked him.

"Didn't stop to ask," replied Harry. "I just stepped on the gas and kept my foot right there for the next ten miles."

To protect themselves against these gentry the drivers usually go armed, and I know of one very thorough operator who used to send out his trucks prepared for any contingency. There were two gunmen with each truck; one sat in front with a sawed-off shot-gun to repel attack with buckshot, and the other sat behind with a Winchester rifle to fight a rear-guard action by putting a bullet through the tyres or radiator of a pursuing car, or perchance through the driver, should the necessity arise.

In the early days of prohibition there was an enterprising man who made a good deal of money out of his fellow-citizens before his little game was discovered.

He used to get the whiskey run ashore in a boat and store it in a barn near the beach, and the men from the city would come down to buy from him. They paid over the cash, loaded the cases on their trucks, and the genial vendor would give them a drink all round to speed them on their way.

"I hear the Government men have been seen on the south road today; better keep clear of it. Goodbye, boys, and good luck. Come again soon," he would say to them as they left.

As soon as the truck had lumbered out of his yard he would go to the telephone and call up some friends at a place twenty-five miles away on the north road, and give them the registration number of the truck.

All would go well with the rum-runners until they reached this place, which was a lonely spot in the woods. Here they would be stopped by a gang of gunmen who used to tie them up and throw them in the bushes. The hijackers would then drive the truck back to the place it had come from, unload the cases, and put them back in the store once more, ready to be sold again to the next customer, who would suffer a similar fate. The truck was either driven into a river or hidden away somewhere or perhaps taken into some other State and sold.

To guard against this sort of thing cautious drivers often carry several sets of number plates and stop to change them every hour or two.

American officials as a rule do not wear a uniform beyond a silver badge on their waistcoat pocket underneath their coat, and hijackers often get hold of real or imitation badges and pretend be revenue men, policemen, or prohibition officers. It gives them a most unfair advantage over the rum-runner, who will usually shoot a hijacker on sight if he gets a chance (and quite rightly too), but hesitates to shoot a Government man.

In all my experience I have never known an authentic case of a rum-runner firing at a Government boat, or even attempting to defend himself when attacked on the sea. On land the Government men sometimes get hurt, but in many cases they deserve what they get; they may be taking advantage of their uniforms by trying to blackmail the rum-runners, or perhaps they are mistaken for hijackers. Or maybe they make a fierce attack on the rum-runners, who have the alternative of allowing themselves to be knocked about or of defending themselves like men.

I have met coastguards and prohibition agents who have been shot at, and in some cases wounded, at sea. They return to their base with a lurid tale of "a battle with the rum-runners." But in every instance I have come across so far, the firing has been by some of their own men who mistook them for rum-runners, or else a gun went off accidentally, and they quite reasonably concluded that a bullet fired by a desperate rum-runner would bring them more in the way of glory and pension than an accidental shot from one of their own people.

# CHAPTER XXVIII

## JUDGES

THREE of us were sitting in a little eating-house: the prosperous Jew bootlegger with his diamond ring, the big burly rum-runner who worked for him, and myself.

The rum-runner had finished his business with the Jew, and having taken a drink or two was in an expansive mood, and glad to find in me a listener who would not try to cap all his stories. The conversation drifted over many lands and topics, and finally got on to the subject of the courts, of which he had much experience and had much to say.

"Yes, sir. Some of them high-up judges is real bard-boiled guys, and I'll bet you don't keep more expensive ones, not even in London, England. You can't slip 'em a grand to put the decision your way. No, sir! It can't be done like that. It has to be done much more diplomatic. I can fix most anyone from a senator to a bell-hop, but some of them big judges is sure tough babies, and to fix them it takes a guy what can wear a Tuxedo and talk turkey to them over the nuts and wine.

"How is it done? Well, I don't say as it always can be done. They do say as how there is judges as can't be fixed at all, though I don't believe it myself.

"How do you go to work?

"Well, I'll tell you how some friends of mine did it last month.

"It was them Baumgarten boys, who got in wrong over their income tax. They was in a real bad jam, and it looked like as if they would be put away for five years apiece, so they saw their attorney and told him that it would be worth nine grand to him if they won their case, and they would pay up and ask no questions. So the attorney went to work and made up to a fellow named Jake Rubens that he knew was a special friend of the judge who was to try the case.

"He asked him to dinner, and gave bouquets to his wife, candy to his kids, and all that sort of bunk, until Jake Rubens was as good as feeding out of his hand.

"Then one day the attorney says to Jake—

"'Jake,' he says, 'that is a nice little corner lot you have down there on Main Street; what might you be asking for it? There's some parties I know what might be interested in buying that for a movie house.'

"And Jake he says, 'I guess it's worth all of four grand.'

"Then the attorney he says, 'Well, Jake, it's like this; I can't let you know nothing definite at present, but I knows some folk as might be willing to pay more than that. These parties are being mixed up in a case. If they lose they won't have the spare dough to buy nothing, but if they win, I might persuade them to put their spare brass into a real estate deal; guess I could stick them eleven grand.'

"'That sounds all right,' says Jake; 'when does their case come off?'

"'It's them Baumgarten boys, and Judge O'Honey is trying it in a few days.'

"'Well,' answers Jake, 'seeing as you and me are such good friends, I'll do this for you; you put up the eleven grand in escrow tomorrow, and I'll give you an option on the land until the end of the month gratis free for nothing. If your people win the case, then they will have the money to buy the land; if they lose, they won't be able to afford it, so I will release the money.'

"You get Sam Dwyer to assess the land as an independent valuer, and I'll see that he puts it at eleven thousand, and it's worth it too, a fine corner lot like that.'

"Next day the attorney phones up the boys to come round to see him. He tells them that he can fix the case for eleven grand if they win, and nothing if they don't.

"They had to figure out quick whether they would win anyhow without paying the graft. But they thought they wouldn't, so they told him to go ahead.

"Well, although all the evidence seemed to be against them, they won out.

"The judge got five grand, Jake got six grand for the corner lot (which was worth three), the attorney got the corner lot, and everyone was pleased, except the boys who had paid the money. They kept kicking themselves with the idea they might have won anyhow, and had been suckers to pay away all that good dough.

"Now I guess that was a pretty slick sort of a deal, because nobody couldn't never prove nothing. Why! the boys and their attorney never even saw the judge!

"Of course, for all those Sheeny boys knew, Jake never said a word to the judge, but meant to pay back the dough if they lost, and pouch it if they won, him standing to win one way and lose nothing the other. That's one of the chances you've got to take in that sort of business; but they were lucky to pick on a real 100 percent honourable attorney for a job like that.

"Yes, sir, justice is sure an expensive article in this country.

"Personally, I like dealing in a straightforward way without using the attorneys and fixers and all the other crooks. Give me the District Attorney, and let me meet him face to face as man to man.

"'Listen here, brother,' I says to him, 'there's ten centuries in it for you if this case gets throwed out.'

"He doesn't make no promises, but I trusts him to do his best for me, and he trusts me to pay up if I win. Knowing that he can twist my tail if I don't, I pays up pronto like one gentleman to another."

Up to the present I have successfully avoided making the acquaintance of any judges, so cannot say whether the picture painted by my rum-runner friend is an accurate one or not; but I do know that it reflects the views of a considerable portion of the community about their courts of justice.

# CHAPTER XXIX

## STRIKE-BREAKING

PAT is first and foremost a man of violence, and whatever he does is done by violence backed by six foot and sixteen stone of bone and muscle, a pair of sparkling dark eyes, and a voice which brings down the plaster from the ceiling. A tougher customer than Pat it would be hard to find; intolerant, passionate, hectoring, and possessed of a flow of language which would make a Thames bargee blush to his boots.

He naturally makes a host of enemies, but he is as straight as a die, full of pluck, generous and big hearted, so he also makes a host of friends, of whom I count myself one.

He is about forty, so was an able-bodied man before Mr. Volstead opened up the field of adventure on which Pat now expends his energies, and I had often wondered how he employed himself before then, for it was difficult to imagine Pat labouring either with hands or head.

"What did you do before you took to booze-running, Pat?" I once asked him, as we sat in front of the fire in my apartment.

"Strike-breaking," he answered.

"How did you work it?"

"Well, I'll tell you all about it," he said. "I worked with a guy who built up a big organisation for breaking strikes in any trade in any part of the country.

"We had an office in the city with dozens of girls sitting there in front of card index drawers, and some of them little Janes was quite easy to look at too. They had the names and addresses and telephone numbers of most every workman in the country all tagged off in districts and trades.

"Supposing there was a strike anywhere, we would send off fifty, or a hundred, or a thousand men of the trade that was wanted, and my part of the job was to boss the strong-arm squad. I used to have

201

my boys all round the works, and inside too, watching the strikers' pickets, and if they interfered with our men we used to sock them on the nut with a piece of lead pipe, or anything else that came handy.

"Sometimes in rough places we used to have gun fights, and as that meant extra pay, the rougher the play the more we liked it."

"But how did you manage to get the skilled labour in trades where all the men belonged to the unions?" I asked.

"Nothing easier," answered Pat. "Supposing it was the printing business that was on strike—and I say the printing business because I never had nothing to do with it; all our work was very confidential-like, and I wouldn't care to give away the affairs of any folk I had been connected with. Supposing it was the printers, I say, we would offer 50 percent or a 100 percent over the standard pay to the men that worked for us; we go to Philadelphia and pick up a lot of strikers there and take them to work at Boston, and we pick up some of the Boston strikers and take them to Pittsburgh, and the Pittsburg men we take to Philly, and so on.

"Of course, if that worked out exactly, they would all keep their new jobs at double pay, but they don't all fall for it, and those who do want to get back to their homes after a while; besides, when all is said and done, that is only a sort of rough idea of how we worked things.

"If the strikers tried any rough stuff, they used to find they weren't no tougher than me and my babies. We was as gentle as sucking doves, and never hurt anyone unless they began the racket, and then the guys who started trying to put anything over us found us 100 percent red-blooded he-gorillas, and darned well wished they had left us alone. If there was any heads being broke, you could bet the last button on your pants that it wasn't ours."

And that I could quite believe, for it would be hard to imagine anything more unpleasant to run up against than Pat with a revolver in one hand and a piece of lead pipe in the other.

"Did you make any money out of it?" I asked Pat.

"Sure thing we did. That's what we were in the business for. Plenty of dough there was, and dough is dough whether there's smiles or blood on it. We never started no rough play; we always waited for the other guys to do that, and if they didn't want to, we'd tickle them up a bit until they did. If there's some of them planted in the marble orchard after trying to rough-house my boys, that's their bad luck.

"Of course, when a strike went bust quickly, we didn't make much on it, what with all the overhead expenses and one thing and another. If it showed signs of tuckering out too quick, I used to send a few of my boys, disguised as unionists, among the strikers just to

202

stir them up a bit and make them carry on longer. Of course, the strikers never won in the long-run, but it wouldn't be reasonable to expect us to go to all the expense and trouble we did just for a two or three day strike, would it?

"Say, Barby, when you and me is through with running booze, what about us starting a real stick-up hundred percent strike-breaking joint in London, England?

"Your unions in England has the employers and the Government all bull-dozed, and if you told the big bosses about me, I reckon they'd be real glad to have me over there.

"I'd take across thirty or forty of my toughest gorillas with guns, blackjacks, lead pipes, riot guns and all, and we'd pick out a hundred real he-men and train them to our ways.

"You wouldn't hear much about 'intimidation' after we'd been taking care of a strike for a few days: the strikers would be that humble they'd be buying safe-passes to the union meetings from the blacklegs!"

"Well, Pat," I answered, "it's a kind offer of yours and I'll bear it in mind. But the upper classes in England have lost their pep, and if there are heads to be broken, it's the heads of the police and the men who want to work."

It will be seen that strike-breaking is a highly organised business in the United States, and, as in the case of most things they do, they consider the end rather than the means.

I once ran across the head of a big employers' association, and for all I know he was the man who had employed Pat as his strong-arm boss. He told me of some amazing coups he had pulled off, but whether he was telling the truth or not, I never had the opportunity of finding out.

He said that on one occasion he was called in to break a strike which was engineered by a union leader whose personality was largely responsible for keeping the thing going.

By some means this man was enticed into a fashionable restaurant for a meal, and on leaving he had to pass a table where there was a merry party enjoying themselves; as he walked by they all stood up round him, and there was the blinding flash of a photographer at work.

Next day over the whole of the disturbed area there were scattered hundreds of thousands of pictures showing the strike leader in the midst of the gay dinner party, the table heaped with choice foods and champagne bottles, and several beautiful ladies smiling at him with languishing glances.

*"How your leader spends his time while you are starving,"* was the

line written underneath, and the collapse of the strike quickly followed.

The same man told me that he had some scores of private detectives employed exclusively in watching and reporting on the activities of the individual trades union officials. When they made themselves objectionable to the employers he was usually able to bring up something to damage their reputations, either in the eyes of the law, or in the eyes of their fellow-unionists. Maybe it was true and maybe untrue, but it was all the same to him so long as it did the trick.

One time a leading trade union official had been pilfering the union funds, and unbeknown to his fellow-workmen had bought himself a pleasing little estate in another part of the country, where he used to spend his week-ends and his money. He was quite flattered when an admiring tourist one day took a snapshot of him as he stood in the garden, discussing with his chauffeur and an architect about the erection of a larger garage.

But he was not at all pleased when, some months later in the midst of a strike he was engineering, this charming little picture was broadcasted among the workpeople with the title:—

"Bill S— at home.

"Two years ago he was a workman, and you know what his wages were.

'Now he is a trade union secretary, and you know what his salary is.

"Where does the money for this come from?

"Ask him!"

They did ask him, and he lost his job.

# CHAPTER XXX

## THE BOMBARDMENT OF THE *EASTWOOD*[1]

In the quaint old harbour of Lunenburg, in the year nineteen hundred and twenty-six, on the coast of Nova Scotia, the whole population was busy fitting out the fishing fleet for its annual voyage to the "Banks"; scores of little two-masted schooners of all sizes from twenty-five to a hundred and fifty tons were lying alongside the docks with dories, bedding, stores, sails, and fishing gear being stowed away for a voyage of many weeks.

Amongst these fishing schooners there was a large four-masted vessel with carpenters, riggers, and other workmen moving about her decks—not fitting her out for a fishing trip, but repairing holes large and small in her hull, deck, masts, sails, and running gear; it was a strange sight for these peaceful times, for a closer examination showed that she had been through a bombardment from machine-guns and artillery. The adventure of the good ship *Eastwood* has already been told and retold among the fishermen of Nova Scotia, but the true story is known so far only to the inner circle of adventurers who use Lunenburg as the base for their voyages.

Having heard various rumours in the smoke-room of the local hotel, I wandered down the railway dock and stepped on board the ship, and making my way through the busy workmen to the spacious cabins aft, found the master, Captain John Spindler, warming his back against the stove. He was a typical Lunenburg skipper, large and powerfully built, with a healthy round face burned brick-red from exposure to the weather, and steady eyes which surveyed the world serenely through a pair of large round tortoise-shell spectacles.

We talked of many matters of interest to those who go down to the sea in ships, and I steered the conversation round to the subject

---

[1]This is the only chapter in the book where the names of men, ships, and places have not been altered, while the affadavits and photographs mentioned are in my possession.—Author

of his last voyage. We walked about the ship together, and the yarn was chiefly told by his pointing out bullet and shell-holes with the stem of his pipe, a few scant words being thrown in here and there by way of explanation, for the world does not contain a more hardy or less emotional breed of men than the Nova Scotian fishermen; their lives are spent in meeting hardships and dangers such as fall to the lot of no other sailors, and a bombardment at point-blank range by an armed ship seemed to have disturbed this solid skipper no more than a stiff breeze of wind.

Here is the story.

The *Eastwood*, a four-masted British schooner of 399 tons gross; registered at Le Have, Nova Scotia, left the port of Lunenburg on the 20th December, 1925, having cleared for Havana, Cuba, with a cargo of wines and spirits. She had twin motors and twin propellers which take her at about seven knots, and she carried a crew of nine men all told, every one of them Nova Scotian.

She arrived at lattitude 40" 17' north and longitude 73" 29' west, which is a spot in the open Atlantic, out of sight of land and some twenty miles from the nearest shore, where she lay at anchor awaiting orders. As she lay there a United States Revenue cutter, the *Seneca*, came out and cruised about near her, evidently fearing lest some thirsty Americans, in search of good cheer for Christmas, should come out to visit her. The cutter was a white steamer, with a crew of some fifty or sixty armed men, and guns on deck, forward and aft.

But the *Eastwood* was over twenty miles from land, and had no communication with the shore, so according to international law, and even under the new treaty between Great Britain and the United States, she was free to come and go on the high seas as she liked, so the cutter could not molest her.

Just before midnight on the 17th January, a seaman named Howard Wilson was on watch, and there were no lights in sight except those of the *Seneca*; he saw the cutter steam up, and suddenly she poured a hail of machine-gun bullets on the deck of the *Eastwood*, then steamed away into the night. The next day numbers of nickel-cased bullets were found embedded in the port side of the ship, several had gone right through the mizzen-mast, an oil-tank was smashed, and loose bullets were picked up on the deck. A less sturdy crew after such an experience would have pulled up the anchor and made for home, but the *Eastwood* just remained in position according to her orders.

For the next few weeks she lay at anchor waiting for the instructions which were delayed in coming, but nothing of any note occurred;

the *Seneca,* aided by several "seventy-five footers," continued to prowl round. They did not molest the *Eastwood* in any way, except on one occasion when one of the smaller craft came alongside and hurled a torrent of abuse and filthy language at the Nova Scotians, making various insulting remarks about the Royal Family. They hoped to make the Canadians retaliate in some way so that they might have an excuse to attack them; but the crew of the *Eastwood* kept silent, because the coastguardsmen, as is often the case, were drunk.

On 16th February, about 10 A.M., the *Seneca* steamed up and placed a small floating target in the water about twenty-five yards from the *Eastwood,* and steaming away for a distance of about a quarter of a mile, hoisted a red flag, blew her whistle, and began firing with a machine-gun and a one-pounder, striking the schooner with both bullets and shells, and doing her considerable damage.

She ceased fire and steamed across the bows of the schooner after taking down the red flag; Donald Cook, the chief engineer of the *Eastwood,* took a red ensign from the cabin, and went forward to hoist it; there were no halliards for this purpose, so he climbed up the rigging to the mast-head, and tied the flag to the mast, as many a British seaman has done before him.

Feeling secure now that the flag was up, the captain and crew came on deck to examine the damage, but the *Seneca,* now about one hundred yards away, again blew the whistle, hoisted the red flag, and began firing once more. The angles of the shell-holes and bullet-holes which I examined show that the big ship was so close that the gunners had to depress their guns below the horizontal in order to hit the schooner, which was lower in the water than they were.

The cutter ceased fire, steamed round the stern of the other ship, and for the third time opened fire; one shell crashed into the cabin and missed the captain's head by a few inches, others ripped up the deck, smashed the gasolene tank in the forward engine-room, broke the engine-room skylight, while several pierced the hull near the waterline and exploded among the cargo.

While the firing was going on, the officers of the cutter could be seen plainly, standing on the bridge and watching the effect of the shots through their glasses.

Fortunately for the *Eastwood* an oil-tank steamer hove into sight, and the cutter, evidently fearing to continue with a witness of her deeds, ceased fire and drew away. During the bombardment the crew had taken shelter in the engine-room between the engines, and fortunately none of them was hurt.

"Well, captain," I remarked at this point of the story, "this was where you slipped your cable and beat it?"

"No, sir," was his reply, "we didn't slip our cable; we had a brand-new anchor and a hundred and fifty fathoms of chain out, so we pulled it up; it took an hour and a half before the hook came out of the water."

Here was a crew of nine men anchored in a little wooden ship on the ocean; for over an hour they had been bombarded with machine-gun bullets and explosive shells, without the means of retaliating; their hull was pierced and leaking, the sails and rigging were damaged, and they were lucky to have escaped with their lives. As long as the tanker was there as a witness they were safe, and the obvious thing to do was to slip the anchor and get away with the other ship.

But that anchor and chain was new and had cost eighteen hundred dollars, so the thrifty skipper, with that dogged tenacity which, up till now, at any rate, has enabled us to rule the waves remained there for another hour and a half while the little twelve horse-power motor in the bow chugged and spluttered away as it pulled up the great clanking chain link by link. The men in the meantime glanced over their shoulders occasionally to see if the cutter showed any signs of making a fresh attack, after the tanker had steamed out of sight.

The cutter kept hanging about in the offing, and when the schooner had pulled up her anchor and started northwards, she followed for about a mile, when she was joined by three other cutters, the *Crescent* and C.G. *122* and the C.G. *205*. The *Seneca* then steamed away, and the other three followed the *Eastwood* until midnight, when they left her. She was making water through the shell-holes, and there was considerable damage done to the running gear, but fortunately the weather was fine, and she reached Lunenburg on the evening of 18th February.

The owner of the ship showed me the affidavits signed by the captain and crew; the report on the ship made by Lloyd's surveyor and the Port Warden and a shipwright, which assessed the damage at eighteen hundred dollars; myself I heard the captain's story and saw the condition of the ship, and the owner showed me several dozen pieces of shell and bullets which the carpenters had removed from the wood. They were mostly fragments of one-pounder shells, and there was one shell intact, which had failed to explode; many of the pieces bore the marks of U.S.A. naval ammunition.

There is no doubt whatsoever as to the accuracy of the story, even if similar attacks had not taken place on other British vessels on the high seas. These have not been officially reported, but I am personally acquainted with men on two other ships which have fired upon by U.S.A. cutters without any justification but no official protest has been made owing to the fact that the owners feared that such a course would only lead to retaliation on the part of the cutters.

Thus ended one of those incidents which the American papers euphemistically describe as "Battle with Rum-Runner," a "battle" which consists in a heavily-armed vessel and crew bombarding defenceless sailors in an unarmed ship or boat; for it can be stated as an absolute fact that there has been no case of any British vessel ever firing a shot at a U.S.A. craft, however great the provocation, and it is extremely doubtful if there has been an authentic case of even the American rum-runners firing on a coastguard boat in self-defence, in spite of the "battles" in which the coastguards state they have taken part, although there is plenty of real fighting between the rum-runners and the pirates, or hijackers, who prey on them.

"What are you going to do now, captain?" I asked, before leaving.

"Going back as soon as the repairs are done," he answered.

"Will you be able to get a crew who will go down?"

"The same crew are going down again," he replied, "except the engineer and three of the men who had engaged to go on a fishing trip this month before they started on the last voyage."

I took leave of him, and stepped ashore.

A grizzled old fisherman was standing on the dock smoking his pipe, and watching the carpenters repairing the shell-holes.

He spat in the water and remarked, "What I want to know is where the hell is the British Navy? When I was in the navy in 1885, we'd have been across here long ago and blown that g— d— cutter out of the water.

"These owners here will have to do what they are doing on the West coast, and transfer their ships to Jap registry; there's lots of Jap ships in the game, but who ever heard of the Yankees touching one of them? How come? Because they are scairt of the Japs, and they think they can do what they like with the English, and you will take it lying down. England sure was foolish when she made that 'One hour sail' treaty; them Yanks is like niggers; treat 'em half-decent and they think you is scairt of them.

"What for did the cutter want to fire on the *Eastwood* when they knew quite well that lots of that booze would go to senators and judges, and as like as not to the President himself?

"And what is the good of being British if any drunken Yankee coastguard can shoot up the Union Jack and get away with it?"

He again spat into the Atlantic and walked off. Protests were made by Sir Esme Howard, the British Ambassador at Washington, and that is the last I ever heard about the affair.

# NOTES

WHILE travelling on trains, schooners, and steamers in North America, the Pacific, and the Atlantic, I jotted down this account of my doings, leaving blank spaces for the names in case any of the loose sheets of paper on which I wrote should go astray.

Since my return to England I have had them typed and read them through; after doing this I realise that as a story it is hopeless; there are crises that never came to a head, incidents that are never explained (because I do not know the explanation myself), while people drift in and out of the story without rhyme or reason, few of them altogether good or altogether bad.

But it is just a slice of life as it was handed to me by the gods, with the currants cut in half and holes where the cherries ought to be, so I have not written it up into a story as a journalist friend of mine advised me to do. Perhaps, however, in years to come it will be more interesting as a record of smuggling in the twentieth century than it would be as a novel.

Did I so wish I could give the names, addresses, and telephone numbers of everyone who has been mentioned, except those careful folk who can only be found by inquiry from the owner of some cigar stand, pool-room, or speakeasy.

Now that I am home again, those of my friends who know what I have been doing usually ask me one or other of the following questions:—

"How could you bring yourself to hinder the Americans in their plucky efforts to cope with one of the greatest of present-day evils?"

My reply is that if they were making a genuine effort, nothing would have induced me to go into the business. But prohibition is a gigantic farce which is being used by hundreds of thousands of Americans for enriching themselves. Go to the houses of any prominent politicians or senators in Washington (with the exception of the White House and Mr. Taft's house), and in eight out of ten of them you will be pressed to drink whiskey, gin, or champagne with an insistence to be found in no European country.

Go to the annual police dinner in New York and see if the amount of drink consumed would not put the whole force under the table were they not hardened to it by much practice.

Even the clergy are not above taking a drink now and then. My friend Mr. D—— offered his bishop a glass of Scotch and soda, or a "highball" as the Americans call them, and the good cleric, rubbing his chin contemplatively, replied, "Well, it's a temptation which so seldom comes my way that I hardly feel justified in refusing it."

The Americans as a nation are determined to have "hard liquor," and when they can't get the real thing they poison themselves with evil substitutes which they kid themselves into believing came "straight from the ship," or "from the cellar of a man who is selling up his pre-prohibition stock." A glance at the hospital statistics for the whole country will show how the deaths from alcoholic poisoning are steadily on the increase.

So who can blame an Englishman for joining in a game which provides the American nation with good liquor instead of bad, and himself with adventure and profit?

The second question is, "What do you think about prohibition?"

I think quite a lot about it, but what I think is not much good to other people; to my mind nobody should form an opinion until they have been to America and seen things for themselves. But in case they interest anyone, here are my views for what they are worth.

The abolition of saloons, *for the United States*, is probably a very good thing, as there are so many people there who cannot pass a saloon when the door is open, or leave it while they have the price of a drink in their pockets.

Prohibition, too, may be a good thing for the United States if it could be enforced; but it cannot be enforced with public opinion as it is, and the premature attempt to do so has led to an increase in the very evil it was meant to stop.

But it must be remembered that the abolition of saloons and prohibition are two separate and distinct questions, which the "Drys" have skillfully bound together as one in order to strengthen their position.

In my humble opinion the statistics published by both the "Wets" and the "Drys" are often equally unreliable, and the attitude of the propagandists on both sides may be characterised by an utterance of Mr. Pussyfoot Johnson at a public meeting not long ago, "I have told enough lies for the cause to make Ananias ashamed of himself."

Only one thing counts, and that is the evidence of a man's own eyes, ears, and nose, which will prove to anyone of intelligence that there is more drinking to excess in America than in any European country, especially among the women; and that the bulk of this drunkenness is caused by alcoholic drinks made in the United States, and not imported.

The third question is, "Do you think we shall ever get prohibition in England?"

Personally I cannot imagine Constable Macintosh arresting Sandy MacDougal for drinking his tot of whiskey in front of his own fire-side, or Constable Hodge taking Farmer Giles to the police station for drinking a bottle of bass behind his barn, or the country J.P., with the aroma of his luncheon sherry still hovering round his moustache, sending the pair of them to gaol.

Still, with an increase in the present crop of theoretical politicians, there is no knowing what is going to happen.

And if prohibition were brought in, who would be better pleased than I? In six months I would be living in Park Lane (or Portland).

My last word is that there are no "interests" behind this book: to my mind there is little to choose between the Wets and the Drys, while the "Liquor Interests" and the extreme reformers should both be debarred from legislating for the good of the masses.

# PUBLISHER'S AFTERWORD

*The Confessions of a Rum-Runner* was written by Englishman Eric Sherbrooke Walker, using the pen name James Barbican. Walker's veiled account of his liquor smuggling career covers the period between 1924 and 1926.

Chief among Walker's reasons for not using his true identity—or that of others—was that Prohibition was still being enforced at the time of the book's release. Repeal, in the form of the 21st Amendment, would not be ratified until December 1933.

The son of a minister, Eric Sherbrooke Walker graduated from Oxford University and served as personal secretary for Robert Baden-Powell, the founder of the Scouting movement. As a major in the Royal Flying Corps during the First World War, he spent time in a German prisoner-of-war camp but managed to escape. He also fought for the White Army against the Bolsheviks during the Russian Civil War, 1918-1920. Walker returned to England and became engaged to the daughter of the Earl of Denbaugh. Needing money to get married, Walker turned to rum running, while his fiancée, Lady Bettie, went to work as social secretary at the British Embassy in Washington, D.C.

At the time, the British government turned a blind eye toward rum running. Britain was in the grips of a depression following the Great War, and both the liquor industry and the shipping industry needed a boost. Rum running was even considered a sport of sorts. Enterprising individuals would openly advertise for "public participation in smuggling adventures into the United States," promising a 25 percent return. Among the most notable of these entrepreneurs was Sir Broderick Cecil Hartwell, who was called the "booze baronet" or "rum running baronet." He solicited investors and purchased the steam yacht *Istar* to deliver his products to Rum Row. In Walker's confession, Hartwell is called Brisbane Swivel.

In Walker's description, it is clear that Swivel's yacht *Mermaid* was actually the British-registered steam yacht *Istar*. The 319-foot vessel was built in 1897 in Glasgow, Scotland, as the private yacht *Nahma* for New York banker and real estate tycoon Robert Goelet. The vessel served in the U.S. Navy in World War I as the USS *Nahma II*. In 1919 she was decommissioned and returned to her owner. Around 1921 she was purchased by the British rum running syndicate and registered with the home port of London. It was estimated that *Istar* could carry 160,000 cases of liquor. Depending on the price on Rum Row, a single cargo could have been worth as much as $8,000,000.

According to U.S. Coast Guard sighting reports, the *Istar* became a regular presence on Rum Row in February 1923. In April 1923 a *New York Times* reporter accompanied Prohibition officials on board the Coast Guard cutter *Manhattan* on a fact-finding tour of Rum Row. Coming upon the *Istar*, the cutter found her officers in uniform and the crew lining the rails. The reporter noted: "From a distance the *Istar*, with her graceful lines, stood out as a queen among beggars, but as the *Manhattan* approached, those aboard the cutter could see that the black paint has been chiseled off the *Istar*'s sides by the waves. The fundamental red showed through here and there, giving the craft a pock-marked appearance. Her superstructure was a dingy gray, her bowsprit was gone, and altogether she looked as dismal as a summer camp in winter."

The *Istar* disappeared from Rum Row in mid-1925. According to Coast Guard scuttlebutt, her owners had earned a fortune and decided to quit while they were ahead. However, Sir Broderick Hartwell declared bankruptcy because of losses due to liquor seizures at that time, so she may have been withdrawn due to lack of profits. The yacht was said to have been consigned to a wrecker's yard in Britain.

In an ironic sidenote, the *Istar* was a near sister ship to the presidential yacht USS *Mayflower*, used by Presidents Warren G. Harding and Calvin Coolidge during Prohibition. The *Mayflower* was the former yacht of Robert Goelet's brother Ogden, and she would go on to serve as a U.S. Coast Guard cutter in World War II.

Because he disguised the locations of his adventures with names like "Cape Ozone" and "Hawkes Bay," it is difficult to determine where Walker operated. While it is most likely that New York City was his primary base of operations, his descriptions could be Long Island, the New Jersey Coast, even the Virginia Capes region. Coast Guard reports and newspaper sightings show that the *Istar* was active off New York City; Montauk Point, Long Island; Sandy Hook, New Jersey; and Norfolk, Virginia.

In May 1923 the *Washington Post* reported that Coast Guard officials in Norfolk expressed concern that the *Istar* carried a gun mounted on her after deck. "The gun," according to Captain D. F. A. Deotte, in command of the Coast Guard Norfolk division, "has been

The steam yacht *Istar,* or the *"Mermaid"* was the "Queen of Rum Row." The former yacht of New York banker Robert Goelet, she saw service in World War I as the USS *Nahma II.* Following the war she was purchased by a rum running syndicate and placed under British registry. She was the semi-sister ship of the presidential yacht USS *Mayflower.* *(U.S. Coast Guard Photo)*

A contact boat and the Canadian schooner *Catherine M.* on Rum Row. The *Istar,* or *"Mermaid"* can be seen in the background. *(U.S. Coast Guard Photo)*

215

seen by officers on board cutters which have been on patrol near the yacht and is believed to be either a six-pounder or a three-inch rifle. "Under international law," Captain Deotte said, "yachts are permitted to carry guns for saluting purposes, but such guns," he added, "usually are one-pounders and are mounted forward."

Chapter XXX, "The Bombardment of the *Eastwood*," is the only section of the book where Walker uses actual names and places. According to U.S. Coast Guard reports, on February 15, 1926, 18 miles south of Long Island, the cutter *Seneca* did engage in target practice in the vicinity of the *Eastwood*, a well-documented rum-runner. In April 1926 the crew of the *Seneca* was absolved of the charge by the U.S. Department of Treasury in a report that noted that the firings on the *Eastwood* must have been made by a rival liquor craft. The case created a great deal of correspondence between American and British officials, but the objections were dropped in March 1927 when it was proven that the *Eastwood* was under the control of a ring of American bootleggers operating out of New York and New Jersey.

Eric Sherbrooke Walker's rum running days were cut short in 1926 when he was shot and badly wounded by a corrupt state trooper (in an episode he writes about in the book). He fled to Canada and later returned to England. In July 1926 he and Lady Bettie were married.

Having amassed a sizeable sum of money from his smuggling efforts, Walker and his wife moved to Kenya, Africa. In 1928 they opened the Outspan Hotel in the Aberdere Range, in the shadow of Mt. Kenya. In 1932 they established the adjacent Treetops Hotel, a safari viewing platform literally built into the tops of trees. Throughout his life Walker maintained his great friendship with Robert Baden-Powell, who lived out his final years with Walker in Kenya. When he died 1941, Baden-Powell was buried on the grounds of the hotel.

Treetops made its international reputation when Princess Elizabeth and her husband, the Duke of Edinburgh, visited on the evening of February 5, 1952. That night Princess Elizabeth learned of the death of her father, King George VI, and that she had become Queen Elizabeth II. Walker later commented that never before had anyone climbed a tree as a princess and come down as a queen.